# Edited by Nick Pulford

## Contributors

Richard Birch
Mark Brown
Marcus Buckland
James Burn
Tom Collins
Dave Edwards
Nick Freedman
Ben Hutton
Pietro Innocenzi

David Jennings
Paul Kealy
Andrew King
Richard Lowther
Kevin Morley
Justin O'Hanlon
Dave Orton
Tom Park
Maddy Playle

Graeme Rodway
Tom Segal
Brian Sheerin
James Stevens
Alan Sweetman
Kitty Trice
Sam Walker
Tom Ward
Nick Watts

## Designed by David Dew
### Cover artwork by Samantha Creedon

Published in 2019 by Racing Post Books, Raceform Ltd, 27 Kingfisher Court, Hambridge Road, Newbury, RG14 5SJ
Copyright © Racing Post 2019

ISBN 978-1910497975

Printed by Buxton Press Limited

O F ALL the obstacles that lie in wait for trainers and punters alike on the way to the Cheltenham Festival, nobody was expecting an outbreak of equine flu and a six-day shutdown of British racing with just a month to go until the biggest four days in jump racing.

There were even fears that a prolonged emergency could lead to the festival being lost, as it was during the foot-and-mouth outbreak of 2001, but swift action averted the crisis and put racing back on track.

To have lost the 2019 festival, which is so rich in promise, would have been a disaster. We would have missed Buveur D'Air v Apple's Jade in the Champion Hurdle – the hat-trick seeker against the first lady of jump racing – Native River's bid for a Gold Cup repeat against a host of up-and-coming chasers led by Presenting Percy and Altior's latest step towards the pantheon of all-time greats.

And we would have been denied the opportunity to see which stars would rise and which would fall in the unforgiving festival atmosphere – Paisley Park, Champ, Al Dancer, Fakir D'Oudairies, Le Richebourg, Lalor, Santini, Delta Work and Sir Erec are among those who could light up the championship meeting.

Our aim, as always, is to make the Racing Post Cheltenham Festival Guide 2019 the most comprehensive punting companion with a full range of opinion and insight from the unrivalled Racing Post team.

This 208-page guide is modelled as a 'Cheltenham preview night in book form' and once again the first half of the book features the views of tipsters and bookmakers, along with Racing Post Ratings, Topspeed, Raceform's examination of the key trials, trainer analysis and much more.

In the second half, Racing Post betting editor Paul Kealy provides his extensive race-by-race guide with forthright opinions and profiles of more than 100 of the top runners, along with key trends.

Racing's back in full swing, the festival's almost here . . . what could be better?

**Nick Pulford, Editor**

## VIEWS FROM THE SPECIALISTS
# 4

The Racing Post's top tipsters and form experts, along with the major bookmakers, pick their fancies and debate the big issues

## RACE-BY-RACE GUIDE
# 114

In-depth form guide to the main contenders by Racing Post betting editor Paul Kealy, with all the key trends

# THE SPECIALISTS

The Racing Post's team of experts reveal their festival fancies and the major bookmakers discuss the big issues in our Q&A

# Bank on Percy for Gold

**By Richard Birch**

PREVIEWING a four-day Cheltenham Festival is like taking your child into a sweet shop – there is something to satisfy every punter's taste from a bewildering assortment of goodies.

Let's start with **Presenting Percy**, who has long had my juices flowing for the Magners Cheltenham Gold Cup. He looked every inch the winner of the 2019 race when storming up the hill last March to slam Monalee by seven lengths in the RSA Chase.

After jumping and travelling beautifully, Presenting Percy *(right)* really stamped his authority between the final two fences. The vibe he gave out that afternoon was one of a potential champion and nothing has happened since to reduce confidence in his chance.

Only eight and still relatively lightly raced, Ireland's latest big hope can improve past the older guard of Native River, Might Bite and Thistlecrack.

Clan Des Obeaux has never struck me as a horse who would go through the pain barrier

in any race – let alone the Gold Cup – so I make Presenting Percy one of my bankers of the week.

Not too many horses enhance their claims for Cheltenham by finishing only third in a Grade 1 trial for the RSA Chase as 11-10 favourite, but that's exactly what **Santini** *(top)* did in Kempton's Kauto Star Novices' Chase over Christmas.

A strong, relentless stayer, he clearly wasn't suited by the demands of a sharp 3m. However, the manner in which he kept on from the last behind La Bague Au Roi – who enhanced the form with another Grade 1 win at Leopardstown – suggests he will hit a mighty peak confronted with the famous Cheltenham climb.

Nicky Henderson's seven-year-old boasts significantly low mileage and could well develop into a leading Gold Cup contender in 2020.

**Belargus** produced the standout trial for the Boodles Juvenile Handicap Hurdle when beating Zafar by a length and a quarter at Ascot in January, the body language of rider Leighton Aspell suggesting his mount had far more in hand than the winning margin suggests. Beat The Judge, who was 15 lengths back in third, rates a fair yardstick to the form and it looks like the JP McManus-owned Belargus has been plotted up for Cheltenham by Nick Gifford.

**First Assignment** started a hot favourite to land a Grade 3 handicap hurdle at Haydock in November on the back of a ridiculously easy success in a Cheltenham Listed hurdle the previous weekend.

Ian Williams' stayer couldn't cope with Paisley Park in receipt of 12lb, but the subsequent Grade 1 and Grade 2 achievements of the winner – now as short as 15-8 market leader for the Grade 1 Sun Racing Stayers' Hurdle and officially rated 168 – makes First Assignment of considerable interest if he tackles the Pertemps Handicap Hurdle off a mark of 142.

Likewise **Ok Corral** smacks of 'must bet' material if he goes for the National Hunt Chase instead of wading into the deeper waters of the RSA Chase.

The booking of leading Irish amateur rider Derek O'Connor for Ok Corral's super-slick Warwick success in January suggests Nicky Henderson is very much leaning towards the four-miler.

Ok Corral produced a speed figure at Warwick that had people who attach importance to such matters drooling and he

seems to have the perfect blend of stamina and class for the festival's longest race.

I wouldn't be in the least bit surprised if Ok Corral romped home in the National Hunt Chase and in 12 months' time held a position near the top of the Gold Cup market.

**Al Dancer** had reportedly been flying up Nigel Twiston-Davies's gallops before the Betfair Hurdle and, although he had to wait his chance due to the equine flu shutdown, he duly landed the rearranged race by three and three-quarter lengths at Ascot.

The way in which he quickly put distance between himself and his rivals in a Cheltenham handicap before Christmas strongly suggests he is the one to beat in the Sky Bet Supreme Novices' Hurdle and he is readily preferred to Angels Breath, Getaway Trump and Elixir De Nutz.

Racegoers may not see too much of **Penhill** on the racecourse these days but Willie Mullins certainly knows how to get a tune out of him when he does turn up.

Confined to just two runs in 2018, Penhill landed the Stayers' Hurdle by two lengths from Supasundae prior to a creditable second behind a revitalised and rampant Faugheen in the Punchestown equivalent.

The hugely progressive Paisley Park may be the name on most lips now, but I'm backing Penhill to make a successful defence of his crown. He's a class act.

*Al Dancer: strong candidate for the Supreme Novices'*

4

# 3/1 OFFER
## UP TO £50 FREE BET WITH EVERY WINNER AT 3/1 OR MORE

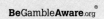

*Uradel: Cesarewitch runner-up (left) can go well in the Coral Cup*

# Apple's ripe for Champion

## By David Jennings

YOU would have got a lot bigger than 9-4 about **Apple's Jade** running in the Unibet Champion Hurdle at the end of January, never mind winning the race, but she was so impressive in the BHP Insurance Irish Champion Hurdle at Leopardstown on February 2 that she is now Buveur D'Air's biggest danger. She can beat the defending champion too.

You can safely put a line through her defeats at Cheltenham and Punchestown last season as she was badly in season on both occasions. When you erase those two disappointments, finding holes in her form is almost impossible.

Some say she could struggle with the early tempo of a Champion Hurdle and point to the fact she will most certainly get taken on up front. That doesn't matter, however. Take a look at the Hatton's Grace Hurdle at Fairyhouse in December when Wicklow Brave, a former Irish St Leger winner, tried to annoy her up front. She responded with arguably the best performance of her career.

If she's in front on the home turn, it is hard to envisage Buveur D'Air getting by her. And you must remember he has to concede 7lb to her as well. Nothing could give weight away

to Annie Power in 2016 and it could be a similar story in 2019.

Apple's Jade's absence from the OLBG Mares' Hurdle, along with the likely defection of Laurina, means the door is wide open for **Benie Des Dieux** to defend her crown. She is in an entirely different league to any of the likely runners and, while her current odds of 2-1 might appear skimpy, they could look terrific value on the day as I wouldn't be one bit surprised were she to be sent off odds-on.

Ok Corral is the right favourite for the National Hunt Chase but he is plenty short enough, so an each-way play on the Joseph O'Brien-trained **Mortal** is advised.

He is a progressive staying chaser who is crying out for a stamina-sapping test. He was good enough to beat Any Second Now in his beginners' chase, was about to give Delta Work a massive scare in a Grade 1 at Leopardstown over Christmas but for making a mess of the last and don't be fooled by the fact he was last to La Bague Au Roi in the Flogas last time. He ran so much better than his finishing position suggests over an inadequate trip.

Speaking of **Delta Work**, he looks the most professional novice chaser we have seen anywhere this season and should be outright favourite for the RSA Chase instead of Santini.

Would Santini, or anyone else in the line-up for that matter, be able to beat Le Richebourg over 2m4f at Fairyhouse? I wouldn't think so. He stays too, as we saw in last year's Pertemps Final when he dug deep to see off Glenloe.

On that topic, **Glenloe** could gain compensation for last season's near-miss if connections decide the Kim Muir is the right race for him.

He has been to Plumpton to get a handicap mark from the British assessor and there was plenty to like about his recent display at Fairyhouse behind Real Steel. He is a natural jumper who could have more than a few pounds in hand over fences.

Willie Mullins and owner Luke McMahon teamed up to take the 2018 Coral Cup with Bleu Berry and lightning could strike twice with **Uradel**.

The 102-rated stayer on the Flat caught the eye when fifth in the Ladbrokes Hurdle at Leopardstown. That was over two miles on the inside track, so imagine what he could do over 2m5f with an uphill finish at Cheltenham.

He has a mark of 132 in Ireland, so if he gets another 4lb or 5lb in Britain that would be great as Mischievious Max sneaked in last year off a mark of 135. There will be no better-handicapped horse than Uradel in the Coral Cup if he gets in, and his jumping is slick too.

Presenting Percy is the right favourite for the Magners Cheltenham Gold Cup but he is very short for what he has done and **Bellshill** looks better value each-way at 14-1.

Bellshill has long been the apple of Willie Mullins' eye and his jumping was a joy to watch around Leopardstown when he edged out Road To Respect in the Irish Gold Cup. He only started last season on February 24 and almost won an Irish Grand National before going on to beat Djakadam and Road To Respect at Punchestown.

He has had an uninterrupted prep this season and it is hard to envisage him finishing out of the first three given how well he jumps.

*Bellshill: jumping prowess a big asset in Gold Cup*

'Presenting Percy is the right favourite but he is very short for what he has done and Bellshill looks better value each-way'

# Rather an attractive bet

## By Nick Watts

THE Brown Advisory & Merriebelle Stable Plate looks like it might be the festival destination for Nicky Henderson's **Rather Be** and it's a race that should suit him perfectly.

He was just touched off at this meeting last season in the novice handicap chase won by Mister Whitaker and is one of those horses who thrives in big-field handicaps.

This season hasn't quite gone to plan for him. He was brought down when travelling well in the BetVictor Gold Cup and then was a slightly lacklustre fifth behind Frodon in the Caspian Caviar Gold Cup the following month.

However, those two performances mean he starts the spring part of his campaign off a mark of 148 – 1lb lower than when he began the season. The last two winners of the Plate, Road To Respect and The Storyteller, won off marks of 145 and 147 respectively, so he is bang where he needs to be on handicap ratings, which he wouldn't have been if he had completed in the BetVictor, as he was in the perfect position and ready to strike when he was brought down four out.

He performs well in the spring – he won a big-field handicap hurdle at Aintree's Grand National meeting in 2017 – and should get a perfect tow into the race courtesy of the front-running Siruh Du Lac.

In recent weeks Henderson has suggested he might try Rather Be over three miles. If this was the case, it would bring in the Ultima Handicap Chase on the first day. Much may depend on what sort of ground we get at Cheltenham, but he would be a player in whichever race he contests.

Alan King has won the Grand Annual before and he has another interesting candidate this year in **Ballywood**. He could have a few options during the week but this race may be the pick of them and a fast-run two miles could be ideal for him.

He's been a revelation this season for such a young horse, beating the useful Capeland at Taunton, following up at Doncaster and then running second to Dynamite Dollars in a Grade 2 at Doncaster.

He is in the Arkle but that might be flying too high. His handicap mark of 140 makes this a more attractive option and he could be potentially better than his mark.

I like the fact he has won over 2m2f, so he should be strong at the finish. While his running has been done in small fields, he is a sound jumper who shouldn't be fazed by a big-field handicap and he did win an 11-runner race in France before coming over to King. He is around 20-1 for the Grand Annual and is definitely on my radar.

Since the advent of the Dawn Run Mares' Novices' Hurdle, Willie Mullins has achieved a clean sweep, winning three out of three. However, that might change this season with Henderson's **Elusive Belle** fancied to break the hegemony.

She was a useful bumper horse in Ireland (Listed placed) before a big-money transfer into the ownership of Robert Waley-Cohen. She made her debut for new connections – and her hurdles debut at the same time – at Wincanton in January and hosed up by 19 lengths.

There was merit to the form, with dual hurdles winner Thistle Do Nicely back in second, and she was never out of third gear for the whole race.

Henderson has always treated the mares' division more seriously than most, even if festival results don't show that, and he could have hit upon the perfect type to give him a first festival success in this category.

If **Out Sam** goes for the Kim Muir he could be worth an investment. He went off favourite for the 2016 Ultima and did well to finish seventh after not jumping particularly well. His career looked to be on the slide after that but he has been revived by Gordon Elliott and his form has been good this season.

He won the Cork Grand National over 3m4f in November and was by no means disgraced in the Thyestes last time out when fourth behind the Gold Cup-bound Invitation Only.

Elliott likes the Kim Muir, having won with Cause Of Causes in 2016 and had a place last season with Squouateur, and he has access to all the top amateur riders. This is a real staying race often run at a frenetic pace, putting the emphasis on stamina, and that would suit Out Sam, whose top price of 25-1 looks too big based on his decent efforts of late.

*Out Sam: Kim Muir test would suit revived chaser*

## DATES

The 2019 Cheltenham Festival takes place over four days from Tuesday, March 12 to Friday, March 15.

## TICKETS

Except for the Friday of the festival, which is all ticket, badges and tickets can be bought at the entrances subject to availability, although savings can be made by booking in advance. To book tickets call 0344 579 3003 or buy online at cheltenham.thejockeyclub.co.uk.

Club is the most exclusive enclosure with the best viewing and refreshment facilities. A Club day badge allows access to all the facilities within Tattersalls. Tue-Thur day badges £86 in advance up to March 10, £90 on the day; Gold Cup day £111 in advance.

Tattersalls offers extensive grandstand views, a wide choice of betting and refreshment facilities, and access to all the bookmakers in the betting ring. There is also access to the Centaur, paddock and unsaddling enclosure, Hall of Fame and the trade stands in the tented village. Tue-Thur £56 in advance up to March 10, £60 on the day; Gold Cup day £80 in advance.

The Best Mate Enclosure, directly opposite the main stands, is the cheapest option, with betting, food and bars and entertainment. Tue-Thur

## RACING POST

- Everything you need for Cheltenham – web, app and newspaper
- Unrivalled cards, form, previews and tips
- Guiding you through all the action in our daily Postcasts
- Replays, results and analysis
- Live blog keeps you up to date with all the news and colour from the track from 8am daily
- Raceday Live with all the up-to-the-minute punting news, live tipping and insight
- Alastair Down heads the best reporting team in the business

£41 in advance up to March 10, £45 on the day; Gold Cup day £65 in advance.

## BY CAR

The course is situated on the A435 north of Cheltenham. The postcode is GL50 4SH for use with GPS equipment, although racegoers are strongly advised to follow the yellow temporary signs when entering Cheltenham and the local area and not the brown permanent signs. Car parking at the racecourse is £12 in advance (£20 on the day).

## BY RAIL

Trains from London to Cheltenham Spa generally run hourly and take about two hours. Trains from Birmingham generally run every half an hour and take about 35 minutes. From Bristol, trains leave every

hour and take about 35 minutes. It is a ten-minute taxi ride from the station.

## WATCH AND LISTEN

ITV will show the first five races live each day, starting at 1pm, with The Opening Show at 9.30am every morning on ITV4. Racing TV will show all 28 festival races live and there will be a live preview show from Cheltenham every morning until racing starts.

Cheltenham Radio broadcasts within a five-mile radius of the course on 87.7FM, with traffic information, previews, interviews, news, commentaries and results. Radio earpieces are available to purchase at the course from racecard kiosks, subject to availability.

## PREVIEW EVENING

For early arrivals among the many thousands who stay in and around Cheltenham during festival week, there is the opportunity to see a preview evening in The Centaur at the racecourse on Sunday, March 10 at 7pm. Admission is £6.

## ■ SECOND-LAST FENCE

A BHA review into last year's six festival fatalities has led to a number of changes, including the resiting of the second-last fence on the Old course (used on the first two days of the meeting).

Having been moved twice before, in 2010 and 2016, the fence has now been placed another ten yards past the final bend, equating to two horse strides. That leaves a gap of 110 yards between the final two fences.

Clerk of the course Simon Claisse said: "We felt if we moved that first fence in the home straight jockeys would have a better chance to get their horses balanced. I don't think anyone would take the view that by giving the horses a little bit further off the turn before they jump the fence it could make things worse. It can only make things better. There are racecourses where the final two fences are closer together than ours are now."

## ■ GRAND ANNUAL FIELD

Three of last year's fatalities were in the Grand Annual Handicap Chase and it was announced in December that the maximum field size for the two-mile race would be reduced from 24 to 20. Last year the race had 22 runners after two withdrawals but there had been 24 in the previous two runnings.

## ■ FRIDAY SWAP

The closing race of the festival will now be the Martin Pipe Conditional Jockeys' Handicap Hurdle (5.30 Friday). In recent years it has been the sixth race on the card, followed by the Grand Annual Handicap Chase as the finale, but the two races have now been switched. This means races open to senior professional jockeys will be concluded with the sixth race, which will help with the presentation of the leading jockey award.

## ■ TUESDAY SWAP

The Tuesday card will have a slightly different feel too, with the sixth and seventh races swapping round. The Close Brothers Novices' Handicap Chase becomes the sixth race (4.50) and the National Hunt Chase is now the seventh and final contest (5.30).

Cheltenham boss Ian Renton said: "We already have an amateurs' race as the last on the card on Thursday, which works well, allowing the professional jockeys to conclude their day after the sixth race. We will now have a similar order of running with the National Hunt Chase on the Tuesday and the Martin Pipe on Friday as the concluding races."

*Blow By Blow lands last season's Martin Pipe Hurdle, which becomes the last race of the festival from this year*

## TOP JOCKEYS
Festival award winners

|  |  | |
|------|--------|---|
| 2018 | **Davy Russell** | 4 |
| 2017 | **Ruby Walsh** | 4 |
| 2016 | **Ruby Walsh** | 7 |
| 2015 | **Ruby Walsh** | 4 |
| 2014 | **Ruby Walsh** | 3 |
| 2013 | **Ruby Walsh** | 4 |
| 2012 | **Barry Geraghty** | 5 |
| 2011 | **Ruby Walsh** | 5 |
| 2010 | **Ruby Walsh** | 3 |
| 2009 | **Ruby Walsh** | 7 |

Total festival winners

**Ruby Walsh** 58
**Barry Geraghty** 36
**Richard Johnson** 23
**Davy Russell** 22
**Tom Scudamore** 10
**Bryan Cooper** 8
**Paul Townend** 8
**Jamie Codd** 7
**Nico de Boinville** 7
**Sam Twiston-Davies** 7

## TOP TRAINERS
Festival award winners

|  |  | |
|------|---------|---|
| 2018 | **Gordon Elliott** | 8 |
| 2017 | **Gordon Elliott** | 6 |
| 2016 | **Willie Mullins** | 7 |
| 2015 | **Willie Mullins** | 8 |
| 2014 | **Willie Mullins** | 4 |
| 2013 | **Willie Mullins** | 5 |
| 2012 | **Nicky Henderson** | 7 |
| 2011 | **Willie Mullins** | 4 |
| 2010 | **Nicky Henderson** | 3 |
| 2009 | **Paul Nicholls** | 5 |

Total festival winners

**Willie Mullins** 61
**Nicky Henderson** 60
**Paul Nicholls** 43
**Jonjo O'Neill** 26
**Gordon Elliott** 22
**Philip Hobbs** 19
**Edward O'Grady** 18
**Nigel Twiston-Davies** 17
**Alan King** 15
**David Pipe** 15

### ■ MARTIN PIPE CHANGES
The race conditions of the Martin Pipe Conditional Jockeys' Handicap Hurdle have been altered to remove all weight-claiming allowances for riders in an attempt to encourage connections to secure the services of the most experienced jockeys.

Last year seven of the 23 riders had an allowance, although the first six finishers were ridden by jockeys without a claim.

### ■ ONE DECLARATION
From this year, connections will not be able to declare a horse to run in any race at the festival if the same horse has already been declared for another race or has already competed in another race at the meeting.

This development is an extension of the change introduced in 2016 preventing horses from being declared to run in any of the ten festival handicaps if they had already been declared for another festival handicap that had yet to take place.

Although some trainers questioned the latest change, Cheltenham believes it will provide greater certainty about running plans for racegoers, the media, the off-course betting market and the international audience.

### ▪ BUVEUR D'AIR

Nicky Henderson's star hurdler will be bidding to join the elite band to have won three Champion Hurdles and is the bookies' favourite to write his name alongside Hatton's Grace, Sir Ken, Persian War, See You Then and Istabraq. There are those who question whether he belongs in the same class, having beaten Melon by just a neck last year in a weak division, and the negative voices grew louder after he lost his 11-race unbeaten record to stablemate Verdana Blue in the Christmas Hurdle. In between, however, he dismissed young pretender Samcro with ease in the Fighting Fifth at Newcastle to show just what he can produce at his best. Now his date with destiny awaits.

### ▪ APPLE'S JADE

Standing in Buveur D'Air's way is Gordon Elliott's superstar mare, who has dazzled all season long and set up a mouthwatering showdown on Cheltenham's opening day with a 16-length romp in the Irish Champion Hurdle. That career-best performance took her ahead of Buveur D'Air on Racing Post Ratings, factoring in her 7lb mares' allowance, and finally appears to have persuaded connections to reroute her to the Champion Hurdle instead of the Mares' Hurdle. Her Cheltenham record is a source of concern but she has moved into a

different league this season and looks ready to give Buveur D'Air a great race.

### ▪ ALTIOR

Nicky Henderson's outstanding two-miler will bid to take his unbeaten record over jumps to 18 when he lines up in the Queen Mother Champion Chase, the Wednesday feature he won last year. That was his third festival success, having followed the classic route to the top via the Supreme

Novices' Hurdle and Arkle Chase, and he has once again stood head and shoulders above the rest this season. He was ranked eighth in the recent Racing Post series on the top two-mile chasers of all time and if he is to challenge erstwhile stablemate Sprinter Sacre – who was no.1 in the list and is 7lb ahead on Racing Post Ratings – he needs to be given a serious race. Whether his rivals can muster a stiff

*Star quality: (from left) Native River, Kemboy and Buveur D'Air*

in Cheltenham Gold Cup history, having won with the incomparable Arkle (1964-66), Prince Regent (1946) and Fort Leney (1968), and Paul Nicholls will join him on five winners if Clan Des Obeaux can follow up his King George VI Chase victory by landing another championship contest. Nicholls, who has won with See More Business (1999), Kauto Star (2007 and 2009) and Denman (2008), would also become only the second trainer to win the Gold Cup with four different horses – Fulke Walwyn achieved that feat with Mont Tremblant (1952), Mandarin (1962), Mill House (1963) and The Dikler (1973).

## ■ KEMBOY

Willie Mullins has never won the Gold Cup and perhaps Kemboy could make his name as the one who succeeds where Florida Pearl, Hedgehunter, Sir Des Champs, On His Own and Djakadam all fell short as runners-up. The seven-year-old has stepped up massively this season, winning the Clonmel Oil Chase before following up with a highly impressive victory in the Grade 1 Savills Chase. That win gave him an RPR of 172, up 9lb from his season-opening mark and 2lb higher than the best achieved by Gold Cup favourite Presenting Percy. With solid form in the book, Kemboy might just be the one for Mullins.

challenge remains open to question.

## ■ NATIVE RIVER

Colin Tizzard's stable star stepped up from third place in 2017 to land the Cheltenham Gold Cup last year and now he will bid to become the first to retain the crown since Best Mate's hat-trick in 2002-04. The record of returning winners since then is 22FP35P and another indication of the difficulty of the task is that only half of the previous

year's winners have managed to line up for a title defence. Native River should at least make it back to Cheltenham despite having had to miss his intended prep in the Denman Chase when it was rerouted from Newbury to Ascot and Tizzard didn't like the shorter gap to the festival and the switch to a right-handed track.

## ■ CLAN DES OBEAUX

Tom Dreaper is the most successful trainer

# 'I expect Presenting Percy to

## Who do you fancy for the Gold Cup?

**Richard Birch** Presenting Percy has been the one for me ever since his impressive RSA Chase victory last year. He's still unexposed, jumps well and has no stamina doubts.

**Brian Sheerin** All you need to do is go back and watch last year's RSA Chase to realise we're dealing with something special in Presenting Percy and I fully expect him to show he's the real deal in the Gold Cup. I wouldn't rule out Native River as the Gold Cup test is exactly what he needs but, apart from him, the British form looks a bit windy to me.

**Nick Watts** Bellshill. His Cheltenham record might be slightly misleading and there are definite signs he's coming of age. A win at left-handed Leopardstown last time has convinced me he goes that way around. He's a strong stayer, goes on any ground and is normally a good jumper. Having won five Grade 1s he has the requisite class too.

**David Jennings** Presenting Percy is the most likely winner but at the prices Bellshill is better value. His jumping was a joy to watch around Leopardstown when narrowly denying Road To Respect in the Irish Gold Cup.

**Graeme Rodway** Kemboy gave one of the most impressive performances of the season when bolting up in the Savills Chase at Leopardstown over Christmas and has been underestimated in the market. The race was falsely run but he couldn't have done it any

*Presenting Percy: RSA Chase winner is two from two at Cheltenham*

# show he's the real deal'

easier and is improving rapidly. At the prices he could be the value.

**Ben Hutton** Excuses have been put forward but it's fair to say things could have gone better this season for last year's one-two Native River and particularly Might Bite, whereas Presenting Percy fans have far less to worry about even though he bypassed the Red Mills Chase. He's two from two at Cheltenham and stands out as the likeliest winner, with Elegant Escape and Definitly Red appealing each-way options at bigger odds.

## Can Buveur D'Air complete the hat-trick in the Champion Hurdle?

**Nick Watts** Yes. While Apple's Jade has been brilliant this season, she was a beaten favourite at the festival last year in the Mares' Hurdle and didn't even finish second. In Buveur D'Air she's taking on a Cheltenham specialist who probably wasn't at his best in the Champion Hurdle last season but still got the job done. At his best his jumping is amazing and will mean he can keep tabs on Apple's Jade while holding enough back to attack in the home straight.

**David Jennings** No. The more you study Buveur D'Air's form, the less impressed you are. Apple's Jade has been a revelation this season and I don't think he can give her 7lb.

**Richard Birch** The 7lb mares' allowance is huge – we all saw that with Annie Power three years ago. Buveur D'Air is a better Champion

Hurdle winner than a lot of people give him credit for, but can he concede the weight to Apple's Jade at the top of her game? Somehow I doubt it. That victory in the Irish Champion Hurdle was Cheltenham-defining in my mind.

**Ben Hutton** Buveur D'Air wasn't totally convincing in last year's Champion Hurdle and he looks vulnerable against Apple's Jade, who has taken her form to the next level this season. Sharjah is another who would be preferred over Buveur D'Air.

**Graeme Rodway** This is ground dependent. Buveur D'Air was devastating when slamming Samcro in the Fighting Fifth on testing ground at Newcastle and, while he handles it quicker, he might be more effective on slower ground at this stage of his career. In contrast, Apple's Jade has recorded her three highest Racing Post Ratings on good or good to yielding ground and, while she handles it slower, she produces her best on better going. If good is in the description she can upset Buveur D'Air. Espoir D'Allen has loads of pace and is a lively outsider.

**Brian Sheerin** Full credit to Buveur D'Air for winning two Champion Hurdles but he's been mopping up in a weak division. He's in for a real test against Apple's Jade and Laurina and I'd marginally favour the former.

## What do you make of the Champion Chase?

**Nick Watts** There's not much to say here. Altior can sometimes race a bit lazily as he did in this race last season but he switches on when he has to and is unstoppable up the hill.

**David Jennings** It's over. Altior wins it, easily. He's almost as good as Sprinter Sacre. Min to chase him home again.

**Richard Birch** Altior is a monster, one of the best two-milers I've seen. The fact he has started odds-on for 11 of his 12 runs over fences tells you everything about his level of superiority in this division.

**Brian Sheerin** Altior's one of the best in training, if not the best, and I don't think there's anything in Ireland that will get near him.

**Graeme Rodway** Altior is head and shoulders above the opposition and has beaten all the main contenders with ease bar Footpad, who has been disappointing this season.

**Ben Hutton** Altior has been as good as ever this season and it's very difficult to look beyond him. If anything is going to put it up to him, last year's easy Arkle winner Footpad is the likeliest and there's each-way mileage in his price if it remains at 7-1 or 8-1.

## Who is your pick for the Stayers' Hurdle?

**Graeme Rodway** This race is about stamina and Paisley Park has that in abundance. He often hits a flat spot but when he reaches top gear nothing can live with him.

**Richard Birch** Penhill obviously isn't easy to train but he has a massive engine and his festival form – two out of two, both Grade 1s – gives him the edge. This looked a weak division until Paisley Park exploded on to the scene and I would question the quality of opposition he has faced in four victories this season.

**David Jennings** Paisley Park has been awesome but his Cleeve win looked too good to be true. I thought Black Op went after the two tearaways and helped the pack more than himself. I wouldn't be surprised to see him going well. It's a very weak division.

**Brian Sheerin** Paisley Park looks the best of the British by some way but I'd be hopeful Willie Mullins will have one or two too good for him. Defending champion Penhill sets the standard and Faugheen can't be underestimated, but I'd rather back Bacardys at a massive price each-way and hope for the best. He was in with a big chance when falling at the last a year ago and could get involved again.

**Ben Hutton** Apple's Jade is unlikely to line up but would be a standout favourite, which is a pointer to 2015 Champion Hurdle winner Faugheen, who was two lengths behind the mare and clear of the rest when falling two out in the Grade 1 Christmas Hurdle at Leopardstown.

# 'Kemboy and Clan look the most exciting'

## Who do you fancy for the Gold Cup?

**Bet365 Pat Cooney** There's no value at the top end of the market, so I'll go for Elegant Escape at a price. He's in good hands and still improving.

**Betbright Gavin Geraghty** Bellshill. I liked his two runs this season and I think there's more to come. It would need to be heavy ground for Native River to retain his title. Presenting Percy is probably the best horse in the race but his lack of jumping experience in top-class company puts me off at his price.

**Betfair Niall O'Reilly** I fancy Presenting Percy and I think the market has it right. Al Boum Photo looks the each-way bet – he's a really strong stayer and I can see the Gold Cup test suiting him really well.

**Betfred Matt Hulmes** Native River is the one to beat. His King George run can be upgraded considering he never travelled a yard and, while it's unfortunate he missed his intended prep, he has proved he goes well fresh. At a price Definitly Red can go well. Brian Ellison says he's better than ever and will come on a bundle for his Kelso match defeat.

**Betway Alan Alger** Presenting Percy looks a worthy favourite but he's probably opposable at the prices. Of the up-and-comers Kemboy and Clan Des Obeaux look the most exciting. It takes a special horse to win back-to-back Gold Cups and you'd have to be against Native River unless it came up soft. Might Bite could be overpriced at around 20-1 after a wind op.

**BoyleSports Alan Reilly** I find it difficult to fancy anything that has run in the race before and therefore would be against Native River. Kemboy is the interesting each-way bet. He's improving, comes into the race fresh and was impressive at Leopardstown over Christmas.

**Coral Andrew Lobo** Presenting Percy has to go close after winning at the last two festivals. He has no ground preferences and should be fine whatever the conditions.

*Rising stars: Clan Des Obeaux (above) and Kemboy*

**Ladbrokes Matt Trounce** Presenting Percy has oozed class at the last two festivals and is by far the most likely winner. Bellshill has had his whole season built around the Gold Cup and I can see him running a big race.

**Paddy Power Daniel Collins** There don't look to be many out-and-out Gold Cup sloggers in the field, so the front two deserve their places at the head of the market. At a price I quite like Al Boum Photo, for all he has stamina doubts.

**Sky Bet Richard Horner** Unless the ground rides very soft I'd side with Presenting Percy as his trainer seems as good as anyone at getting one ready for the big day.

**Sporting Index Charles Hitchings** Native River is only nine and if it's on the soft side he seems the most solid. Clan Des Obeaux probably hasn't been given enough credit for winning the King George and looks a bit of value.

**William Hill Jamie McBride** I wouldn't be keen on the chances of Native River following up unless it comes up heavy again. Kemboy probably hasn't had the credit he deserved for his win at Christmas and can run a big race, and so can Frodon at a bigger price.

### Can Buveur D'Air complete the hat-trick in the Champion Hurdle?

**Bet365** I keep changing my mind after each run but on balance he's no bargain at current prices. The 7lb mares' allowance is the key to the race and I take Laurina and Apple's Jade to fight out the finish. At a big price Brain Power is a possible outsider having proved he can win at Cheltenham last time.

**Betbright** Buveur D'Air is very good but the form of the last two Champion Hurdles wouldn't be good enough to win this year's renewal. If they can get Apple's Jade to Cheltenham in top form she'll win, but it's a big if as they've struggled to keep her from coming into season in the last two springs. If Willie Mullins feels Laurina is up to it, that says a lot.

**Betfair** Having been against Buveur D'Air for most of the season, mainly due to his price, I'm starting to think he'll end up being the bet on the day. I have doubts about Cheltenham being the ideal track for Apple's Jade, particularly over two miles.

**Betfred** Buveur D'Air is the one to beat but giving 7lb to two fantastic mares won't be easy and at the prices Laurina may be the one to side with. At a bigger price I think Espoir D'Allen can run well. Other than one poor run as a juvenile at Leopardstown he has done nothing wrong.

**Betway** Buveur D'Air is a class act but Apple's Jade is potentially better than anything he's come up against and I'd have to be with her. I don't think Sharjah has had the credit he deserves for his two Grade 1 wins this season and he could cause an upset.

**BoyleSports** Undoubtedly the current champion sets the standard but having to concede the mares' allowance to Laurina and Apple's Jade makes his task all the more difficult. We'd be happy to take him on if the mares turn up.

**Coral** Buveur D'Air could be value if Apple's Jade runs as the market is likely to swing her way. Her running style could set it up for the reigning champion. Silver Streak could be each-way value if the ground comes up good.

**Ladbrokes** I'd have a slight preference for Apple's Jade with the 7lb mares' allowance. She was devastating when dropping back to two miles at Leopardstown and it'll take a personal best from Buveur D'Air to topple her. Melon hasn't been great so far this season but that was also the case last year and I can see him improving to hit the frame again.

**Paddy Power** Apple's Jade has been so impressive this season that it's hard to see her not going off favourite on the day.

**Sky Bet** It's going to be tough for Buveur D'Air to give 7lb to two classy mares but he loves Cheltenham whereas Apple's Jade hasn't always run to form at the track. With the ground likely to be at its softest on the first day, I'd prefer to take a chance on Laurina at the prices.

**Sporting Index** This will be a tougher test than last year for Buveur D'Air but he always seems to get the job done and I wouldn't want to oppose him. If it's soft Laurina would be huge value at current prices.

**William Hill** I marginally favour Buveur D'Air over Apple's Jade given his solid course form. At a big price Saldier is something of a forgotten horse as he would probably have beaten Espoir D'Allen when last seen but is currently a bigger price.

## What do you make of the Champion Chase?

**Bet365** It looks a penalty kick for Altior but this is racing and anything's possible. He won't be beaten on merit, that's for sure, but perhaps Sceau Royal, given his ground, could be the one to follow him home.

**Betbright** Altior looks untouchable barring accidents as he has beaten his rivals numerous times already.

**Betfair** Altior is unbeatable barring injury or a fall. For an each-way bet I'd probably back Footpad, who can jump with the best. Arkle winners have an excellent record in the race on their first season out of novice company.

**Betfred** Altior is imperious. He gave the others a glimmer of hope last season when not travelling at his best but still bolted home. I'd love to see Simply Ned and Lady Buttons go well for the north and pick up place money.

**Betway** Altior is in a league of his own and should win easily.

**BoyleSports** Altior is such a fantastic champion and the ultimate professional.

**Coral** Altior looks rock solid and has no flaws.

**Ladbrokes** Altior's in a different class and nothing will be able to go with him when he hits the turbo. Sceau Royal is solid for a place if he gets his favoured fast ground.

**Paddy Power** Min, one of the best chasers of recent years, has been beaten seven lengths on both occasions he has faced Altior at the festival. That just about sums up the race.

**Sky Bet** Altior looks the British banker. If Willie Mullins gets Footpad there 100 per cent on the day he can be the main challenger and pick up the pieces if Altior underperforms.

**Sporting Index** Altior is exceptional and should win barring accidents. At a big price I could see Lady Buttons running into a place.

*Class of his own:
Altior is expected
to be back in the
winner's enclosure*

**William Hill** Altior eventually won well last year but Min arguably travelled more smoothly through the race and he can make him pull out all the stops. Lady Buttons could reward each-way support.

## Who is your pick for the Stayers' Hurdle?

**Bet365** It's hard to knock the claims of Paisley Park but he's no value. Faugheen's win at Punchestown last April is the best form line and he'd be my pick if he runs.

**Betbright** Paisley Park is improving with every run similar to the year that Thistlecrack annihilated the field.

**Betfair** Paisley Park looks clear of the field after his Cleeve Hurdle demolition job. If Samcro takes up his entry, which Gordon Elliott suggested is a possibility, he could be the fly in the ointment.

**Betfred** Paisley Park hit a flat spot in the Cleeve Hurdle but was well on top at the end and is hard to look past. At a price Bacardys, who was staying on when falling at the last behind Penhill last year, can hit the frame.

**Betway** It's hard to overlook Paisley Park, who looks like he stays all day. If Penhill makes it, he'll be a big threat.

**BoyleSports** I hope Samcro runs as it would inflate the price of Paisley Park, who's a good thing.

**Coral** Paisley Park is short enough. Penhill won last year off a break and I'm sure his trainer will have him spot on again.

**Ladbrokes** I'm happy to take on Paisley Park at the prices. I'd take a flyer on Bacardys, who was running a big race last year and will be well suited by a truly run race.

**Paddy Power** Paisley Park is impressive and looks much the best of the British. If the race is as slowly run as last year, and the ground is better, I'd give Supasundae a chance of staying if he's aimed here. Samcro would be an interesting curveball if he turned up.

**Sky Bet** Paisley Park was impressive in the Cleeve Hurdle and from what looked a wide-open division we now have a clear and worthy favourite.

**Sporting Index** I can't see any value in Paisley Park's price. I'd go for Supasundae each-way as I think this is his best trip.

**William Hill** In a division lacking depth it's hard to get away from Paisley Park. He'd be our worst result of the meeting ante-post, and perhaps a rejuvenated Samcro could come and save us.

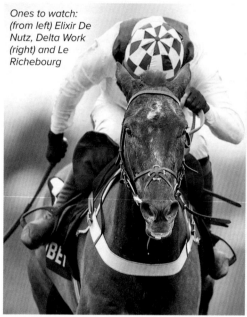

Ones to watch: (from left) Elixir De Nutz, Delta Work (right) and Le Richebourg

### ■ ELIXIR DE NUTZ

The Supreme Novices' Hurdle was 4-1 the field with less than a month to go and arguably Elixir De Nutz is still underestimated in the market despite having strong form lines. Second to Thomas Darby on his reappearance, the Colin Tizzard-trained grey won his next two starts at Cheltenham before landing the Grade 1 Tolworth Hurdle at Sandown – the race used as a stepping stone to the Supreme by last year's winner Summerville Boy. Elixir De Nutz's economical jumping and genuine attitude make him one to watch in the festival opener.

### ■ LE RICHEBOURG

The Arkle Chase has gone to Ireland in four of the past five years and Joseph O'Brien has their strongest candidate on form this time with Le Richebourg, who has won four out of five over fences – including two Grade 1s over 2m1f – and been beaten only by RSA fancy Delta Work at the longer trip of 2m4f. This good-ground specialist was well beaten in the County Hurdle on soft last year but has improved with every start over fences to an RPR of 160 and, with the favourite having won six of the last seven runnings of this race, he looks the one to beat.

### ■ CHAMP

It is four years since Tony McCoy signed off at the festival with a memorable Ryanair Chase victory on Uxizandre and now the horse named after the 20-time champion jump jockey arrives with a big chance in the Ballymore Novices' Hurdle. After gaining valuable experience by winning two novice hurdles in the summer, he overcame keenness to land a deep handicap at Newbury on his return in December and then stepped into Grade 1 novice company to win the Challow Hurdle, quickening away from Getaway Trump and Kateson in good style. Cheltenham will pose a different test but raw ability is incredibly important in the top races and he looks one of the best from Nicky Henderson's strong team of novices.

### ■ LOSTINTRANSLATION

Lostintranslation improved to be Grade 1-placed at the end of his novice hurdle campaign and his first few runs over fences suggest he will be winning a top-flight contest before too long, quite possibly in the JLT Novices' Chase. After two decent efforts behind the rock-solid mare La Bague Au Roi, the Colin Tizzard-trained gelding stepped up with a stylish win in the Grade 2 Dipper at Cheltenham in January when getting the better of Defi Du Seuil. That rival reversed the result in the Grade 1 Scilly Isles at Sandown but it would be no surprise if Lostintranslation landed the knockout blow in round three.

### ■ DELTA WORK

Festival form is a key factor when it comes to assessing Cheltenham chances and Delta Work ticks that box, having won the Pertemps Final last year. He has been flawless in three runs over fences this season, including when beating Arkle candidate Le Richebourg in the Grade 1 Drinmore at Fairyhouse, and could follow Presenting Percy in adding the RSA Chase to his Pertemps success. The Gordon Elliott-trained stout stayer is likely to be partnered by Presenting Percy's jockey Davy Russell, who rides Cheltenham particularly well, and he could prove too strong for the British challengers.

### ■ DERRINROSS

Celebrations would be tinged with poignancy if Derrinross won the Albert Bartlett Novices' Hurdle for trainer Philip Dempsey and his family. The eight-year-old was owned by Dempsey's late father Des, who died a few weeks before this late developer won his first race under rules in a Grade 3 at Cork in December, and he has continued to lift the family by following up in a Grade 2 at Limerick. Given the injury problems that delayed his emergence, Derrinross won't be risked on anything other than soft ground, but provided it's safe at Cheltenham he'll line up as a lively outsider.

# 'He's one of my strongest fancies of the entire week'

## What do you fancy for the novice hurdles?

**Nick Watts** Elixir De Nutz loves Cheltenham and there was nothing wrong with his win in the Grade 1 Tolworth Hurdle when he beat Grand Sancy by half a length. The latter franked the form by taking the Kingwell Hurdle and Elixir De Nutz should really be single figures for the Supreme. I much prefer Champ to Battleoverdoyen in the Ballymore, while Relegate would have a chance in the Albert Bartlett. Her jumping has been ordinary but a longer trip will help and she has a hell of an engine when she gets going. Downtown Getaway is interesting each-way for either of the longer races.

**David Jennings** Mister Fisher is one of my strongest fancies of the week in the Supreme; I think he's better than stablemate Angels Breath. Champ looks rock solid in the Ballymore. Sir Erec is a worthy favourite in the Triumph but I could see Coeur Sublime running a massive race. It'll be the first time he's had a race run to suit.

*Mister Fisher: could outrun stablemate Angels Breath in the Supreme*

**Ben Hutton** Nicky Henderson has strong contenders with Angels Breath in the Supreme and Champ in the Ballymore. The stamina test of the Albert Bartlett should suit the Noel Meade-trained First Approach, while Dinons showed significant promise for Gordon Elliott last year. Sir Erec looks short enough in the Triumph and the lightly raced Carlo Biraghi catches the eye, having been an easy winner at Punchestown on his hurdles debut.

**Richard Birch** Al Dancer looked tailor-made for the demands of the Supreme when landing a Cheltenham handicap before Christmas. He has a high cruising speed and explosive turn of foot, as he showed again in the Betfair Hurdle. I think Quel Destin is underrated in the Triumph Hurdle market; he's more than just a battler.

**Graeme Rodway** I've backed Al Dancer for the Supreme and he has a massive chance, but if Fakir D'Oudairies goes for the race instead of the Triumph he would be my idea of the winner. Champ cruised all over a smart field in the Challow at Newbury and should win the Ballymore. Nadaitak is a lively outsider for the Albert Bartlett. He's just the type who might thrive when faced with this sort of test and is open to improvement in cheekpieces. Sir Erec is the right favourite for the Triumph.

**Brian Sheerin** Sir Erec has been the most impressive novice this season and he'll take the world of beating in the Triumph. If I was to back one at a bigger price I'd be concentrating on Elusive Belle for the Mares' Novice Hurdle.

### Which novice chasers stand out?

**Nick Watts** I would really fancy Defi Du Seuil in the Arkle but connections seem determined to keep him at 2m4f, probably due to the emergence of Le Richebourg. That sways me back towards Lalor, who was mustard at Cheltenham on his chasing debut and didn't run badly at Sandown considering he may not have liked the ground and track. Lostintranslation will outstay Defi Du Seuil in the JLT and I think Santini has too much class for Delta Work in the RSA.

**Ben Hutton** Lalor was impressive at Cheltenham on his chase debut and got bogged down on soft ground at Sandown. Granted a better surface, he'll be an entirely different proposition at the festival. Defi Du Seuil has been rejuvenated this season and has leading claims in the JLT. Some outsiders catch the eye in the RSA – Drovers Lane and Talkischeap should be suited by the attritional nature of the race, while northern challenger Top Ville Ben impressed on his first two chase starts before jumping to the left at right-handed Ascot.

**Richard Birch** Santini has been my Cheltenham banker since his impressive winning debut over fences at Newbury. Kempton didn't suit him, yet I still thought he emerged from his Christmas third there with enormous credit. He'll win the RSA. Le Richebourg looks the one to be on in the Arkle.

**Graeme Rodway** Lalor has the potential to be a superstar and, although he comes with question marks, he'll be hard to beat if at his best and the going is quick. The RSA is probably the best renewal of the race in many years and, although I narrowly prefer Santini of the big three, there's no value. Defi Du Seuil and Lostintranslation set the standard in the JLT. La Bague Au Roi would be interesting if she lined up but trainer Warren Greatrex has yet to commit to a Cheltenham bid.

**Brian Sheerin** I'm a big fan of Le Richebourg but I'd rather side with Cilaos Emery in the Arkle. He was a better hurdler and was awesome on his chasing debut at Gowran. Paloma Blue could go close in the JLT, while Delta Work looks the most likely RSA winner. Ballyward has been a big improver over fences this season and should give Patrick Mullins a cracking spin in the National Hunt Chase.

**David Jennings** I'm leaning towards Kalashnikov in the Arkle, although Paloma Blue could run well if his jumping improves. The JLT looks between Defi Du Seuil and Lostintranslation, unless Topofthegame shows up there. Delta Work has been my idea of the RSA winner ever since he got up to beat Le Richebourg in the Drinmore at Fairyhouse.

## What do you fancy for the novice hurdles?

**Bet365 Pat Cooney** JP McManus has plenty to look forward to with Fakir D'Oudairies (Supreme), Champ (Ballymore) and Sir Erec (Triumph) all perfectly reasonable selections. The Albert Bartlett is usually a race for the bookmakers, with three 33-1 winners in the last nine renewals, so I'll probably back a couple at big prices each-way on the day.

**Betbright Gavin Geraghty** Sir Erec looks head and shoulders above all the other juveniles. The Ballymore is probably the hardest to call but I'll plump for Battleoverdoyen. He has loads of ability, is not short of speed and will improve again.

**Betfair Niall O'Reilly** I like Getaway Trump and Fakir D'Oudairies in the Supreme. With his allowance Fakir D'Oudairies barely needs to improve at all on what he showed at Cheltenham to go close in an average year. Champ is the banker of the week for the Ballymore. I couldn't have been more impressed with Allaho at Clonmel and he looks a big player in the Albert Bartlett.

**Betfred Matt Hulmes** For the Supreme I like Elixir De Nutz, who is taking the Summerville Boy route, has track and trip winning form

# 'Champ my banker of the week in Ballymore'

and looks gutsy. Brewin'upastorm, who still looked to have plenty left when tipping up on trials day, and City Island, who has gone quietly about his business in Ireland, are the two for me in the Ballymore. Commander Of Fleet looks a worthy favourite for the Albert Bartlett on his Leopardstown win and Allaho impressed at Clonmel.

**Betway Alan Alger** Relegate was a big eyecatcher last time out and if she brushes up her jumping she could be well suited to the Albert Bartlett.

**BoyleSports Alan Reilly** The Triumph looks

like a potential one-two for Joseph O'Brien and JP McManus with Sir Erec and Fakir D'Oudairies, but the latter would be favourite for the Supreme if they take that option. McManus could also land the Ballymore with Champ, who was impressive in the Challow Hurdle. The Albert Bartlett looks wide open.

**Coral Andrew Lobo** The Supreme looks a strong race and Fakir D'Oudairies has possibly been overbet. Thomas Darby should appreciate the Supreme test and is a good each-way bet. In the Ballymore I fancy Battleoverdoyen and in the Albert Bartlett I think Geordie B and Highland Hunter are

big prices. Sir Erec should be hard to beat in the Triumph.

**Ladbrokes Matt Trounce** I'm interested in Thomas Darby and Itchy Feet for the Supreme at big prices – both have some nice course form and should appreciate a truly run race. In the Triumph I wouldn't given up on Tiger Tap Tap as an each-way alternative against Sir Erec. I wouldn't be surprised if something

*Champ: impressive Challow winner*

improved past Champ in the Ballymore and I'd be interested in stablemates Angels Breath or Birchdale if they got redirected to that race.

**Paddy Power Daniel Collins** I wouldn't give up on Vision D'Honneur for the Supreme on ground with more ease, Champ looks solid in the Ballymore if the festival pace helps him to settle and in the Albert Bartlett I like Downtown Getaway.

**Sky Bet Richard Horner** I'd like to see Fakir D'Oudairies go for the Supreme as he'd be a fascinating runner getting a weight allowance. Battleoverdoyen is my Ballymore pick and I'd be interested in Carefully Selected in the Albert Bartlett if Willie Mullins can get a run into him. Sir Erec is the obvious one for the Triumph after his impressive win at Leopardstown.

**Sporting Index Charles Hitchings** The Supreme looks tricky but I'll go with Al Dancer. Champ is a deserved short-price favourite in the Ballymore. Carefully Selected is an interesting contender in a tough Albert Bartlett and in the Triumph Sir Erec has the look of an Irish banker.

**William Hill Jamie McBride** I'd be very keen on Fakir D'Oudairies if he goes for the Supreme and takes advantage of his age allowance. Relegate could go well in the Albert Bartlett if she can brush up her jumping.

## Which novice chasers stand out?

**Bet365** There seems plenty of depth to all the races but I give Santini the best chance in the RSA. I liked his chase debut win at Newbury and there was much to like about his run at Kempton even though he was beaten. I'll take Lostintranslation to reverse Sandown form with Defi Du Seuil as the left-handed track will suit him better. I was taken by Cilaos Emery's chase debut win at Gowran Park and he's my Arkle choice.

**Betbright** I've been impressed with Topofthegame for the RSA. I liked Cilaos Emery on his chasing debut but the boat may have been missed on his price.

**Betfair** I was blown away by Lalor earlier in the season at Cheltenham and he'd be my tentative pick for the Arkle, although I'm worried by his Sandown run and the fact we haven't seen him since. I really like Lostintranslation in the JLT and Santini would be my pick for the RSA, although I'd like to see him get another run before the festival.

**Betfred** The Arkle could be the race of the festival. Le Richebourg is an outstanding jumper for a novice but I'm keeping the faith with Kalashnikov, who has a potent mix of speed and stamina. I'm still a big fan of Vinndication for the JLT as he hated the sticky Sandown ground last time. The RSA looks tailor-made for Topofthegame, who gave Defi Du Seuil a 20-length head start at Exeter but was only beaten three lengths and has proven festival form.

**Betway** I like the look of Paloma Blue in the Arkle as he won well last time despite a poor round of jumping. He's in the right hands to improve and has clearly got an engine on him. I'm surprised Topofthegame isn't favourite for the RSA. He got left at the start first time out but still finished second in a good race and his Kempton run, where he was in front of Santini, has been nicely franked by La Bague Au Roi.

**BoyleSports** Le Richebourg for the Arkle after winning the Irish equivalent very easily and Ok Corral will be considered as banker material in the four-miler.

**Coral** I'm not a fan of the British form line at the top of the market in the JLT and will be backing whatever the Irish bring over. The RSA looks a belter and Topofthegame looks overpriced to confirm form with Santini.

**Ladbrokes** If he gets there I like Champagne Classic in the JLT. He ran a massive race on his chase debut off a long layoff and is a previous festival winner. Delta Work will be hard to beat in the RSA and I prefer him to the British-trained pair. I also prefer the Irish in the National Hunt Chase, where Ballyward looks the pick. I'd worry about Ok Corral's lack of experience.

**Paddy Power** If Lalor bounced back to the

form of his course-and-distance success he'd be tough to beat in the Arkle but it's hard to have much confidence given his preparation since then. La Bague Au Roi has put up some really good performances but by all accounts will be heading to Aintree.

**Sky Bet** I was impressed with Cilaos Emery at Gowran and he should go well in the Arkle for the Mullins-Walsh team, who know what's required for this race. Defi Du Seuil at 4-1 looks fair in the JLT as a lot of the horses high up the betting will be going elsewhere. Topofthegame at 7-1 looks the last bit of value in the RSA after his good second to La Bague Au Roi.

**Sporting Index** I like Cilaos Emery in the

Arkle. His hurdling form reads extremely well and he was impressive on his chase debut. For the JLT it's between Defi Du Seuil and Lostintranslation and I prefer the latter, especially at the current prices. Topofthegame lost little in defeat to La Bague Au Roi and should have won first time out, and he looks the value in the RSA.

**William Hill** Le Richebourg jumps really well but I think Lalor may just turn out to be the more talented horse. Defi Du Seuil and Lostintranslation don't look to be as far ahead of some others in the JLT as the betting suggests and we can hopefully get a result in that race. At the prices I'd much rather be with Topofthegame for the RSA.

*Cilaos Emery:
plenty of votes
for the Arkle*

# DID YOU KNOW YOUR DREAM HOME IS ONLY A 5% DEPOSIT AWAY?

**Already being on the property ladder you may not have known, but you too can use Help to Buy* to step up into a bigger and better family home with Crest Nicholson.**

In 3 simple steps you could move into a brand new home that requires no DIY, meaning you will have the spare time to do the things you love!

Discover the right move for you today!

**So what does that mean to you?**

- All you need is as little as a 5% deposit
- You will need to take out a 75% mortgage
- The government loans you the remaining 20%

## 4 BEDROOM HOMES FROM £340,000

THE

*Ridings*

Marconi Drive | Waterwells Business Park
Hardwicke | Gloucester | GL2 2A

ww.crestnicholson.com/theridings

01452 646030

### ■ RIDERS ON THE STORM

'Into this world we're thrown' is a lyric in The Doors song that shares a name with this Tom Taaffe-trained six-year-old, who could be thrown into the Close Brothers Novices' Handicap Chase. His first two runs over fences suggested Graded company may be slightly beyond him but his victory in a Punchestown rated novice chase in February was a sign of real potential in the handicap arena. He has a similar profile to the 2017 Close Brothers winner Tully East, albeit a year younger, and looks the type to make good on his untapped potential.

### ■ GIVE ME A COPPER

Since joining Paul Nicholls in 2016, this nine-year-old has seen the track just six times and his unexposed profile makes him a prime candidate for the Ultima Handicap Chase. On his reappearance after a 446-day break at Sandown in February he produced an excellent performance when fourth of 16 in a 3m handicap chase despite giving weight to all but two rivals. He has a touch of class, having once been seen as an RSA Chase contender, and almost certainly there is improvement to come.

### ■ LA SORELITA

The Boodles Juvenile Handicap Hurdle is always a puzzle but the big trainers have done well with their lesser lights and it could be Willie Mullins' turn this year with this filly. She was 3-1 favourite on her first start for Mullins in a Grade 2 at Leopardstown over Christmas but was beaten just over six lengths into fourth. She was then sent off at prices of 7-4 and 7-2 on her next two starts, only to disappoint a little, leading to the feeling that handicapping may be the option for her now. Any Mullins horse who carries that sort of market confidence in three successive starts in her debut season surely is not a complete flame-out and she could be on a good mark for Cheltenham.

### ■ MALL DINI

This Pat Kelly-trained nine-year-old might well feature on a list of the most frustrating jumps horses in training but could be about to shed that tag. Undoubtedly talented yet winless since taking the Pertemps Final in 2016, this stablemate of Presenting Percy was a close second in the Fulke Walwyn Kim Muir Handicap Chase at last year's festival and, judging by his light race schedule this season, that looks to be his target again. His liking for Cheltenham makes him one to consider.

Riders Onthe Storm (left) and Dallas Des Pictons make plenty of appeal

## ■ WHATSWRONGWITHYOU

Trainer Nicky Henderson has joked in the past that the name of this horse is indicative of his character – in so far as he has talent but has not always been keen to show it. Sent over fences after starting off this season in the Listed Gerry Feilden Hurdle at Newbury in December, this lightly raced eight-year-old has taken to chasing with aplomb and looks a decent candidate for the 2m Grand Annual Handicap Chase. A keen-going type who pulled hard in his first two starts over fences in small fields, he was third in last year's Imperial Cup over hurdles and may well show more off the frantic pace at which the Grand Annual is usually run.

## ■ DALLAS DES PICTONS

Gordon Elliott has won the past two renewals of the 2m4½f Martin Pipe Conditional Jockeys' Handicap Hurdle and he may hold another ace with this Gigginstown-owned six-year-old. He started his career with progressive performances in three maiden contests, winning the last of them over 2m4f, and then stepped up to 3m for a battling Leopardstown victory on his first start in handicap company. That distance looked something of a stretch for him and Elliott, who is so good at shuffling his festival pack and playing his cards right, indicated the Martin Pipe could be the target.

# 'Great value – that's Fact'

**Give us a value bet for the festival**

**Bet365 Pat Cooney** Fact Of The Matter at double figures in the Cross Country Chase. He'll need to find a few pounds to win but has jumped well over the course and looks a decent each-way bet.

**Betbright Gavin Geraghty** Uradel is a general 10-1 for the Coral Cup. No matter what the British handicapper does, he'll remain a well-handicapped horse and would be one of the strongest bets of the week.

**Betfair Niall O'Reilly** Whatswrongwithyou looks a good-value bet in the Grand Annual at 16-1. His trainer has suggested that's the target and he looks one who will be ideally suited by the race.

**Betfred Matt Hulmes** Fact Of The Matter appears underestimated in the Cross Country considering he has been second and first in two starts this season. At double-figure odds he's great each-way value.

**Betway Alan Alger** Discorama at 16-1 for the National Hunt Chase. He was staying on well and had every chance when coming down last time out. Extreme trips could be the making of him.

**BoyleSports Alan Reilly** Kemboy each-way in the Gold Cup at 8-1 or bigger.

**Coral Andrew Lobo** Geordie B in the Albert Bartlett or Thomas Darby in the Supreme.

**Ladbrokes Matt Trounce** Thomas Darby has been trained for the Supreme and looks a

*Fact Of The Matter (left): double-figure odds for the Cross Country*

# THE X7.
## LUXURY WITHOUT LIMITS.

BAYERISCHE MOTOREN WERKE

**The new BMW X7 - luxury without limits.**

Effortlessly sumptuous, its interior space brings new meaning to first class, while the exterior combines scale with beauty.

Revel in driver-focused technology that tackles the roughest terrains with the calmest tranquillity.

Three rows of seats as standard.

The new BMW X7 will arrive at Cotswold Cheltenham in April.

For more information call 01242 335 335 or register your interest at cotswoldcheltenhambmw.co.uk.

## COTSWOLD CHELTENHAM
Corinthian Way, Cheltenham GL51 6UP

01242 335 335

big price at 20-1. A keen-going sort, he's only had a strong pace to aim at once this season and that was when he was an impressive winner over subsequent Grade 1 winner Elixir De Nutz.

**Paddy Power Daniel Collins** The Storyteller ran a nice enough race in the Irish Gold Cup but surely connections cannot pass up his hurdles mark of 142. He'd look thrown in if he took his chance in the Coral Cup and he's a 20-1 shot in places.

**Sky Bet Richard Horner** I'd be very interested in The Storyteller at 20-1 for the Coral Cup as he has a much lower hurdles mark and I could see him going off favourite. Fine Brunello ran a nice Fred Winter trial at Cheltenham last time out and should go well at 16-1 if he's given a fair mark.

**Sporting Index Charles Hitchings** Ok Corral will surely take all the beating in the National Hunt Chase with Derek O'Connor aboard.

**William Hill Jamie McBride** Lethal Steps looks to have been campaigned by Gordon Elliott with the Fred Winter in mind. I'd expect to see some headgear refitted for the big day and if the ground isn't too soft he'll be well suited by the relative test of speed.

## What's your best festival bet?

**Bet365** Nicky Henderson to be top trainer at the meeting. He's already 1-0 up with Altior surely?

**Betbright** Tiger Roll. He's being primed for the Cross Country and a repeat victory in the Grand National, which he won off a biggish weight. He's head and shoulders above the opposition, loves

*Ok Corral: fancied for the National Hunt Chase*

the course and will be better on the likely good ground.

**Betfair** I love Lostintranslation and I think he's capable of reversing form with Defi Du Seuil back around Cheltenham. He's a magnificent jumper who will have most of them under pressure from a fair way out and I'm hopeful he'll be able to run the finish out of Defi Du Seuil.

**Betfred** Honeysuckle in the Dawn Run Mares' Novices' Hurdle.

**Betway** Topofthegame for the RSA.

**BoyleSports** Paisley Park in the Stayers' Hurdle.

**Coral** Presenting Percy in the Gold Cup.

**Ladbrokes** Tiger Roll looks different class to the rest of the Cross Country field and can win the race for the second year in a row.

**Paddy Power** Gigginstown have had a lot of success in the Martin Pipe in recent years and Dallas Des Pictons looks absolutely ideal for it. He only won by a neck last time but the way he travelled through the Leopardstown race marked him out as well ahead of his mark.

**Sky Bet** Defi Du Seuil at 4-1 for the JLT Chase as the race looks like cutting up with six of the top ten in the betting likely to head elsewhere. His price looks sure to contract and, given he's proven on the track as well as on good or soft ground, he looks sure to run a big race.

**Sporting Index** I'd have to go with Sir Erec. If I was having an each-way Lucky 15 to try to win big I'd have Topofthegame, Ok Corral, Supasundae and Give Me A Copper.

**William Hill** I'm very pleased to be on Fakir D'Oudairies at 10-1 for the Supreme, non-runner money back.

*Last year seven festival winners had run at Cheltenham that season, with two winning and three others placed. Here we look at some likely types this year*

### ■ CUBOMANIA

Gordon Elliott has become famed for his success in the Cheltenham Festival handicaps and he entered Cubomania on trials day in order to get an idea of what mark the handicapper would allocate his course winner. Cubomania's 147 rating is 5lb higher than his Irish equivalent, but he was rated 143 when landing a novice chase at Cheltenham's Showcase fixture in October and is fairly treated off only 4lb higher, having run solid races in defeat in handicaps in Ireland since. Two of his last three runs have been staying-on seconds over 2m1f but his course win came over 2m4f and there are two handicaps over that distance at the festival. A strongly run 2m might also suit and the Grand Annual could also be a target.

### ■ BUN DORAN

Tom George's improving eight-year-old has appeared only twice this season and both runs came at Cheltenham for the two highest Racing Post Ratings of his career. Bun Doran needs a strongly run 2m on decent ground and looks made

for the Grand Annual. He appears to have been trained for the race as he hasn't run since being beaten by Ozzie The Oscar in a tactical race on the New course in December and has been kept fresh for the bid. That is a wise move as Bun Doran's form figures after breaks of 50 days or more are an impressive 11336231.

### ■ DEFI DU SEUIL

The 2017 Triumph Hurdle winner's Cheltenham form figures over hurdles and fences read 111152 and he confirmed his liking for the venue when second to Lostintranslation in the Dipper Novices' Chase on New Year's Day. Philip Hobbs's gelding traded at the minimum 1.01 in running on Betfair when swooping past Lostintranslation on the run-in but failed to see it out.

Defi Du Seuil reversed that form on 3lb better terms at Sandown next time and will return to his favourite track to bid for the Grade 1 JLT Novices' Chase on the Thursday of the festival.

### ■ JANIKA

This improving six-year-old joined Nicky Henderson after completing a hat-trick in France for Guy Cherel and has continued his progress. Beaten only by the talented Hell's Kitchen on his British debut at Ascot, Janika failed by just a head to give the progressive Siruh Du Lac 19lb in a Grade 3 over 2m4½f on trials day at Cheltenham and that rival was completing a hat-trick. The front two pulled nine lengths clear of the third Ballyhill, who is a solid type, and that gives the form a strong look. Janika is up 6lb and that will make life tough in the Brown Advisory

Course specialists:
(clockwise from top left)
Bun Doran, Cubomania,
Defi Du Seuil and Janika

& Merriebelle Stable Plate but he is also in the Ryanair and looks a lively outsider.

### ■ BREWIN'UPASTORM

It hasn't been profitable to back last-time-out fallers at the festival but statistics are there to be broken and there won't have been many fallers who went into Cheltenham on the back of as good an effort as Brewin'upastorm. Olly Murphy's novice hurdler was travelling like the winner in front in a Grade 2 on trials day at the course and probably needed only to jump the last to secure an easy victory over Birchdale. He was matched at 1.26 in running on Betfair but met the final flight wrong. Birchdale went on to win by a whopping 18 lengths and impressive Listed course winner Jarveys Plate was

among those in behind. That is strong form and Brewin'upastorm can take revenge on Birchdale if they both run in the Ballymore.

### ■ CHAMPAGNE CITY

Tom George's six-year-old has yet to win at Cheltenham but loves the place and form figures of 3334 in competitive handicap hurdles at the course mark him out as an interesting one from an each-way perspective at the festival. He has run only twice this winter and both outings came at Cheltenham. He was no match for Supreme hope Al Dancer and subsequent winner Not That Fuisse in

December but still finished third at 25-1. He followed that with a good fourth on trials day when he was in front at the last and had been matched at evens in running only to lose three places on the run-in behind Benny's Bridge, who was given an inspired waiting ride by Paddy Brennan. Champagne City is usually sent off at decent prices and his consistency means he shouldn't be underestimated by punters.

# Percy can take Native's crown

By Sam Walker

## ■ GOLD CUP

Native River (178) sets the standard on RPR after last year's unforgettable victory, but he may not repeat those heroics under different conditions and I'm looking to take him on with the younger brigade.

Everything went right for Native River last year. He had a flawless preparation, the soft ground made it a real stamina test and Richard Johnson rode the race perfectly to keep the pressure on Might Bite. This time he faces new challengers and the ground may not be as testing, which would put less of an emphasis on stamina. He sets the standard but probably won't run to 178 unless it comes up soft.

Presenting Percy is certainly one who could improve to win a Gold Cup and he has been high on my list since his impressive win in last

year's RSA Chase. He stayed and jumped well that day to earn an RPR of 170, which is the second highest achieved by an RSA winner in the last ten years.

Trainer Pat Kelly was perhaps overly patient with his stable star this season, as we had to wait until January to see him again, but the eight-year-old looked as good as ever in his comeback win over hurdles at Gowran Park.

That effort earned him his best hurdles RPR of 158, which bodes well as he attempts to hit new heights back over fences at Cheltenham. We're working on limited evidence with him but what we've seen is good and he looks the most likely winner.

Another one with potential is Kemboy (172). He wasn't the top novice last year but he has improved into the leading second-season chaser after winning the Grade 1 Savills Chase at Leopardstown in December.

### GOLD CUP

| This year's top rated | RPR |
|---|---|
| Native River | 178 |
| Bristol De Mai *(right)* | 177 |
| Clan Des Obeaux | 177 |
| Frodon | 176 |
| Balko Des Flos | 174 |
| Might Bite | 174 |
| Thistlecrack | 174 |
| Bellshill | 172 |
| Kemboy | 172 |
| Anibale Fly | 170 |
| Presenting Percy | 170 |
| Road To Respect | 170 |

#### How the past ten winners rated

| Year | Winner | Win RPR | Pre-race RPR |
|---|---|---|---|
| 2018 | Native River | 178 | 174 |
| 2017 | Sizing John | 171 | 168 |
| 2016 | Don Cossack | 182 | 181 |
| 2015 | Coneygree | 178 | 168 |
| 2014 | Lord Windermere | 170 | 157 |
| 2013 | Bobs Worth | 181 | 174 |
| 2012 | Synchronised | 173 | 171 |
| 2011 | Long Run | 181 | 181 |
| 2010 | Imperial Commander | 182 | 177 |
| 2009 | Kauto Star | 185 | 184 |

**10yr winning average RPR: 177**

### CHAMPION HURDLE

| This year's top rated | RPR | |
|---|---|---|
| Apple's Jade* | 175 | |
| Buveur D'Air | 173 | |
| Sharjah | 168 | |
| Laurina* *(right)* | 167 | |
| Melon | 166 | |
| Supasundae | 165 | |
| Call Me Lord | 164 | |
| Samcro | 163 | |
| Verdana Blue* | 163 | |
| Global Citizen | 160 | |
| Brain Power | 159 | *Includes |
| Silver Streak | 159 | 7lb mares' |
| Wholestone | 159 | allowance |

#### How the past ten winners rated

| Year | Winner | Win RPR | Pre-race RPR |
|---|---|---|---|
| 2018 | Buveur D'Air | 167 | 171 |
| 2017 | Buveur D'Air | 170 | 159 |
| 2016 | Annie Power | 162 | 164 |
| 2015 | Faugheen | 170 | 169 |
| 2014 | Jezki | 173 | 167 |
| 2013 | Hurricane Fly | 173 | 173 |
| 2012 | Rock On Ruby | 171 | 166 |
| 2011 | Hurricane Fly | 171 | 169 |
| 2010 | Binocular | 172 | 172 |
| 2009 | Punjabi | 165 | 164 |

**10yr winning average RPR: 170**

Optimism is often tempered when a horse wins a slow-pace Grade 1 in Ireland because the form doesn't always translate to a furious tempo at Cheltenham, but in this instance his success seems to have been underplayed.

He travelled really well throughout, suggesting a stronger pace is well within his range, and he had everything in trouble turning in before pulling well clear from the last to score by seven and a half lengths.

Every aspect of his performance suggested there could be more to come and if he clicks at Cheltenham he looks a player.

Clan Des Obeaux (177) improved his RPR by 9lb to beat Thistlecrack (174) in the King George VI Chase. He would take some beating if he could improve again but he's been beaten on all four starts at Cheltenham and on both starts over distances beyond 3m.

Bellshill (172) jumps and stays and could plug on into the places.

### ■ CHAMPION HURDLE

I like Apple's Jade (175*) in the match of the season. She is enjoying one of the best seasons of any horse and she can put it up to Buveur D'Air (173) as he bids for a third win in the Tuesday showpiece.

The Irish mare has won four times in open company since November, at distances ranging from 2m to 3m, by margins of 11 to 26 lengths. She has simply looked untouchable.

She has been beaten at Cheltenham in the past, including in the Mares' Hurdle last year, but she was in season for that race and she had won it the previous year.

The most important thing with Apple's Jade, though, is that she is operating at a completely different level this season and has recorded her three best career RPRs on her last three starts.

Buveur D'Air may well go off favourite, as

it is hard to ignore that he has won the last two Champion Hurdles and has been beaten just once since the 2016 festival.

He looked better than ever when beating Samcro in the Fighting Fifth in December but he ran below that when beaten by stablemate Verdana Blue on his next start, returning an RPR of just 164.

Apple's Jade will receive a 7lb mares' allowance from Buveur D'Air, giving her a 2lb advantage on RPR, and that could make all the difference.

The other one worth a mention is Sharjah (168), who has recorded big victories over Faugheen and Supasundae in Grade 1s this season. He flopped at Cheltenham last year but has improved this term and could make his presence felt with his sharp turn of foot.

I don't fancy Laurina over 2m on better ground. She's been dominant against the mares but these are just not her conditions.

## ■ CHAMPION CHASE

This is all about Altior. If he was a year older or had shown even the tiniest crack in the armour it could be worth a look elsewhere but he's been as strong as ever this season and goes to Cheltenham with sky-high expectations.

He's 17 from 17 over fences and hurdles and has run out an easy winner at the last three festivals. He has produced RPRs of 178-180 on all three starts this season and the only Champion Chase winners to run bigger figures in the past decade were Sprinter Sacre (190) and Altior himself last year (183).

If he runs below his best we will be looking to Willie Mullins to fill the void with Min (176) or Footpad (172).

Min has recorded two strong wins in Ireland this season and remains clear second best in the division, but he was seven lengths behind Altior in last year's Champion Chase and in the 2016 Supreme. You have to wonder how he is going to close the gap.

Footpad hacked up by 14 lengths in the Arkle last year and looked a real danger to Altior but he has failed to win in two starts this season.

## CHAMPION CHASE

| This year's top rated | RPR |
|---|---|
| Altior | 183 |
| Min | 176 |
| Un De Sceaux | 174 |
| Politologue (right) | 173 |
| Footpad | 172 |
| Fox Norton | 172 |
| God's Own | 166 |
| Saint Calvados | 165 |
| Diego Du Charmil | 164 |
| Sceau Royal | 164 |
| Simply Ned | 164 |

### How the past ten winners rated

| Year | Winner | Win RPR | Pre-race RPR |
|---|---|---|---|
| 2018 | Altior | 183 | 177 |
| 2017 | Special Tiara | 170 | 170 |
| 2016 | Sprinter Sacre | 176 | 173 |
| 2015 | Dodging Bullets | 169 | 173 |
| 2014 | Sire De Grugy | 173 | 174 |
| 2013 | Sprinter Sacre | 190 | 178 |
| 2012 | Finian's Rainbow | 175 | 167 |
| 2011 | Sizing Europe | 176 | 166 |
| 2010 | Big Zeb | 172 | 171 |
| 2009 | Master Minded | 169 | 186 |

**10yr winning average RPR: 175**

Fox Norton (172) has good form at Cheltenham and is worth a look at bigger odds.

## ■ STAYERS' HURDLE

The staying hurdles division is typically weak and when a good horse comes along they can dominate. Paisley Park is a good one.

He's on a roll with four wins out of four this season and he tops the RPRs after running out an impressive 12-length winner of the Cleeve Hurdle in January. There was a true festival-style pace that day and he stayed on much the best at the business end to win by daylight.

That win earned him a huge career-best RPR of 172, which ranks him up with the best staying hurdlers of the last ten years. In the last ten years just two Stayers' Hurdle winners earned higher RPRs than that – and they were the thoroughly dominant pair Thistlecrack (178) and Big Buck's (176).

# Injured Jockeys Fund

We provide appropriate support in a prompt and sympathetic manner to those jockeys, past or present, who are injured, unable to ride, or generally in need.

As a not-for-profit, self funding organisation we are reliant on the support and generosity of our supporters.

To find out how you can become involved and support the Injured Jockeys Fund or make a donation please visit us at:

# www.ijf.org.uk or call: 01638 662246

**Compassion • Care • Support**

The Injured Jockeys Fund (Registered Charity No. 1107395)

**Brough Scott** MBE
Chairman - Injured Jockeys Fund

## STAYERS' HURDLE

| This year's top rated | RPR |
|---|---|
| Apple's Jade* | 175 |
| Paisley Park | 172 |
| Faugheen | 171 |
| Melon | 166 |
| Supasundae (right) | 165 |
| Samcro | 163 |
| Agrapart | 162 |
| Penhill | 162 |
| Benie Des Dieux* | 159 |
| Coquin Mans | 159 |
| Wholestone | 159 |

*Includes 7lb mares' allowance

### How the past ten winners rated

| Year | Winner | Win RPR | Pre-race RPR |
|---|---|---|---|
| 2018 | Penhill | 162 | 158 |
| 2017 | Nichols Canyon | 164 | 166 |
| 2016 | Thistlecrack | 178 | 172 |
| 2015 | Cole Harden | 168 | 158 |
| 2014 | More Of That | 172 | 161 |
| 2013 | Solwhit | 166 | 165 |
| 2012 | Big Buck's | 170 | 175 |
| 2011 | Big Buck's | 162 | 176 |
| 2010 | Big Buck's | 174 | 176 |
| 2009 | Big Buck's | 176 | 166 |

**10yr winning average RPR: 169**

## RYANAIR

| Top rated | RPR |
|---|---|
| Cyrname† | 181 |
| Frodon | 176 |
| Min | 176 |
| Balko Des Flos | 174 |
| Un De Sceaux | 174 |
| Waiting Patiently | 174 |
| Politologue | 173 |
| Bellshill | 172 |
| Footpad | 172 |
| Fox Norton | 172 |
| Kemboy | 172 |
| Road To Respect | 170 |

†Needs to be supplemented

**10yr winning average RPR: 171**

## RSA

| Top rated | RPR |
|---|---|
| La Bague Au Roi* | 161 |
| Delta Work | 160 |
| Topofthegame | 160 |
| The Worlds End | 159 |
| Drinks Interval* | 157 |
| Santini | 157 |
| Ok Corral | 156 |
| Top Ville Ben | 156 |
| Drovers Lane | 154 |
| Spiritofthegames | 154 |
| Vinndication | 154 |
| Talkischeap | 153 |

*Includes 7lb mares' allowance

**10yr winning average RPR: 164**

Faugheen (171) is likely to arrive as the second best on RPRs judged on his big victory over Penhill in the Champion Stayers Hurdle at Punchestown in April, but he is getting on now and has run below that level in two starts this season.

Penhill (162) has a great Cheltenham record but still has something to prove on the ratings. They went a steady pace when he won last year's Stayers' Hurdle and it turned into a sprint. He may be capable of better off a strong pace but Paisley Park sets a high standard.

### ◼ RYANAIR CHASE

Cyrname (181) needs to be supplemented but he would be the number one pick after trouncing Waiting Patiently (174) at Ascot in February.

Prior to that meeting Waiting Patiently had looked a budding star over this intermediate trip but Cyrname's 17-length victory makes him the new kid on the block.

Min (176) would be interesting if he tackled the race as he does stay this far but he may run in the Champion Chase.

Footpad (172) has not had a great season but last year's Arkle win was hugely promising and he has hurdles form over this trip.

### ◼ NOVICE CHASES

Delta Work (160) is the one to beat in the RSA Chase after landing the Grade 1 Neville Hotels Novice Chase at Leopardstown by eight lengths.

That contest is often a good trial for Cheltenham, with Bostons Angel (2011) and Don Poli (2015) doubling up in the RSA, Back In Focus taking the National Hunt Chase (2013) and Shattered Love going on to win the JLT (2018).

Delta Work was more impressive than those past Leopardstown winners and he has a festival win in the bag already (the 2018 Pertemps Final over hurdles).

Topofthegame (160) looks the leading British hope despite losing both starts over fences this season. In fairness he was left at the start on his chase debut before staying on for an unlikely second and then he finished a good second to La Bague Au Roi in a Grade 1 at Kempton.

*Arkle players: Lalor has a big shout if he can bounce back to the form of his debut over fences; Ireland's best hope appears to be Le Richebourg (below)*

## ARKLE

| Top rated | RPR |
| --- | --- |
| Lalor | 160 |
| Le Richebourg | 160 |
| Kalashnikov | 158 |
| Knocknanuss | 158 |
| Ornua | 157 |
| Winter Escape | 157 |
| Defi Du Seuil | 156 |
| Glen Forsa | 155 |
| Diakali | 154 |
| Duc Des Genievres | 153 |
| Hardline | 152 |
| Us And Them | 152 |

**10yr winning average RPR: 167**

## BALLYMORE

| Top rated | RPR |
| --- | --- |
| Fakir D'Oudairies** | 156 |
| Al Dancer | 152 |
| Grand Sancy | 151 |
| Champ | 150 |
| Dinons | 148 |
| Birchdale | 147 |
| Brewin'upastorm | 147 |
| Felix Desjy | 147 |
| Aramon | 146 |
| Rhinestone | 146 |
| Salsaretta** | 146 |
| Commander Of Fleet | 145 |
| Easy Game | 145 |
| City Island | 145 |
| Angels Breath | 144 |
| Battleoverdoyen | 144 |
| Getareason | 144 |
| Getaway Trump | 144 |
| Honeysuckle** | 144 |
| Klassical Dream | 144 |
| Robin De Carlow** | 144 |

*\*\*Includes age/ sex allowance*

**10yr winning average RPR: 156**

He was a decent hurdler, having finished second in last year's Coral Cup, and he is built to be a better chaser. He should improve again and looks the best bet against Delta Work, with Santini (157) looking a silly price and La Bague Au Roi (161, with her mares' allowance) having a poor Cheltenham record and unlikely to turn up.

The Arkle looks highly competitive. With Dynamite Dollars out for the rest of the season, the leading six contenders on RPR are separated by just 3lb. The ten-year average stands at 167, with a high of 176 and a low of 161, so whatever wins will probably need to improve.

Le Richebourg (160) is the clear pick of the Irish after comfortably landing Grade 1 events at Leopardstown in December and February. He needs to improve again but he is heading the right way and a better pace could see him step up.

Lalor (160) would be a player if he can bounce back from his dire performance at Sandown, where something was clearly amiss. Connections blamed the ground that day but he has plenty of form on soft in the past, so whether that is the only explanation is open to doubt. If there was a valid excuse that day a good case could be made for him based on his monster debut success at Cheltenham, where he earned an RPR of 160.

### ■ NOVICE HURDLES

Champ (150) looks a rock-solid favourite for the Ballymore. He is the only likely runner with an RPR of 150 or over and the way he travelled in the early stages of his two races at Newbury in December suggests there could be even more to come off a stronger pace.

The ten-year average RPR for winners of the Ballymore Novices' Hurdle stands at 156 and most winners tend to go into the race with a mark around 151.

Connections have held on to the 'Champ' moniker for a while. They were saving it for a special horse and nothing in the novice ranks will live with him if he puts in the sort of performance he has threatened.

Second favourite Battleoverdoyen (144) is unbeaten but the form of the Grade 1 he won at Naas was not brilliant and he will need to find more.

In the shorter races Joseph O'Brien could be king as he has the three highest-rated contenders for the Triumph Hurdle. He may not throw all his four-year-olds at the Triumph, so the question becomes where each of them will run.

Fakir D'Oudairies (147) is his number one. He is very professional for his age, with experience in France, Ireland and Britain. He is also a slick jumper and proved himself up Cheltenham's hill when charging away to win the Grade 2 Triumph Trial by 13 lengths in January.

Judged on that effort he could easily take the Triumph but he is also entered in the Supreme, where he would receive an 8lb concession from the older horses. That would make him the number one contender for that race too.

The ten-year average RPR for Supreme winners stands at 157 and, if you add on his four-year-old weight concession, Fakir D'Oudairies effectively sits on 155.

Sir Erec (146) is O'Brien's next best on RPR. He is very different from his stablemate as he is all raw talent, unproven off a strong pace but with huge potential.

The ten-year average RPR for Triumph winners is 151 and the way he won the Spring Juvenile Hurdle suggested that is well within his range. He isn't as experienced as his higher-rated stablemate and is likely to be kept to his age group at Cheltenham.

If O'Brien doesn't send Fakir D'Oudairies to the Supreme, the Willie Mullins-trained Klassical Dream (144) could be the one. He will need to improve to hit the normal standard but he travelled really well on both starts in Ireland and there should be more to come.

Al Dancer (152) is the leading British-based novice hurdler and looks the home team's best hope for the Supreme after his impressive Betfair Hurdle success.

In the Albert Bartlett I like the Gordon Elliott pair Commander Of Fleet and Dinons. Commander Of Fleet (145) took a big step forward to win a Grade 1 at Leopardstown and is entitled to improve for the step up in trip.

Despite being an outsider, Dinons is actually top-rated for the Albert Bartlett on RPRs. He stays forever and has loads of experience, including at Cheltenham.

He had loads of excuses when beaten at Navan in November (drop in trip, sprint finish, hampered, seventh run in four months) and at the price (28-1) I'm more than happy to overlook that defeat considering his earlier strong form over 3m.

Fakir D'Oudairies: top juvenile hurdler

| SUPREME | |
| --- | --- |
| Top rated | RPR |
| Fakir D'Oudairies** | 155 |
| Al Dancer | 152 |
| Grand Sancy | 151 |
| Gardens Of Babylon** | 149 |
| Brewin'upastorm | 147 |
| Felix Desjy | 147 |
| Aramon | 146 |
| Commander Of Fleet | 145 |
| Easy Game | 145 |
| Surin** | 145 |
| Angels Breath | 144 |
| Battleoverdoyen | 144 |
| Getaway Trump | 144 |
| Klassical Dream | 144 |
| Triplicate | 143 |
| Come To Me | 142 |
| Jetez | 142 |
| Mister Fisher | 142 |
| Relegate** | 142 |
| **Includes age/ sex allowance | |
| 10yr winning average RPR: 157 | |

| TRIUMPH | |
| --- | --- |
| Top rated | RPR |
| Fakir D'Oudairies | 147 |
| Sir Erec | 146 |
| Gardens Of Babylon | 141 |
| Pic D'Orhy | 138 |
| Adjali | 137 |
| Quel Destin | 137 |
| Surin* | 137 |
| Torpillo | 136 |
| Chief Justice | 135 |
| Tiger Tap Tap | 135 |
| Coeur Sublime | 133 |
| Got Trumped | 132 |
| *Includes 7lb mares' allowance | |
| 10yr winning average RPR: 151 | |

# Buveur set to land hat-trick

**By Dave Edwards**

### ■ GOLD CUP

A Topspeed rating of at least 157 has been needed to lift the Gold Cup in eight of the last ten years and the same number of winners had achieved a pre-race figure in excess of 150.

Although Native River set some punishing fractions in front 12 months ago his effort was perfectly judged by Richard Johnson and the defending champ looks the one to beat again. He has run a couple of solid races in defeat this term at Haydock and Kempton and will relish a return to Cheltenham.

Might Bite, a gallant runner-up last year, has plenty to prove now after a couple of lacklustre

efforts. King George winner Clan Des Obeaux will deservedly have his supporters, but leading fancy Presenting Percy has a personal best of just 106 and has questions to answer on the clock.

### ■ CHAMPION HURDLE

Although dual winner Buveur D'Air had his wings clipped by stablemate Verdana Blue at Kempton in December he looks on course to retain his crown. Only three of the last ten winners had a pre-race figure below 150 and the 160 he clocked in 2017 has been bettered just twice in the past decade. He recorded his best figure (147) since then in defeat at Kempton and got back to winning ways at Sandown in February. The majority of his

## GOLD CUP

| Topspeed figures | Career best | Season best |
|---|---|---|
| Native River | 167 | 152 |
| Might Bite | 162 | 127 |
| Anibale Fly | 158 | 97 |
| Clan Des Obeaux | 157 | 157 |
| Balko Des Flos | 156 | 95 |
| Bristol De Mai | 156 | 156 |
| Thistlecrack | 155 | 155 |
| Minella Rocco | 155 | - |
| Road To Respect | 154 | 82 |
| Blaklion | 153 | 103 |

### How the past ten winners rated

| Year | Winner | Win TS | Pre-race TS |
|---|---|---|---|
| 2018 | Native River | 167 | 154 |
| 2017 | Sizing John | 158 | 146 |
| 2016 | Don Cossack | 167 | 165 |
| 2015 | Coneygree | 169 | 152 |
| 2014 | Lord Windermere | 144 | 123 |
| 2013 | Bobs Worth | 144 | 164 |
| 2012 | Synchronised | 164 | 151 |
| 2011 | Long Run | 157 | 163 |
| 2010 | Imperial Commander | 180 | 173 |
| 2009 | Kauto Star | 172 | 176 |

## CHAMPION HURDLE

| Topspeed figures | Career best | Season best |
|---|---|---|
| Buveur D'Air | 160 | 147 |
| Apple's Jade* | 157 | 157 |
| Petit Mouchoir | 152 | 118 |
| Verdana Blue* | 149 | 147 |
| Brain Power | 148 | 123 |
| Supasundae | 147 | 139 |
| Melon | 145 | 132 |
| Cilaos Emery | 143 | - |
| Samcro | 143 | 143 |
| Mohaayed | 142 | 142 |
| Sharjah | 140 | 140 |
| Silver Streak | 140 | 140 |
| Wholestone | 139 | 139 |

*Includes 7lb mares' allowance

### How the past ten winners rated

| Year | Winner | Win TS | Pre-race TS |
|---|---|---|---|
| 2018 | Buveur D'Air | 145 | 160 |
| 2017 | Buveur D'Air | 160 | 143 |
| 2016 | Annie Power | 154 | 139 |
| 2015 | Faugheen | 132 | 141 |
| 2014 | Jezki | 160 | 151 |
| 2013 | Hurricane Fly | 135 | 161 |
| 2012 | Rock On Ruby | 167 | 160 |
| 2011 | Hurricane Fly | 149 | 153 |
| 2010 | Binocular | 163 | 158 |
| 2009 | Punjabi | 155 | 160 |

rivals look pretty exposed but Apple's Jade threw down the gauntlet when she left her rivals standing in the Irish Champion Hurdle and rates as the obvious stumbling block. She is a class act and the 7lb mares' allowance is an added bonus.

Laurina has not put a foot wrong in five starts since joining Willie Mullins but a lifetime-best speed figure of 133 leaves her with plenty to find. She has been in her comfort zone so far and it will be interesting to see if her jumping holds up amid the usual frenetic pace of a Champion Hurdle.

*Big match: Buveur D'Air (facing page) and Apple's Jade*

## CHAMPION CHASE

| Topspeed figures | Career best | Season best |
|---|---|---|
| Altior | 159 | 159 |
| Footpad | 158 | 147 |
| Un De Sceaux | 158 | 113 |
| Politologue | 154 | 138 |
| Min | 153 | 136 |
| Fox Norton | 153 | 151 |
| God's Own | 150 | 130 |
| Simply Ned | 148 | 148 |
| Forest Bihan | 147 | 147 |
| Doctor Phoenix | 146 | 131 |
| Sceau Royal | 145 | 145 |

### How the past ten winners rated

| Year | Winner | Win TS | Pre-race TS |
|---|---|---|---|
| 2018 | Altior | 152 | 154 |
| 2017 | Special Tiara | 154 | 156 |
| 2016 | Sprinter Sacre | 159 | 165 |
| 2015 | Dodging Bullets | 144 | 159 |
| 2014 | Sire De Grugy | 152 | 158 |
| 2013 | Sprinter Sacre | 153 | 165 |
| 2012 | Finian's Rainbow | 159 | 154 |
| 2011 | Sizing Europe | 146 | 166 |
| 2010 | Big Zeb | 168 | 159 |
| 2009 | Master Minded | 161 | 185 |

## STAYERS' HURDLE

| Topspeed figures | Career best | Season best |
|---|---|---|
| Apple's Jade* | 157 | 157 |
| Faugheen | 152 | 132 |
| Petit Mouchoir | 152 | 133 |
| Top Notch | 150 | 107 |
| Supasundae | 147 | 139 |
| Melon | 145 | 132 |
| Yanworth | 145 | - |
| Old Guard | 144 | 144 |
| Lil Rockerfeller | 144 | 118 |
| Samcro | 143 | 143 |
| Paisley Park | 141 | 141 |
| Wholestone | 139 | 139 |
| Penhill | 138 | - |

*Includes 7lb mares' allowance

### How the past ten winners rated

| Year | Winner | Win TS | Pre-race TS |
|---|---|---|---|
| 2018 | Penhill | 93 | 138 |
| 2017 | Nichols Canyon | 145 | 156 |
| 2016 | Thistlecrack | 158 | 133 |
| 2015 | Cole Harden | 151 | 135 |
| 2014 | More Of That | 135 | 118 |
| 2013 | Solwhit | 31 | 167 |
| 2012 | Big Buck's | 161 | 154 |
| 2011 | Big Buck's | 119 | 147 |
| 2010 | Big Buck's | 139 | 147 |
| 2009 | Big Buck's | 131 | 147 |

### ■ CHAMPION CHASE

Only the brave or foolish will oppose Altior, who is unbeaten in a dozen starts over fences. The past ten winners all boasted a pre-race rating of 154 or more, although only five of them had to run to that level in the race itself.

Altior suffered an interrupted preparation on his way to last year's race but was still a cut above the opposition with a seven-length victory over Min and it is hard to envisage defeat for Nicky Henderson's polished performer.

Although eased on the run-in, he produced a career-best effort on this timepiece when slamming Fox Norton at Ascot in January and it will take an exceptional performer to lower his colours.

Footpad, who clocked an astonishing time when landing the Arkle 12 months ago, has blotted his copybook in both starts this term but could be a threat at his best, although he also holds a Ryanair Chase entry.

### ■ STAYERS' HURDLE

As the accompanying list of recent winners vividly illustrates, this race often turns into a test more of speed than stamina. That was certainly true last year when Penhill's 93 was the second-lowest winning figure in the race in the past decade.

Surprisingly for a championship race a rating above 150 has been achieved in victory only three times in the last ten years and in the same period just three winners boasted a pre-race figure above that mark. The pre-race ten-year average is a moderate 144 and the race average only 126, and such modest yardsticks mean there are plenty with prospects on paper.

Paisley Park shot to the head of the market when stretching his winning streak to four in a truly run Cleeve Hurdle in January. He has solid claims but it may pay to take a chance

*Waiting Patiently: class act on figures and entitled to improve*

with Faugheen. A dual festival winner in the 2014 Neptune and 2015 Champion Hurdle, he has had his issues but should not be written off at this trip.

### ■ RYANAIR CHASE

It is testament to the quality of this race that a rating above 150 has been required for victory in each of the past ten seasons and only four of the winners had a pre-race rating below that mark.

Waiting Patiently has won six of his seven completed starts over fences – having unseated in the King George when badly hampered – and his Ascot Chase win last season bore the hallmark of class. He was well beaten by Cyrname at Ascot last time but is entitled to improve and it may pay to keep the faith. Ease underfoot is a prerequisite for Ruth Jefferson's stable star, who has yet to race at Cheltenham but is well capable of passing this acid test.

Min, winner of both starts this term, and last season's Arkle winner Footpad merit the utmost respect but trainer Willie Mullins has other options with them at the festival.

## RYANAIR CHASE

| Topspeed figures | Career best | Season best |
|---|---|---|
| Footpad | 158 | 147 |
| Un De Sceaux | 158 | 113 |
| Waiting Patiently | 157 | 134 |
| Balko Des Flos | 156 | 95 |
| Politologue | 154 | 138 |
| Road To Respect | 154 | 82 |
| Fox Norton | 153 | 151 |
| Min | 153 | 136 |
| Sub Lieutenant | 153 | 130 |
| Top Notch | 152 | 152 |
| Aso | 151 | 132 |
| Charbel | 147 | 147 |

### How the past ten winners rated

| Year | Winner | Win TS | Pre-race TS |
|---|---|---|---|
| 2018 | Balko Des Flos | 156 | 139 |
| 2017 | Un De Sceaux | 158 | 155 |
| 2016 | Vautour | 163 | 150 |
| 2015 | Uxizandre | 163 | 130 |
| 2014 | Dynaste | 160 | 127 |
| 2013 | Cue Card | 151 | 156 |
| 2012 | Riverside Theatre | 162 | 160 |
| 2011 | Albertas Run | 157 | 152 |
| 2010 | Albertas Run | 152 | 148 |
| 2009 | Imperial Commander | 159 | 160 |

### ■ TIGER ROLL

Three Cheltenham Festival wins was a rare enough feat for Tiger Roll but adding Grand National victory put him in a similar bracket as Golden Miller, the legendary 1930s chaser who took five Cheltenham Gold Cups as well as the National. Tiger Roll does not have the same class but has had a remarkable journey from Triumph Hurdle victory in 2014 to winning the National Hunt Chase in 2017 and the Cross Country Chase and National last year. A fourth festival success for Gordon Elliott's brave little battler when he returns for the Cross Country would set him up nicely for his National defence.

### ■ BENIE DES DIEUX

The French import was having her first start over hurdles for Willie Mullins when she upset odds-on favourite Apple's Jade in last year's Mares' Hurdle and, with that rival likely to go for the Champion Hurdle this time, she looks the one to beat again. Any doubt stems from her long absence since last year's Punchestown festival, where she won the Grade 1 Mares Champion Hurdle, but Mullins often takes an unconventional route with his mares. Quevega won the Mares' Hurdle at Cheltenham six times, mainly on her seasonal debut, while Benie Des Dieux was campaigned over fences before last year's success.

*Been there and done that: Benie Des Dieux (left) and Tiger Roll*

### ■ SUPASUNDAE

The 2017 Coral Cup winner is set for a fifth consecutive visit to the festival as he bids to go one better than last year's second place behind Penhill in the Stayers' Hurdle. Jessica Harrington has campaigned him in Grade 1s since the Coral Cup and he has proved a capable and consistent performer at that level, winning the Irish Champion Hurdle and Punchestown Champion Hurdle at 2m and finishing a close second on all three starts at 3m.

### ■ PACHA DU POLDER

A storming finish up the hill by Pacha Du Polder in the Foxhunter has become a festival staple and the grand old campaigner might well come alive again as he tries to complete a hat-trick at the age of 12. His first bid under Victoria Pendleton saw him finish a close fifth in 2016 but he triumphed by a neck under then amateur Bryony Frost the following year and did it again in 2018, by the same margin, for Harriet Tucker (*right*), who remarkably got him home despite a "half-dislocated" shoulder that prevented her from using her whip.

## ■ FOOTPAD

No other Grade 1 winner at last year's festival came close to the margin of victory recorded by Footpad as he surged to a 14-length success in the Racing Post Arkle Chase and, while he has had a couple of setbacks this season, a return to that form would make him a dangerous contender. Altior, his predecessor as Arkle winner, would stand in the way in the Queen Mother Champion Chase but Willie Mullins could opt to step him up in trip for the Ryanair Chase.

## ■ THE STORYTELLER

Last season ended in memorable fashion for The Storyteller, who landed a huge gamble in the Brown Advisory & Merriebelle Stable Plate at the festival and then scored a dramatic Grade 1 win in a Punchestown novice chase. This season the Gordon Elliott-trained eight-year-old has form figures of 5463 but a strong pace could be what he needs and he might be an outsider to watch in the Ryanair Chase. Alternatively, Elliott could send him back over hurdles in the Coral Cup off a similar mark to last year's chase win and over the same trip.

**Racing Post analysts Richard Lowther and Dave Orton assess the winter action**

# Kemboy can strike Gold

### ■ GOLD CUP

Presenting Percy has been solid near the head of the market all season for the Magners Cheltenham Gold Cup despite being kept out of the fray in the major chases. The RSA winner did not have an outing until January and then it was over hurdles, in a Grade 2 event at Galway, although there was plenty to like about Presenting Percy's victory. He had won the same race on the way to last year's festival, with his final warm-up coming in the Red Mills Chase at Gowran Park, but this time he sidestepped that Grade 2 over fences.

All in all, a most unconventional build-up.

The five runners in the Betfair Chase at Haydock in November were all making their first appearances of the season, among them Native River and Might Bite, who had fought out a compelling Gold Cup finish in March. Native River had a pleasing comeback, staying on steadily for a four-length second behind Bristol De Mai, who had won the previous year's Betfair by no less than 57 lengths. Might Bite, however, found little for pressure and finished a tired last, Nicky Henderson reporting that the gelding had been left

*Kemboy: one of the young improvers in the Gold Cup field*

## VITAL STATISTICS
## Races with the 'festival factor'

**BetVictor Gold Cup**

Cheltenham, November 17, 2018, 2m4f, good

1 **Baron Alco** 7 10-11 Jamie Moore 8-1

2 **Frodon** 6 11-12 B Frost 16-1

3 **Guitar Pete** 8 10-2 B Hughes 12-1

4 **Mister Whitaker** 6 11-3 A Heskin 6-1f

Trainer: Gary Moore

Distances: 2l, 8l, ¾l; 18 ran

*Festival pointer This has been one of the better races for finding a festival winner and last year Le Prezien took the Grand Annual after finishing third here, while winner Splash Of Ginge and fourth-placed Ballyalton finished second and fourth in the Stable Plate at 25-1 and 16-1. Four of the first five Ryanair winners came out of this race (and the other was a former winner of this race) but it has not had the same influence in recent years*

🏇*Four festival winners have come out of this race in the past ten years*

**Betfair Chase**

Haydock, November 24, 2018, 3m1½f, good

1 **Bristol De Mai** 7 11-7 D Jacob 13-2

2 **Native River** 8 11-7 R Johnson 5-2

3 **Thistlecrack** 10 11-7 T Scudamore 10-1

Trainer: Nigel Twiston-Davies

Distances: 4l, 1¾l; 5 ran

*Festival pointer Betfair Chase winners to run in the Gold Cup had finishing positions of 012P3PPF7FF (only Kauto Star in 2006-07 has won both in the same season)*

🏇*Three festival winners in the past ten years*

## VITAL STATISTICS
## Races with the 'festival factor'

**BetVictor Fighting Fifth Hurdle**

Newcastle, December 1, 2018, 2m½f, soft

1 **Buveur D'Air** 7 11-7 B Geraghty 11-8

2 **Samcro** 6 11-7 J Kennedy 6-5f

3 **Vision Des Flos** 5 11-7 R Power 14-1

Trainer: Nicky Henderson

Distances: 8l, 13l; 5 ran

*Festival pointer The key British trial for the Champion Hurdle in recent years, featuring the winners of 2008, 2009, 2010 and 2018, the runner-up in 2011, 2012, 2014 and 2015 and the third in 2013 and 2017 (their respective finishing positions in the Fighting Fifth were 31511113F1). Last year Buveur D'Air became only the second to do the Fighting Fifth-Champion double in the past 20 years (the other was Punjabi in 2008-09)*

🏇*Four festival winners in the past ten years*

**Ladbrokes Trophy Chase**

Newbury, December 1, 2018, 3m2f, soft

1 **Sizing Tennessee** 10 11-3 T Scudamore 12-1

2 **Elegant Escape** 6 11-10 H Cobden 4-1

3 **Dingo Dollar** 6 11-3 W Hutchinson 10-1

4 **Beware The Bear** 8 11-3 J McGrath 14-1

Trainer: Colin Tizzard

Distances: 10l, 7l, 15l; 12 ran

*Festival pointer Six of the past seven runnings of this often informative race have featured a subsequent festival winner, most recently Missed Approach (sixth here, won last year's Fulke Walwyn Kim Muir Handicap Chase). The 2014 Gold Cup winner Lord Windermere had finished eighth here that season; before that Denman (2007-08) and Bobs Worth (2012-13) completed the Hennessy-Gold Cup double and the 2011, 2012 and 2015 Gold Cup runners-up came from this race*

🏇*Seven festival winners in the past ten years*

in "panic mode" by the bigger-than-usual Haydock fences, which attracted criticism on the day. Thistlecrack showed his engine was fully intact in third but was another to have difficulty with the obstacles, while the youngest horse in the field, Clan Des Obeaux, was a promising fourth.

The five Betfair Chase runners reconvened on Boxing Day in the King George VI Chase, with a somewhat different outcome. This time it was Clan Des Obeaux who came out on top, Paul Nicholls' gelding travelling well before finding enough despite idling to beat Thistlecrack by a length and a half. In February Clan Des Obeaux cemented his Gold Cup claims with an impressive defeat of Terrefort in the Denman Chase at Ascot. The

## VITAL STATISTICS

### Races with the 'festival factor'

**Betfair Tingle Creek Chase**

Sandown, December 8, 2018, 1m7½f, soft

1 **Altior** 8 11-7 N de Boinville 8-13f

2 **Un De Sceaux** 10 11-7 R Walsh 7-2

3 **Saint Calvados** 5 11-7 G Sheehan 8-1

Trainer: Nicky Henderson

Distances: 4l, 15l; 4 ran

*Festival pointer The key guide to the Champion Chase. Seven of the 20 to try have won both races since the Tingle Creek became a Grade 1 and the Champion Chase winner had run in the Tingle Creek in 11 of the past 18 years*

🐎 *Six festival winners in the past ten years*

### Caspian Caviar Gold Cup

Cheltenham, December 15, 2018, 2m4½f, good

1 **Frodon** 6 11-12 B Frost 7-1

2 **Cepage** 6 10-5 C Deutsch 12-1

3 **Guitar Pete** 8 10-0 R Day 13-2

4 **Baron Alco** 7 11-0 Jamie Moore 5-1

Trainer: Paul Nicholls

Distances: 1¼l, 15l, 2¼l; 12 ran

*Festival pointer None of the festival scorers to come out of this race in the past ten years had won here, with the latest example being last year's eighth Le Prezien, who dropped in trip to land the Grand Annual. The first three Ryanair Chase winners ran in this race (form figures of 2B3) but none has since and nowadays it is more likely to be a guide to the handicap chases (last season's seventh, third and fourth finished second, third and fourth in the Stable Plate)*

🐎 *Four festival winners in the past ten years*

'Thistlecrack jumped better in the King George than he had at Haydock and ran as well as he ever has over fences'

seven-year-old is improving quickly and has a fine chance on the figures, but Cheltenham will place extra demands on his stamina.

Thistlecrack jumped better in the King George than he had at Haydock and ran as well as he ever has over fences, while Native River, unsuited by the right-handed and relatively sharp circuit, performed right up to expectations in third. The Gold Cup winner missed the Denman Chase in favour of heading straight for Cheltenham after it was delayed a week and moved to right-handed Ascot.

Betfair winner Bristol De Mai was on the deck with a circuit to run in the King George and, although Might Bite completed, it was in last place. He was reported to have bled, while in early January he underwent a wind operation. That hard race in last season's Gold Cup seems to have left lasting marks.

*Battle royal: Clan Des Obeaux (right) beats Thistlecrack in the King George VI Chase*

## VITAL STATISTICS
### Races with the 'festival factor'

**Unibet International Hurdle**

Cheltenham, December 15, 2018
2m1f, good to soft

1 **Brain Power** 7 11-0 N de Boinville 7-1
2 **Silver Streak** 5 11-4 B Geraghty 9-2
3 **Western Ryder** 6 11-0 R Johnson 4-1f
Trainer: Nicky Henderson
Distances: 1¾l, 2¼l; 8 ran

***Festival pointer*** Rooster Booster (2002-03) is the only winner of this race to land the Champion Hurdle since Comedy Of Errors (1974-75) and it has been a poor guide recently, with Katchit (2008) the last runner to have gone on to festival success, although Melon was a neck runner-up in last year's Champion after finishing third here. In the past 20 years, two who were beaten here went on to take the Champion Hurdle crown and four of the last eight winners to line up in the Champion finished in the first three

🐎 *No festival winner in the past ten years*

**32Red King George VI Chase**

Kempton, December 26, 2018
3m, good to soft

1 **Clan Des Obeaux** 6 11-10 H Cobden 12-1
2 **Thistlecrack** 10 11-10 T Scudamore 15-2
3 **Native River** 8 11-10 R Johnson 9-2
Trainer: Paul Nicholls
Distances: 1½l, 12l; 10 ran

***Festival pointer*** Six of the last ten festivals have featured at least one winner who had run here. Desert Orchid (1988-89) was the last to complete the King George/Gold Cup double until 2002-2003, since when the double has been done by five of the 12 to try. Since Desert Orchid, 25 festival winners have come out of this race (in the Gold Cup, Champion Chase or Ryanair Chase)

🐎 *Nine festival winners in the past ten years*

A steady improver in his first season over fences, Willie Mullins' Kemboy made a winning return in the Grade 2 Clonmel Oil Chase in November, when he was rather keen, and then had many of the leading Irish contenders, bar Presenting Percy, behind him in the Grade 1 Savills Chase at the Leopardstown Christmas meeting. Allowed to lead by halfway and stepping up the pace, he went on to prove far too strong

*Apple's Jade: can deny
Buveur D'Air a third success*

for Monalee, Road To Respect and Bellshill. This progressive young chaser will be fresh and well on Gold Cup day.

Winner of the Punchestown Gold Cup in April, Bellshill ran out of steam late on when fourth in the Savills and was fitter when he revisited Leopardstown early in February for the Irish Gold Cup. It looked a cracking edition of the race on paper, but unfortunately it wasn't run on paper but on ground that was rather too quick for some trainers' liking, and the race was devalued by six high-profile withdrawals. Two of the four remaining runners produced an epic struggle, Bellshill digging deep to get past a tremendously game Road To Respect to win by a short head.

**Verdict** Kemboy can beat the big guns and give Willie Mullins his first Gold Cup. Thistlecrack should run a big race *(Richard Lowther)*

## ■ CHAMPION HURDLE

The Unibet Champion Hurdle looks a straight fight between Lambourn's Nicky Henderson and the massed forces of the leading Irish stables, who between them are responsible for the major contenders. At the time of writing there was only one British entry not trained by Henderson quoted at under 33-1.

Buveur D'Air has used the same stepping stones to the festival that he did last season, starting with the Fighting Fifth at Newcastle at the beginning of December, then a Boxing Day date at Kempton, followed by Sandown's Contenders Hurdle in early February. This season's Fighting Fifth was billed as a showdown between the reigning champion and young pretender Samcro, the latter even starting favourite, but it proved an uneven contest. A stirring finish looked on the cards as they locked horns going to the final flight,

## Races with the 'festival factor'

**Unibet Christmas Hurdle**

Kempton, December 26, 2018
2m, good to soft
1 **Verdana Blue** 6 11-0 N de Boinville 11-2
2 **Buveur D'Air** 7 11-7 B Geraghty 1-4f
3 **If The Cap Fits** 6 11-7 N Fehily 7-1
Trainer: Nicky Henderson
Distances: shd, 6l; 5 ran

*Festival pointer* Last season Buveur D'Air became only the second to complete the Christmas/Champion Hurdle double since Kribensis in 1989-90 (the other was Faugheen in 2014-15) and there was another festival winner in the four-runner field with third-placed Mohaayed going on to take the County Hurdle. Four beaten horses in the past 17 runnings have landed the Champion (the most recent was 2011 runner-up Rock On Ruby)

🏇 Six festival winners in the past ten years

---

**Savills Chase**

Leopardstown, December 28, 2018
3m, good
1 **Kemboy** 6 11-10 David Mullins 8-1
2 **Monalee** 7 11-10 N Fehily 11-2
3 **Road To Respect** 7 11-10 S Flanagan 9-4f
Trainer: Willie Mullins
Distances: 7½l, hd; 11 ran

*Festival pointer* Four of the past 13 runnings have featured that season's Gold Cup winner. Two were British raiders who won here (Denman and Synchronised) while the two Irish-trained Gold Cup winners to come out of this race were both beaten here (War Of Attrition was runner-up and Lord Windermere was seventh). Last year Balko Des Flos was second here before dropping in trip to win the Ryanair Chase

🏇 Three festival winners in the past ten years

### VITAL STATISTICS

## Races with the 'festival factor'

**Galliardhomes.com Cleeve Hurdle**

Cheltenham, January 26, 2019
3m, good to soft
1 **Paisley Park** 7 11-6 A Coleman 100-30f
2 **West Approach** 9 11-0 T Scudamore 20-1
3 **Black Op** 8 11-3 N Fehily 11-2
Trainer: Emma Lavelle
Distances: 12l, 2l; 12 ran

*Festival pointer* Principally a Stayers' Hurdle trial (three of the past ten winners did the double, most recently Thistlecrack in 2016) but has been used as a successful prep for a variety of races – the Champion Hurdle, National Hunt Chase and Ultima Handicap Chase (four times in the past nine years, most recently with Un Temps Pour Tout in 2017)

🏇 Eight festival winners in the past ten years

---

**BHP Insurance Irish Champion Hurdle**

Leopardstown, February 2, 2019
2m, good to yielding
1 **Apple's Jade** 7 11-3 J Kennedy 8-11f
2 **Supasundae** 9 11-10 R Power 4-1
3 **Petit Mouchoir** 8 11-10 R Blackmore 12-1
Trainer: Gordon Elliott
Distances: 16l, 5l; 6 ran

*Festival pointer* The most important hurdle race in Ireland before the festival, with eight of the 12 Irish-trained winners in the past 20 runnings of the Champion Hurdle having run here (six won). Last year's winner Supasundae went on to finish second in the Stayers' Hurdle, while the Irish placegetters behind Buveur D'Air in the Champion all ran here (Melon fifth, second in the Champion; Mick Jazz third, third; Identity Thief sixth, fourth)

🏇 Four festival winners in the past ten years

---

but despite a mistake there Buveur D'Air quickly left his rival trailing on the run-in to win easily by eight lengths.

Things didn't go to script in the Christmas Hurdle, though. Normally a slick jumper, Buveur D'Air got the third-last all wrong,

losing little momentum but surely softening him up for the finish. He struck the front two out and was still ahead starting on the run-in but couldn't hold off his stablemate Verdana Blue, who caught him on the line. Verdana Blue hasn't been in action since her Christmas success and Henderson has always stressed that she'd need decent ground to have a realistic chance in the Champion Hurdle.

Buveur D'Air hurdled with his usual fluency in the Contenders and scampered away from Vision Des Flos on the run-in to land odds of 1-5, a thoroughly satisfactory trial against limited opposition and a valuable workout for a gelding who isn't the easiest to get fit.

Brain Power, Henderson's third string, failed to get round three times in his novice season over fences and his chasing career was put on hold in December for him to contest the International Hurdle at Cheltenham. Apparently it was his owner Michael Buckley's idea and it proved a canny move as Brain Power won with something to spare after easing to the front on the home turn. He was getting weight from most of his rivals, however, and finished only eighth in the 2017 Champion Hurdle, so he needs to find considerable improvement.

Apple's Jade has enjoyed a terrific season in Ireland, notching Grade 1 wins over two and a half miles (the Hatton's Grace) and three miles (Leopardstown's Christmas Hurdle) before dropping back to two miles for the first time since the 2016 Fighting Fifth in the Irish Champion Hurdle at Leopardstown in February. Allowed a fairly soft lead, she galloped on strongly to thrash Supasundae by 16 lengths, having beaten him by 20 in the Hatton's Grace. Such is her versatility that Apple's Jade is not a certain runner in the Champion Hurdle, but she has a massive chance if she takes that route.

Laurina's 'trial' this season consisted of an incredibly easy win against a single opponent in a Listed mares' hurdle at Sandown in January. That revealed little about her other than her wellbeing, but she's a festival winner, unbeaten since joining Willie Mullins, and we don't yet know the limit of her potential. If she takes up the Champion Hurdle assignment it would be her first run against male opposition.

**Verdict** Apple's Jade can deny Buveur D'Air a third championship *(Richard Lowther)*

### ■ CHAMPION CHASE & RYANAIR CHASE

Altior is an obvious banker for many punters in the Betway Queen Mother Champion Chase, as he'll arrive at Cheltenham unbeaten in 17 races over jumps, with his most recent defeat having come in a bumper in April 2015. Limited to just a single outing before landing last season's Champion Chase, he'll go there this time with three runs under his belt. He was given a race by Un De Sceaux in the Tingle Creek at Sandown until drawing four lengths clear up the hill, before Diego Du Charmil proved 19 lengths his inferior in the Desert Orchid Chase at Kempton over Christmas. Brought out again for a third run in six weeks, Altior faced just two rivals in Ascot's Clarence House Chase and cruised to a seven-length win over a ring-rusty Fox Norton, with Diego Du Charmil a distant third.

Altior has jumped to his left at times during his career but did so much more obviously at Ascot. Nicky Henderson was unfazed, however, saying: "He was doing nothing in front. It's amazing how many horses you'll see jumping left around Ascot. I don't know

*Star attraction: Altior and Nicky Henderson at the trainer's media day in February*

## VITAL STATISTICS

### Races with the 'festival factor'

**Ladbrokes Hurdle**
Leopardstown, February 2, 2019
2m, good to yielding
1 **Off You Go** 6 11-5 M Walsh 8-1
2 **Jezki** 11 11-0 D O'Keeffe 16-1
3 **Ivanovich Gorbatov** 7 10-10 JJ Slevin 16-1
4 **Eclair De Beaufeu** 5 10-5 J Kennedy 7-1
Trainer: Charles Byrnes
Distances: 1l, ½l, 1½l; 19 ran
***Festival pointer*** *Five of the nine Irish-trained County Hurdle winners in the past 16 years had run in this race (only Final Approach, in 2011, won both) – two of the other three ran in the Betfair Hurdle at Newbury. Xenophon followed up victory here by taking the Coral Cup in 2003 and last year Bleu Berry won the Coral Cup after finishing 17th here*
🐎*Four festival winners in the past ten years*

**Chanelle Pharma Novice Hurdle**
Leopardstown, February 3, 2019, 2m, good
1 **Klassical Dream** 5 11-9 R Walsh 9-4f
2 **Aramon** 6 11-10 P Townend 5-2
3 **Vision D'Honneur** 5 11-9 J Kennedy 3-1
Trainer: Willie Mullins
Distances: hd, 6l; 7 ran
***Festival pointer*** *This race – recently reduced in distance to 2m – produced a festival winner each year from 2002 to 2004 and after a long gap has enjoyed a resurgence with Champagne Fever, Vautour (both won here), Windsor Park (second) and Samcro (won) scoring at the festivals of 2013, 2014, 2015 and 2018. While most winners over the old 2m2f trip since 2000 dropped back to land the Supreme, Windsor Park was a runner-up who stepped up to win the Ballymore over 2m5f (as did the top-class Istabraq and Danoli in the 1990s) and Samcro went up from 2m here last year to take the Ballymore*
🐎*Four festival winners in the past ten years*

why but it certainly doesn't concern me in any way." The hot favourite will be racing left-handed for the first time since last season's festival and, assuming he jumps out that way again, it won't be an issue at Cheltenham.

Second favourite with most bookmakers is Min, but he proved no match for Altior in the 2018 Champion Chase and it wouldn't surprise at all if his connections ducked a rematch. Min has won both starts this season, starting with a straightforward defeat of Shattered Love and Balko Des Flos in the John Durkan Memorial at Punchestown. That was over 2m4f, but he was back in trip at Leopardstown in February when he comfortably accounted for Ordinary World and company in the Dublin Chase. Willie Mullins, Ruby Walsh and owners Susannah and Rich Ricci have yet to decide on Min's Cheltenham target. He's favourite for the Ryanair and open to further improvement at two and a half miles or so.

Mullins has to juggle not only Min but Footpad and Un De Sceaux too. The 2018 Arkle winner Footpad got this season off to

## VITAL STATISTICS

# Races with the 'festival factor'

### Flogas Novice Chase

Leopardstown, February 3, 2019
2m5f, good

1 **La Bague Au Roi** 8 11-3 R Johnson 10-11f
2 **Kaiser Black** 8 11-10 J Doyle 33-1
3 **Hardline** 7 11-10 J Kennedy 7-2

Trainer: Warren Greatrex

Distances: 1¼l, 4¼l; 6 ran

*Festival pointer This has emerged as an excellent guide in recent years, with four of the last ten RSA Chase winners having run here (two won, one was second and the other was third), as well as an Arkle winner who finished second here and then dropped back in trip. Last year The Storyteller (seventh here) went on to land the Stable Plate and Rathvinden (unseated) took the National Hunt Chase*

*Seven festival winners in the past ten years*

### Unibet Irish Gold Cup

Leopardstown, February 3, 2019, 3m, good

1 **Bellshill** 9 11-10 R Walsh 2-1
2 **Road To Respect** 8 11-10 S Flanagan 5-6f
3 **The Storyteller** 8 11-10 D Russell 8-1

Trainer: Willie Mullins

Distances: shd, 7½l; 4 ran

*Festival pointer In 2017 Sizing John became only the third winner since the race's inception in 1987 to land the Gold Cup in the same year, joining Jodami (1993) and Imperial Call (1996). Lord Windermere won the Gold Cup in 2014 after finishing sixth of seven here, while six more have placed in the Gold Cup in the past decade after running in this race (Anibale Fly fell two out last year before finishing third at Cheltenham)*

*Two festival winners in the past ten years*

*Way ahead: Altior storms home in the Clarence House Chase*

an unhappy start with a fall at Naas that left him with a minor injury, which meant ten days or so on the sidelines, and he returned at Leopardstown's Christmas fixture. Sent off evens favourite for the Grade 1 Paddy's Rewards Club Chase, he looked set for a comfortable win when taking the lead before the last, only to succumb to Simply Ned close home. Footpad has questions to answer now, but his novice brilliance lingers in the memory and a step up in trip could unlock more.

Un De Sceaux's only appearance this term is that admirable second to Altior in the Tingle Creek. The 2017 Ryanair winner finished runner-up to Balko Des Flos in that race last year and it's likely he'll be Ryanair-bound again. This remarkable 11-year-old has never finished out of the first two in 17 completed starts over fences.

Cyrname produced a performance of Ryanair quality when trouncing a high-class field in the Ascot Chase, breaking the course record by a second and a half, but the Paul Nicholls-trained gelding has never won on a left-handed track and would have to be supplemented. Seventeen lengths back in second at Ascot was Waiting Patiently, whose attitude under pressure looked questionable. Trainer Ruth Jefferson felt he wasn't at home on the ground, which was the quickest he has encountered.

Henry de Bromhead's Monalee made all in the Red Mills Chase at Gowran Park in February and connections must decide between the Ryanair and the Gold Cup. He's much shorter in the market for the former, which the stable won last year with Balko Des Flos.

**Verdict** With half the Champion Chase entries also in the Ryanair, it's difficult to gauge the make-up of these races. Altior can surely land a fourth festival win, while Footpad would make plenty of appeal if he runs in the Ryanair *(Richard Lowther)*

## ■ STAYERS' HURDLE

For a second successive campaign the staying hurdle division seemed to be wide open. That was, however, until Cheltenham's trials day in January, when Emma Lavelle's hugely progressive Paisley Park took apart a competitive-looking Grade 2 Cleeve Hurdle. Having resumed with back-to-back handicap wins, he made a Grade 1 breakthrough in the Long Walk Hurdle at Ascot in December and the Cleeve provided even more conclusive proof that he is the leading domestic hope for the big one at the festival.

The RPR of 172 he was given for the Cleeve would have been good enough to win seven of the last ten Stayers' Hurdles. He still looked raw there and is only a seven-year-old, so it is highly likely he has more to offer. Most ground comes alike to him.

Colin Tizzard's West Approach has followed Paisley Park home the last twice and, while winless over hurdles since 2016, his liking for Cheltenham makes him each-way material.

Black Op, runner-up to Samcro in last year's Ballymore Novices' Hurdle, finished third in the Cleeve on his return from an aborted novice chase campaign. That was his first run over 3m and arguably a career-best, despite being beaten 14 lengths. He's entitled to get closer but seems happiest when the mud's flying and it's pushing it to think he can win.

Midnight Shadow, tailed off in the Cleeve, had previously impressed when taking the Grade 2 Relkeel Hurdle over 2m4½f on New Year's Day. A return to kinder ground at the festival would really help and Sue Smith's six-year-old is not yet the finished article.

Tizzard has another contender in last season's Grade 1 Albert Bartlett Novices' Hurdle winner Kilbricken Storm. He isn't fully exposed as a staying hurdler, although soft ground seems important to his cause.

Even if Apple's Jade heads for the Champion Hurdle as seems likely, the biggest threat to Paisley Park should still emerge from Ireland and 2018 winner Penhill heads the challengers. The Willie Mullins-trained eight-year-old is 2-2 at the festival, having won the Albert Bartlett as a novice, and seems to peak when fresh, so it's no surprise he has been held back this term. However, it was a messy edition he took last year and that display leaves him with around 10lb to find this time.

If the ground is quicker it's far from certain Penhill will confirm form with last year's runner-up Supasundae. Jessica Harrington's dependable Grade 1 winner has twice been firmly put in his place by Apple's Jade this season, either side of finding Sharjah too sharp over 2m in the Ryanair Hurdle at Leopardstown's Christmas meeting. A sounder surface would help him see out this distance much better, though.

Samcro, last season's top novice, would be a fascinating contender. He was roughed off when respiratory issues emerged after a shock defeat behind Sharjah and Supasundae at Christmas. He has no 3m form under rules but has been pleasing again at home and possesses the class to have a say if he turns up here.

**Verdict** Paisley Park is rated by many as a banker and ought to justify the tag if repeating the level of his demolition job in the Cleeve Hurdle – a pivotal trial. Last year's runner-up Supasundae could prove most troublesome, although if it came up soft Kilbricken Storm would be feared most *(Dave Orton)*

*Festival form: Stayers' Hurdle hope Supasundae wins the 2017 Coral Cup*

# 8th-12th May 2019

## The Private Grounds of Windsor Castle

5★ International Show Jumping · 4★ International Dressage · 2★ Endurance
The Land Rover International Driving Grand Prix · 130 Showing Classes
More than 220 Shops & Restaurants

# ROYAL WINDSOR HORSE SHOW

*In Partnership with*

ook Tickets now · rwhs.co.uk · 0844 581 4960

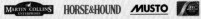

## ■ NOVICE CHASES

With leading form pick Dynamite Dollars missing due to injury, the British challenge in the Racing Post Arkle is led by Lalor. A Grade 1 winner over hurdles, he looked the real deal on his chasing debut at Cheltenham in November when readily taking the Racing Post Arkle trial from Dynamite Dollars.

That form was turned on its head at Sandown in December in the Henry VIII, when deep ground and going right-handed found out Kayley Woollacott's gelding as he toiled in third behind Dynamite Dollars and the Henry de Bromhead-trained Ornua. With the ground not suitable thereafter, Woollacott opted to keep him fresh for the festival. While that's not ideal, he'd relish a sound surface in March and a repeat of the level of his November win would see him go close.

Kalashnikov, second in last year's Supreme Novices' Chase, came unstuck in his quest for a hat-trick over fences behind Dynamite Dollars in the Wayward Lad at Kempton. That form still puts him in the picture but Amy Murphy's stable star then got turned over at odds of 1-4 in the rescheduled Kingmaker at Sandown and supporters are left hoping that a return to a left-handed circuit will do the trick.

Kingmaker winner Glen Forsa made an official mark of 138 look silly with a 19-length romp and, although potentially flattered, his slick jumping will stand him in good stead if he turns up.

The top Irish hope is Joseph O'Brien's Le Richebourg, who has turned up to every dance and lines up with four wins out of five over fences. A comfortable victory over reliable stablemate Us And Them in a Grade 1 at Leopardstown's Christmas meeting was followed by a similar display back there in the Irish Arkle in February. He was never sighted in last season's County Hurdle on his previous visit to Cheltenham, but the ground turned against him and it's hard to say he doesn't like the venue. If the sun shines on the first day, expect a big gamble on him.

Willie Mullins, responsible for three of the past four Arkle winners, has had a quiet

season with novice chasers. However, Cilaos Emery was electric on his chasing debut at Gowran in January after an injury layoff and has some smart hurdles form. He's a potential fly in the ointment.

The only horse to have lowered Le Richebourg's colours this season is the remarkably progressive Delta Work, who beat him a neck in the prestigious Drinmore at Fairyhouse in November. That came over 2m4f and it was only when he faced three

## VITAL STATISTICS

### Races with the 'festival factor'

**Betfair Hurdle**
Ascot, February 16, 2019, 1m7½f, good to soft
1 **Al Dancer** 6 11-8 S Twiston-Davies 5-2f
2 **Magic Dancer** 7 10-3 R Patrick 20-1
3 **Blu Cavalier** 9 11-2 J O'Neill jnr 100-1
4 **Getaway Trump** 6 11-9 H Cobden 4-1
Trainer: Nigel Twiston-Davies
Distances: 3¾l, 2½l, ½l; 14 ran

*Festival pointer One abandonment means there have been only nine runnings of this valuable handicap hurdle in the past decade. The race is a good pointer, although Wicklow Brave (11th in 2015 before landing the County Hurdle at 25-1) is the only winner to emerge since 2010. However, runners from the last eight editions have gone on to take six seconds (including last year's winner Kalashnikov in the Supreme) and five thirds at the festival*

🏇 *Two festival winners in the past ten years*

---

**Betfair Ascot Chase**
Ascot, February 16, 2019, 2m5f, good to soft
1 **Cyrname** 7 11-7 H Cobden 3-1
2 **Waiting Patiently** 8 11-7 B Hughes 11-8f
3 **Fox Norton** 9 11-7 R Power 6-1
Trainer: Paul Nicholls
Distances: 17l, 1¼l; 6 ran

*Festival pointer A good guide to the Ryanair Chase, with four winners having prepped here (two of the last six Ryanair winners took this race first). In the past ten years, first-three finishers from this race have finished 25181316472P7P5 in the Ryanair.*

🏇 *Three festival winners in the past ten years*

miles for the first time as a chaser, in the Grade 1 Neville Hotels Novice Chase, that Gordon Elliott's six-year-old took his form to a new level when winning by eight lengths despite idling. With the promise of more to come over the distance, last year's Pertemps Final winner is by some margin the leading Irish hope for this year's RSA Chase.

Leading the domestic challenge is Nicky Henderson's Santini, a Grade 1 novice hurdle winner at Aintree last season who bettered that level when taking a Grade 2 on his introduction to chasing at Newbury's Ladbrokes Trophy meeting in December.

He then found wondermare La Bague Au Roi and Topofthegame too quick around Kempton in the Grade 1 Kauto Star at Christmas. The track was against him but he stayed on stoutly for third and cemented his place at the head of the RSA market.

La Bague Au Roi is expected to bypass the festival, although runner-up Topofthegame is set to renew rivalry and has to be considered the stronger form pick on that running. He was touched off in last year's Coral Cup over 2m5f and it remains to be seen how he'll take to the much stiffer 3m at Cheltenham in March.

Henderson also has the talented Ok Corral, who made it two out of two over fences in a Listed chase at Warwick in January. He saw off Nicholls' useful Secret Investor by four lengths on good ground, with favourite Rocky's Treasure a further eight lengths behind. Rocky's Treasure had chased home Santini at Newbury, so on form there's little between the stablemates. However, the fact that crack Irish amateur Derek O'Connor did the steering on Ok Corral at Warwick strongly suggests his festival target will be the National Hunt Chase over four miles and he would rightly be a warm order in that.

Each season the JLT is contested by those in between distances and Defi Du Seuil perfectly fits the bill this term. Philip Hobbs's 2017 Triumph Hurdle winner looked a potential Arkle player when second in the Grade 2 Dipper over 2m4½f to Colin Tizzard's Lostintranslation at Cheltenham on New Year's Day. However, he proved his stamina when gaining revenge on that rival in a decent renewal of the Grade 1 Scilly Isles at Sandown in February and looks near certain to head the JLT challenge.

**Verdict** Delta Work rates a confident selection in his bid to emulate last year's RSA winner Presenting Percy, who also took the Pertemps Final the season before. If the ground rides good on the opening day Delta Work's form should be well advertised by Le Richebourg in an open-looking Arkle. Leading owner JP McManus also has standouts with Ok Corral in the National Hunt Chase and Defi Du Seuil in the JLT *(Dave Orton)*

### ■ NOVICE HURDLES

Sky Bet Supreme Novices' favourite Al Dancer cemented his credentials by making it four out of four over hurdles in the Betfair Hurdle in February. Rearranged due to the equine flu saga, that was a below-par renewal but his victory makes him the leading domestic form pick. He is proven at Cheltenham and acts on most ground.

His owner Dai Walters also has Angels Breath, who justified a lofty reputation when winning the Grade 2 Kennel Gate at Ascot in December. The Irish point winner jumped only four hurdles that day due to false ground and his inexperience is a concern. However, the form has substance and he's the apple of Nicky Henderson's eye.

Colin Tizzard's course-and-distance winner Elixir De Nutz bagged a hat-trick when seeing off Grand Sancy in the Grade 1 Tolworth Hurdle at Sandown. That's a leading trial and the form got a big boost when the runner-up landed the Kingwell Hurdle at Wincanton the following month.

Willie Mullins is set to run ex-French Klassical Dream and Aramon in his bid for a fourth win in the race since 2013. That pair fought out the Grade 1 Chanelle Pharma Novice Hurdle, a key trial at Leopardstown in February that was formerly known as the Deloitte, with Klassical Dream scoring by a head. The runner-up arrived having won

the Future Champions Novice Hurdle there at Christmas.

However, on form the strongest Irish challenger in the Supreme is Joseph O'Brien's Fakir D'Oudairies. The four-year-old sluiced in at Cheltenham on trials day in January, having landed a gamble on his stable debut at Cork earlier in the month, and his weight-for-age allowance is a big weapon. He's set to bypass the Triumph Hurdle in an attempt to become the first four-year-old to win the Supreme since Hors La Loi in 1999.

O'Brien has dominated the juvenile division and has a major contender for the Triumph in the shape of Sir Erec. Rated 109 on the Flat, he followed up a narrow win over the Mullins-trained Tiger Tap Tap at Leopardstown's Christmas meeting when impressively making all in the Grade 1 Spring Juvenile Hurdle back there in February. He got an easy lead but was going away at the finish from progressive stablemate Gardens Of Babylon.

That standard puts him clear of main British hope Quel Destin, who landed Grade 1 success for Paul Nicholls in the Finale Hurdle at Chepstow in December and is admirably consistent.

The Ballymore Novices' Hurdle over 2m5f has a more compact look and second-season novice Champ sets a formidable level for rivals. The seven-year-old was quick to get back out this season, having met defeat against the smart Vinndication on his hurdling bow at Ascot last term, and won minor contests at Perth and Warwick in May. His comeback in December saw him land a handicap at Newbury over the intermediate trip, recording an RPR of 150, and he was sent off a warm order for the Group 1 Challow Hurdle back there later in the month.

Jockey Barry Geraghty had to get serious with Champ in between the final two flights but ultimately he landed the four-timer with plenty to spare in what was a solid edition of the race. The form has worked out particularly well.

The Irish challenge is led by Battleoverdoyen, a former point winner who is unbeaten since

joining Gordon Elliott under rules having landed a Punchestown bumper in November and two starts over hurdles.

His Grade 1 win at Naas in January came in a messy contest, with main market rival Tornado Flyer pulled up. However, he was still green and it's hard to knock the form of his previous runs. He's happiest on decent ground, and bred for it too, so any rain in March would be an unknown.

A darker Irish contender is Martin Brassil's City Island, who hasn't looked back since being disqualified after winning at the Galway festival. He came back with success at Leopardstown's Christmas meeting over two miles, comfortably seeing off subsequent dual winner Dallas Des Pictons, and warmed up for the Ballymore with an easy victory at odds of 1-5 at Naas in February when upped to 2m3f. He is yet to tackle Graded races but his form isn't far off the leading contenders and he loves good going.

Willie Mullins is unusually thin on the ground in this division and it's hard to gauge which of his novices will pitch up. However, he has an unexposed sort for the Albert Bartlett over 3m in the Cheveley Park Stud-owned Allaho.

The ex-French five-year-old, runner-up on his hurdling debut in Listed company at Auteuil last year, disappointed on his debut for Mullins in a bumper at Christmas. However, the decision to send him next for a Grade 3 hurdle at Clonmel in February paid off as he relished moving up to 3m and won well. That race has been won by heavyweights such as Don Poli and Monalee in recent seasons.

The top British hope for the Albert Bartlett is Nicky Henderson's Birchdale, who was left clear by the final-flight fall of Brewin'upastorm when winning a Grade 2 on trials day in January. He's a highly regarded former Irish point winner and would relish some decent ground in March.

**Verdict** Champ has outstanding claims in the Ballymore and it's the same story with Sir Erec in the Triumph Hurdle, while Elixir De Nutz offers some value in the Supreme *(Dave Orton)*

■ The big four trainers – Nicky Henderson and Paul Nicholls from Britain and Irish titans Willie Mullins and Gordon Elliott – took their dominance to new heights in 2018 by landing 19 of the festival's 28 races between them.

Their influence has increased with each passing year. Five years ago the big four won seven races between them, a quarter of the total, but their share has been at least 50 per cent at each of the past four festivals.

A total of 70 Grade 1 races have been run at the past five festivals and 39 (56 per cent) have gone to one of the big four. Last year they won nine (64 per cent) of the 14 Grade 1s.

■ One area where the big four trainers have yet to exert a strong influence is in the five handicap chases – they have won only four of the 25 run in the past five years.

Gordon Elliott and Paul Nicholls won one apiece last year but the other three went to Nick Williams, Mick Channon and Warren Greatrex – all with runners priced below 10-1 and in the top three in the betting.

A fancied runner from outside the big stables is always worth a look.

■ Once again ratings proved a good guide to the non-handicap races last year with the winner coming from the top three on official ratings in ten of the 18 races.

'Five years ago the big four won seven races between them, a quarter of the total, but their share has been at least 50 per cent at each of the past four festivals'

Leaving out the four non-handicaps not in the Grade 1 bracket, eight out of 14 winners came from the three top rated, while there were six winners out of nine if you concentrated only on the novice races over hurdles and fences.

■ The importance of coming to the festival with good form was emphasised with 13 of the 28 winners in 2018 having scored last time out, while a further nine had finished second or third. Of the six who hadn't been placed, only National Hunt Chase winner

*Rathvinden (left) bucked a trend last year by winning the National Hunt Chase after failing to complete on his previous start*

Rathvinden bounced back from a non-completion last time out (unseated).

■ Nineteen of the 28 winners had run in the previous seven weeks and the first edition of the Dublin Racing Festival in early February proved a good staging post for Irish hopefuls, with eight of their 17 Cheltenham winners having run there for finishing positions of 1U101372.

■ Seven winners hadn't run in that calendar year, with two having last raced at Cheltenham in December and two more at Leopardstown's Christmas fixture. The longest layoff was 323 days for Stayers' Hurdle winner Penhill and the shortest was 22 days for Martin Pipe Handicap Hurdle scorer Blow By Blow. It will be interesting to see if the British flu shutdown has any impact on the figures.

# Plenty of top-end quality as well as quantity

**By Alan Sweetman**

There was one major negative attached to the collective feats of Irish-trained runners at the 2018 Cheltenham Festival. Failures in the Gold Cup, Champion Hurdle and Champion Chase left a slightly empty feeling at the end of an otherwise superb week that yielded a 17-winner haul, spearheaded by Gordon Elliott and Willie Mullins with eight and seven victories respectively.

Henry de Bromhead and Pat Kelly contributed one winner each in 2018. A year on, Irish prospects will largely depend on the two powerhouse stables, although the publicity-shy Kelly, standard-bearer for the grassroots at the last three festivals, fields the nation's prime Gold Cup candidate Presenting Percy and De Bromhead is responsible for a putative banker, the unbeaten Honeysuckle in the Mares' Novices' Hurdle.

Presenting Percy, last season's RSA Chase winner, was in good shape when making a belated reappearance over hurdles at Gowran Park in January. He remains on course despite having missed an intended run in the Red Mills Chase, heading a lively challenge in which a Mullins-trained trio of Kemboy, Bellshill and Al Boum Photo figure along with Anibale Fly and Road To Respect, best of the raiders behind Native River and Might Bite last season. Kemboy is particularly

*Irish-trained hopefuls: Honeysuckle (main), Min (above left) and Samcro*

attractive on the strength of his victory over last season's RSA Chase runner-up Monalee and Road To Respect in the Savills Chase at Leopardstown in December.

Irish hopes of thwarting a Champion Hurdle hat-trick by Buveur D'Air received a massive boost with the confirmation of Apple's Jade as an intended runner. With all due respect to the defending champion he is hardly in the same league as Persian War, See You Then or Istabraq, the only horses in the past 50 years to have won the race three times. The 7lb mares' allowance is a major positive in favour of Apple's Jade.

While Altior looks unassailable in the Champion Chase, one would imagine Mullins will run at least one high-profile horse against him just in case of accident. If last year's Arkle winner Footpad is given that task, it would leave Min and Un De Sceaux free to take the more appealing option of the Ryanair Chase. De Bromhead, trainer of last year's winner Balko Des Flos, could have a big say again if Red Mills Chase winner Monalee takes his chance here instead of the Gold Cup.

The home side's Paisley Park sets a high standard in the Stayers' Hurdle. It will be quite a training performance if Mullins can get last year's winner Penhill there again in fighting shape, and likewise if Elliott wins the race against time to restore Samcro to full health after a lung infection.

## ■ NOVICE CHASERS

Le Richebourg, winner of four of his five races over fences and second to leading RSA Chase fancy Delta Work in the Drinmore Chase, is a strong Arkle contender for Joseph O'Brien, although one could quibble with the form of two Grade 1 wins achieved at the main expense of stablemate Us And Them. The Mullins-trained Cilaos Emery competed only twice last season and has run just once over fences. He impressed at Gowran in January and seems to retain the ability he showed when beating stablemate Melon in a Grade 1 novice hurdle two seasons ago.

Elliott's 2018 Pertemps Final winner Delta Work is expected to mount a strong challenge for the RSA Chase. Mullins has won run three of the last four editions of the JLT, so the likes of Real Steel, a wide-margin winner of a Fairyhouse beginners' chase, and Camelia De Cotte, a mare who has been mopping up in weak races, are worth looking out for.

Derek O'Connor has been lined up to ride Ok Corral, who would not be out of place in the RSA Chase, for Nicky Henderson in the National Hunt Chase. He is potentially a cut above the opposition, although Ballyward should go well for the Mullins team, who won the 4m event with Rathvinden last year. The form of his Naas win has been boosted in a Grade 2 Navan contest dominated by a pair of RSA Chase hopefuls, Chris's Dream and Champagne Classic.

## ■ NOVICE HURDLERS

Klassical Dream and Aramon, separated by only a head at the finish of the 2m Grade 1 novice hurdle at the Dublin Racing Festival, are the principal Mullins hopes for the Supreme Novices'. The pair have an edge over the Elliott-trained Vision D'Honneur on Leopardstown running.

Perhaps the most intriguing aspect of the Supreme is that Joseph O'Brien could split his juvenile resources by running Cheltenham

*Ballyward: strong contender for the National Hunt Chase*

# THE KNIGHTS OF MIDDLE ENGLAND

# Unique Mounted Experience Days

## Jousting Experience Days

### LEARN HOW TO JOUST

And master the medieval horseback skills: Lancing the Gold Rings, Spearing the Peasant's Heads, Strike the dreaded Quintaine!

Take up lance and experience the trills of riding down the tilt in the jousting field! The Knights of Middle England run Medieval Jousting Experience Days at their Warwickshire Jousting Arena and Medieval themed Hall, which bring to life all the excitement, glamour and challenges of this most fabled equestrian sport.

## Specialist Skills Days

### TRICK RIDING

Come and take part in one of our half day Trick Riding workshops. Within the safety of our enclosed arena on specially trained horses on the lunge you will learn the basics of classical vaulting techniques performing gymnastic manoeuvres on the back of a moving horse.

Then progress on to the authentic Cossack Trick Riding Saddle learning a variety of basic vaults, tricks and stands.

### HORSE ARCHERY

Taught by qualified archery instructors, you will first learn to use your bow from the ground learning to nock and master speed leading your arrow.

Then mount one of our specially trained horses and practise nocking on the move as you ride down the archery run unleashing your arrows upon targets!

- No Riding Experience Necessary
- Open to All Abilities
- 21st Century safety rules apply
- Large private Group Bookings welcome
- Spectators Welcome

For more information, call: 01926 400401 • Email: info@knightsofmiddleengland.co.uk
Like us on Facebook or follow us on Instagram @knightsofmiddleengland

# www.knightsofmiddleengland.com

Grade 2 winner Fakir D'Oudairies in a bid to become the first horse in his age group to win the festival opener since Hors La Loi in 1999, with Sir Erec, the former Ballydoyle-trained stayer who has won his two races over hurdles at Leopardstown, leading the way in the Triumph.

Elliott's unbeaten Battleoverdoyen looks tailor-made for the Ballymore on the strength of a Grade 1 win over 2m4f at Naas. Allaho staked a late claim for Mullins with a Grade 3 Clonmel win and the Martin Brassil-trained City Island is a credible challenger for race sponsor Sean Mulryan.

Leopardstown Grade 1 winner Commander Of Fleet faces a possibly crucial rematch with O'Brien's runner-up Rhinestone in the Albert Bartlett. Philip Dempsey's dual 3m winner Derrinross and the Mouse Morris-trained Sams Profile, second to Battleoverdoyen at Naas, should help to provide depth to the Irish team in this stamina test.

## ■ BEST OF THE REST

Mullins has won the Champion Bumper nine times but never with a four-year-old, a possible negative for impressive Gowran winner Blue Sari. Elliott will fancy his chances with the unbeaten Envoi Allen in the Cheveley Park colours and has solid back-up in the shape of Andy Dufresne, acquired by JP McManus prior to a smooth success at Down Royal in January, and Thatsy, whose Navan win came just in time to book his ticket.

Grand National hero Tiger Roll will be a short price to repeat his 2018 Cross Country win following a sparkling return in the Boyne Hurdle at Navan, although this is no formality with the Enda Bolger-trained duo Auvergnat and Josies Orders in opposition.

Despite a reverse in a point-to-point at Kilfeacle, Bolger's Stand Up And Fight remains a strong Foxhunter candidate along with Elliott's ex-track performer Ucello Conti, whose depth of experience in valuable handicaps should be an asset now that he has retrieved the winning habit.

Bar the inaugural running in 2008, the Mares' Hurdle has been an Irish monopoly. Mullins holds the aces, with Laurina in pole position if she swerves the Champion. Running plans may hinge on whether last year's winner Benie Des Dieux is judged ready to go without having had a prep race. Limini and Stormy Ireland could also be in the mix for Mullins.

The depth of resources among the top stables in recent years has greatly increased the quality of the Irish challenge for the handicaps at the meeting. The likes of Off You Go, Uradel and The Storyteller are potentially appealing in the Coral Cup. The strength of O'Brien's juvenile squad points to Band Of Outlaws and Gardens Of Babylon as Fred Winter possibles. Mall Dini, second for Pat Kelly in last year's Kim Muir, has prospects of going one better, and Elliott's Dallas Des Pictons is fancied for the Martin Pipe as the trainer goes for a hat-trick in what is now the festival finale.

*Battleoverdoyen: tailor-made for the Ballymore*

# Aneata Boote - artisan jeweller

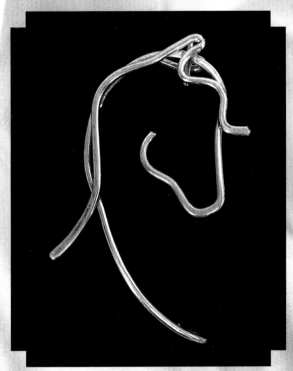

**For The Love Of Horses**
Brooch in Sterling Silver £85

# Angels looks a godsend

**The Racing Post's regional correspondents pick their fancies**

■**LAMBOURN** James Burn

Nicky Henderson has tried to play down the hype surrounding **Angels Breath** but there is no doubt those closest to the promising five-year-old rate him highly, so expect him to start the festival with a bold show in the Sky Bet Supreme Novices' Hurdle.

Henderson is brilliant with two-mile novice hurdlers and Angels Breath, who looked smart when winning a Grade 2 at Ascot before Christmas, ticks plenty of boxes.

The champion trainer can also capture the National Hunt Chase on the opening day with **Ok Corral**, who is a class act and would not be out of place in the RSA.

The four-miler has been the plan for some time and crack amateur Derek O'Connor got a feel for last year's Albert Bartlett Novices' Hurdle runner-up at Warwick in January, when the strapping nine-year-old oozed quality in a six-length Listed win.

Henderson also has a strong hand in the Ballymore Novices' Hurdle but **Emitom** appeals in that. He has always been held in high regard by Warren Greatrex, who knows a good horse when he sees one and, crucially, how to handle one. Any ease in the ground would help the son of Gold Well.

■**WEST COUNTRY** Andrew King

**Defi Du Seuil** looks one of the area's best chances of festival success in the JLT Novices' Chase as he is ideally suited by the 2m4f trip. They are bound to go a good pace and that will play into his hands as he is best when delivered late.

**Native River** has been aimed specifically at the Magners Cheltenham Gold Cup all season and there is no reason why he cannot repeat his success of last March, as he seems to handle most types of ground.

**Give Me A Copper** ran a race full of promise on his seasonal comeback at Sandown in February. He will come on a lot for that outing and is one to keep an eye on in the Ultima Handicap Chase on the first day of the festival.

■**IRELAND** Brian Sheerin

In an era where the powerhouse owners and trainers have made it increasingly difficult for anyone outside the top bracket to unearth a diamond, **Presenting Percy** can strike a blow against them by lifting the Magners Cheltenham Gold Cup for Galway trainer Pat Kelly.

Presenting Percy's story is hardly one of rags to riches – he's owned by successful businessman Philip Reynolds, son of the late Taoiseach Albert Reynolds – but it has captured the imagination of the Irish public. There were huge crowds at Gowran Park to witness his successful reappearance in the Galmoy Hurdle in January and there is sure to be a huge Irish roar if he follows up last year's impressive RSA Chase win with victory in the big one.

While the enigmatic Kelly has sent his stable star along an unorthodox path towards the Gold Cup, there is every chance it will be a successful one. Presenting Percy is a deserving favourite and will take a lot of beating.

The Irish novice chase brigade looks quite strong and the Willie Mullins-trained **Cilaos Emery** could have what it takes in the Arkle, while Gordon Elliott's **Delta Work** has outstanding claims in the RSA Chase.

An outsider for the week? Keep Mullins' **Bacardys** on side in the Stayers' Hurdle. He was running a big race in the Stayers' 12 months ago before coming down at the last and, while chasing hasn't worked out for the second successive season, he could show his big engine back over hurdles.

*Give Me A Copper (right): can go well in Tuesday's Ultima*

### ■ THE NORTH
Ben Hutton

**Definitly Red** may have been turned over at 1-6 at Kelso but that match turned into a sprint and it is worth remembering Zaynar was beaten at 1-14 at the Borders course in 2010 before going on to finish third in the Champion Hurdle. The Brian Ellison-trained ten-year-old should be a different proposition in the Magners Cheltenham Gold Cup and is a value each-way option.

He has shown strong form this season in winning the Charlie Hall and Many Clouds Chases, he is proven at the course, and odds of 33-1 and bigger underestimate his chance.

**Waiting Patiently** would be a player if Ruth Jefferson runs him in the Ryanair, despite his Ascot Chase defeat, while Phil Kirby has two interesting contenders in **Lady Buttons** and **Top Ville Ben**. Lady Buttons would be an each-way player in the Mares' Hurdle or the Champion Chase, and the return to a left-handed track would suit Top Ville Ben in the RSA Chase.

Racing Post experts each give a top tip for the meeting

### ■ TOM SEGAL
**Clan Des Obeaux**
*Gold Cup*

It seems to me everyone is trying to pick holes in Clan Des Obeaux when there simply aren't any. He won the best race run over fences this season with his ears pricked and he is still the Gold Cup contender with the most improvement in him. What was so special about his King George win was his jumping at speed and, while it's true he has never won at Cheltenham, he's run well every time he's been there and he's a much better horse now.

### ■ JUSTIN O'HANLON
**Derrinross**
*Albert Bartlett Novices' Hurdle*

This improving novice's chance is quite dependent on him getting soft ground but you'd think it will arrive eventually and softer going by the end of Cheltenham week is not unprecedented. His improvement has really taken shape since Philip Dempsey stepped him up in trip in December, following a year's absence, and front-running tactics were also key in dour staying performances in Graded contests at Cork and Limerick. With the right conditions he will be tough to pass.

### ■ PIETRO INNOCENZI
**Sharjah**
*Champion Hurdle*

Although he has a fair bit to find on the book, Sharjah appears to be improving fast, having finally got over last season's Leopardstown fall that clearly left its mark. He made Faugheen look second rate in the Morgiana Hurdle in November and quickened much the best to notch his second Grade 1 over Christmas. He remains something of a dark horse and has won on ground ranging from good to heavy.

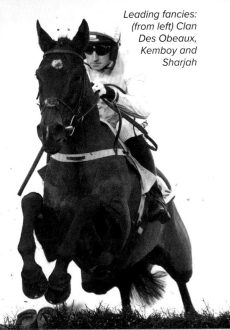

*Leading fancies: (from left) Clan Des Obeaux, Kemboy and Sharjah*

## ◼ GRAEME RODWAY
**Kemboy**
*Gold Cup*

Plenty seem keen to pick holes in Kemboy's Savills Chase victory at Leopardstown on account of the race being run at a slow pace. That's a fair criticism but ignores the fact that Kemboy couldn't have won the race any easier than he did. He was still on the bridle on the approach to the last and stormed away to score by seven and a half lengths. A rapid improver who will be coming here on a five-timer, Kemboy remains open to further progress and doesn't have much to find with the best in this race.

## ◼ TOM PARK
**Elusive Belle**
*Mares' Novices' Hurdle*

This talented five-year-old looked exceptional on her hurdles debut for Nicky Henderson at Wincanton in January, beating dual winner Thistle Do Nicely – who was rated 134 – by 19 lengths. Owner Robert Waley-Cohen, who paid £180,000 for Elusive Belle in November, is the chairman of Cheltenham and played a big part in the introduction of this race three years ago, and he clearly bought this mare with the intention of landing this prize.

## ◼ TOM COLLINS
**Sire Du Berlais**
*Pertemps Final*

This unexposed seven-year-old has been campaigned carefully since joining Gordon Elliott in 2016 and he looks to be primed for another shot at the Cheltenham Festival after last year's fourth place in the Martin Pipe. He hit the line powerfully that day over 2m4½f and looked better than his mark of 144. He has dropped 2lb despite a couple of eyecatching performances and is open to plenty of improvement over this longer trip, having tried it for the first time when sixth in a Pertemps qualifier at Christmas.

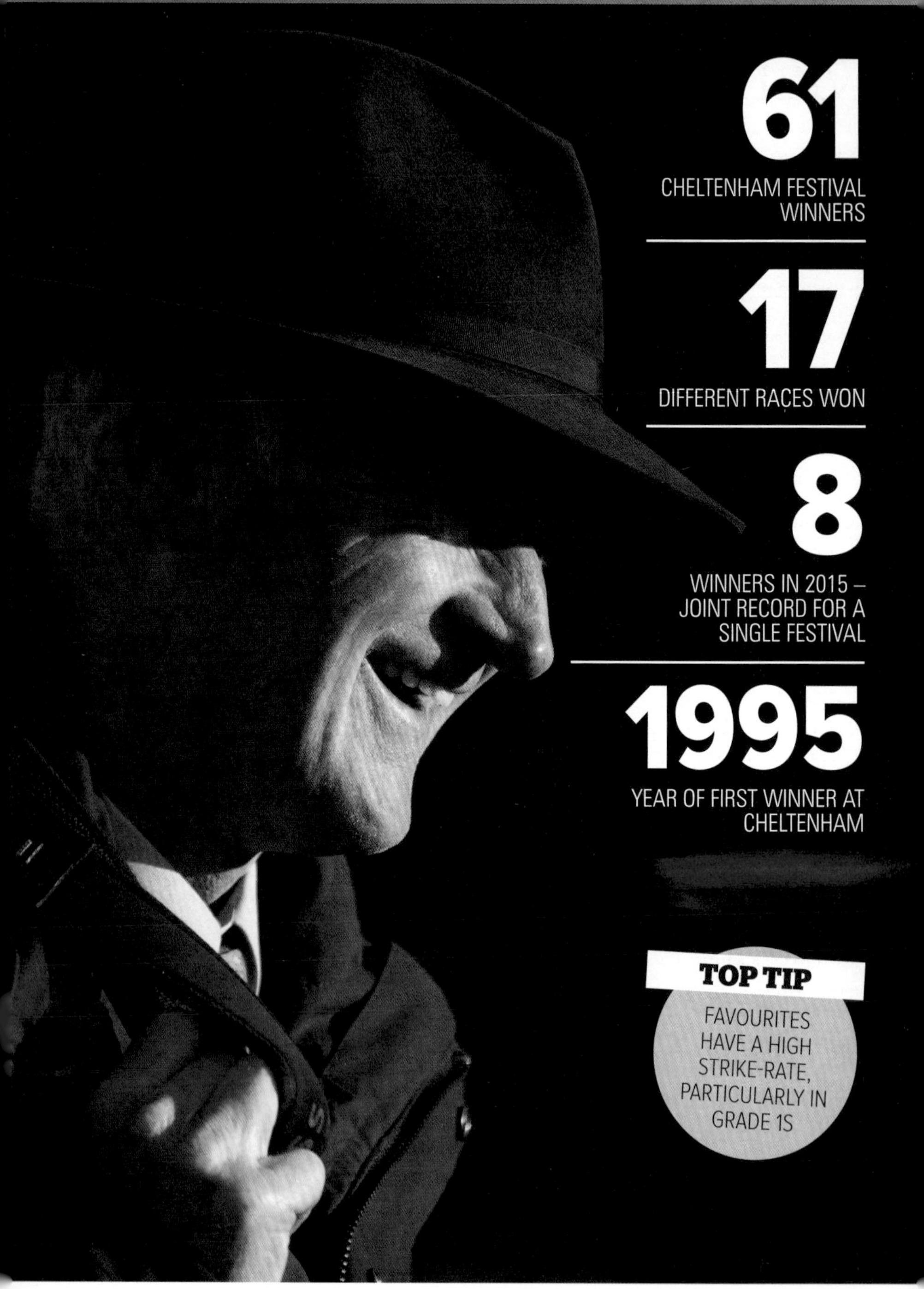

# 61
CHELTENHAM FESTIVAL
WINNERS

# 17
DIFFERENT RACES WON

# 8
WINNERS IN 2015 –
JOINT RECORD FOR A
SINGLE FESTIVAL

# 1995
YEAR OF FIRST WINNER AT
CHELTENHAM

**TOP TIP**

FAVOURITES
HAVE A HIGH
STRIKE-RATE,
PARTICULARLY IN
GRADE 1S

# Market a strong pointer

MULLINS has overtaken Nicky Henderson as the winningmost trainer in festival history, moving one ahead with 61 winners after adding seven more to his total in 2018. That was not enough to give him last year's trainers' award, however, as his great Irish rival Gordon Elliott pipped him by one.

The 11-time Irish champion trainer has exceeded five winners at each of the past four festivals (he had a joint-record eight in 2015). Elliott and Henderson are the only other trainers to have had more than five at a single meeting.

Usually Mullins relies on a big opening day to get him off and running and that was the case again last year when he scored with Footpad in the Arkle, Benie Des Dieux in the Mares' Hurdle and Rathivinden in the National Hunt Chase.

The market tells its story. At the past five festivals, Mullins has had a total of 43 favourites and 19 (44%) have won. Only 13 of his 32 winners in that period did not start favourite (and five of those were second favourite).

Traditionally the stable's main strength in Grade 1 races has been over hurdles, particularly over 2m, but Mullins has won nine Grade 1 chases in the past four

## MOST SUCCESSFUL RACES

**Champion Bumper**
■■■■■■■■■

**Mares' Hurdle**
■■■■■■■■■

**Supreme Novices'**
■■■■■

**Champion Hurdle**
■■■■

**RSA Chase**
■■■■

**Ballymore Novices'**
■■■■

**County Hurdle**
■■■■

**JLT Chase**
■■■■

## WILLIE MULLINS FESTIVAL WINNERS BY RACE TYPE

■ Hurdles **37**
■ Chases **15**
■ Bumpers **9**

years (having not done so since 2009). His most fancied runner is well worth noting in the four non-handicaps for novice chasers (Arkle, National Hunt, RSA and JLT) with a 50 per cent strike-rate in the past four years (8-16, +6.83pts).

He has had eight handicap hurdle winners since 2010 (six at double-figure odds), the latest coming last year with 20-1 shot Bleu Berry in the Coral Cup. Excluding the Fred Winter Juvenile Handicap Hurdle, which he has never won, his strike-rate in that period is 8-72 (+54.5pts) and the key targets have been the County Hurdle (4-26, +53pts) and Martin Pipe Conditional Jockeys' Hurdle (3-17, +9.5pts).

He is always the one to beat in races restricted to mares, having won nine out of 11 in the Mares' Hurdle and all three runnings of the mares' novice hurdle, and is strong in the Champion Bumper where eight of his nine winners were five-year-olds (and six of those had won their sole outing prior to arriving at Cheltenham).

> *County and Martin Pipe handicap hurdles have proved profitable*

> *Thirteen of his 15 chase winners were in novice races*

# String of Grade 1 hopes

THE master of Seven Barrows has 60 festival winners but was overtaken on the all-time leaderboard last year by Willie Mullins, who is now one ahead.

Quality matters as much as quantity for Henderson, whose two winners last year were Buveur D'Air in the Champion Hurdle and Altior in the Champion Chase, with Might Bite going close to the big-race hat-trick with his gallant second in the Gold Cup. Those stable stars had provided his three winners the previous year and, all being well, they will lead the charge again.

As usual Henderson also looks well stocked in the novice hurdles with Angels Breath, Champ and Birchdale among his leading candidates, while Santini heads the novice chasers.

Second-season hurdlers are always worth noting, along with the booking of claiming jockeys — four of Henderson's seven handicap winners since 2009 have had the benefit of a weight allowance.

The quality that runs through his string means the market doesn't always provide an accurate guide and longer-priced runners in handicaps are always worth a look, especially if they are lightly raced. Call The Cops at 9-1 in the 2015 Pertemps Final was the only one of the trainer's 11 handicap winners since 2005 to have been returned shorter than 12-1.

It is also worth noting that eight of those 11 handicap winners since 2005 came over trips of at least 2m4f.

Among Henderson's favourite races is the Triumph Hurdle, in which he holds the record with six wins. In the past decade, when his most fancied runner has been under 10-1, their finishing positions have been 11366164 for a level-stakes

## MOST SUCCESSFUL RACES

**Champion Hurdle**
■■■■■■■

**Triumph Hurdle**
■■■■■■

**Arkle Chase**
■■■■■■

**Champion Chase**
■■■■■

**Stable Plate**
■■■■

**Cathcart Chase***
■■■■

**Supreme Novices'**
■■■

**RSA Chase**
■■■

**Kim Muir**
■■■

*\* No longer held*

## TOP TIP

NEVER ONE TO DISCOUNT IN HANDICAPS AT REWARDING ODDS

**60**
CHELTENHAM FESTIVAL WINNERS

**22**
DIFFERENT RACES WON

**9**
HORSES WHO HAVE WON MORE THAN ONCE AT THE FESTIVAL

**1985**
YEAR OF FIRST WINNER AT CHELTENHAM

profit of 8.5pts, although Apple's Shakira was a costly loser last year as 6-5 favourite.

Overall he has an excellent record of delivering with the hot ones in Grade 1 races. In the past decade he has sent out 25 favourites in that category and 13 have won, returning a level-stakes profit of 10.56pts.

## NICKY HENDERSON FESTIVAL WINNERS BY RACE TYPE

- ■ G1 hurdles **20**
- ■ G1 chases **18**
- ■ Non G1 chases **15**
- ■ Non G1 hurdles **7**

*Profitable record with Grade 1 favourites*

# Watch for single runners

ELLIOTT has been leading trainer at the festival for the past two years, becoming the only one apart from Howard Johnson in 2005 to break the monopoly of Willie Mullins, Nicky Henderson and Paul Nicholls at the last 15 festivals. With Elliott's arrival as a major force, the big three has become the big four.

Elliott's 14 winners at the past two festivals have quickly advanced his total to 22, accumulated at just eight festivals after his breakthrough double in 2011 with Chicago Grey in the National Hunt Chase and Carlito Brigante in the Coral Cup.

He already has a Cheltenham Gold Cup on the list with Don Cossack in 2016 – one of eight Grade 1 wins among the 22 – and that highlights a key strength with staying chasers.

Seven of his nine chase wins have come at distances in excess of 3m, in the National Hunt Chase (three times), the Gold Cup, the Fulke Walwyn Kim Muir Handicap Chase and the Cross Country (twice) – five of them provided by his three-time festival scorers Cause Of Causes and Tiger Roll.

Some of Elliott's 12 successes over hurdles also emphasise the stable's accent

## MOST SUCCESSFUL RACES

**National Hunt Chase**
■■■
**Triumph Hurdle**
■■
**Coral Cup**
■■
**Cross Country Chase**
■■
**Fred Winter**
■■

## GORDON ELLIOTT FESTIVAL WINNERS BY RACE TYPE

■ Grade 1 **8**
■ Non Grade 1 **14**

## FESTIVAL WINNERS BY RACE DISTANCE

■ Below 2m4f **6**
■ 2m4f-3m **9**
■ Above 3m **7**

on stamina, with wins in the Coral Cup (twice), Martin Pipe Conditional Jockeys' Handicap Hurdle (twice), Ballymore Novices' Hurdle and Pertemps Network Final coming at distances of 2m4f-plus.

He also has a notably strong record with juvenile hurdlers, having won the Triumph Hurdle and the Fred Winter Handicap Hurdle twice each (including both races last year). Four of his 15 runners in those races since 2013 have won (at odds of 25-1, 10-1, 33-1 and 9-1, +66pts).

The market is not that good at identifying Elliott's winning chances, with only four of his 15 festival favourites having been successful, but the trainer's selection process is clearly working well as 16 of his 22 winners came in races where he had only one representative.

If punters had restricted themselves to backing Elliott runners when he had only one representative at last year's festival, they would have had four winners from 12 winners for a level-stakes profit of 10.73pts (the profits in the previous two years were 44.5pts and 9.75pts).

The figures may change as multiple representation

becomes more the norm for Elliott, given he has become the principal trainer for Gigginstown, but for now it is a factor worth bearing in mind.

*Look out for single representatives*

*Be wary of favourites*

## 22
CHELTENHAM FESTIVAL WINNERS

## 6
WINS WITH TIGER ROLL AND CAUSE OF CAUSES

## 15
DIFFERENT RACES WON

## 2011
YEAR OF FIRST WINNER AT CHELTENHAM

# Better Grade 1 prospects

THE ten-time British champion was leading trainer at the festival five times in six years between 2004 and 2009 but has not had that accolade since then, with the flood of winners having slowed to a trickle.

In the past two years he has had to wait until the Friday to get on the scoreboard. In 2017 Pacha Du Polder in the Foxhunter was his sole winner and last year he had a brace with Pacha Du Polder's repeat success and Le Prezien's victory in the Grand Annual finale.

Whereas Nicholls used to dominate the Grade 1 races, eight of his last 11 winners (going back to 2013) have been in handicaps. Since the end of the Big Buck's four-timer in the Stayers' Hurdle in 2012, Nicholls' only Grade 1 winner has been Dodging Bullets in the 2015 Queen Mother Champion Chase.

This year he has some decent prospects of a return to Grade 1 success with King George VI Chase winner Clan Des Obeaux in the Gold Cup, and possibly Cyrname if he is supplemented for the Ryanair Chase. His novices include Topofthegame in the RSA Chase and Triumph Hurdle contender Quel Destin.

The key to finding a Nicholls handicap winner at the festival, especially over

*Clan Des Obeaux: bidding to give Nicholls a record-equalling fifth Gold Cup win*

## MOST SUCCESSFUL RACES

**Champion Chase**
■■■■■
**Gold Cup**
■■■■
**Stayers' Hurdle**
■■■■
**Foxhunter**
■■■■
**County Hurdle**
■■■■
**Grand Annual**
■■■■
**Fred Winter**
■■■

hurdles, is to identify a young, lightly raced type yet to be exposed to the handicapper. Eight of his ten handicap hurdle winners were aged four or five, and nine of his 15 handicap winners overall have carried between 10st 10lb and 11st 11lb (two of the three above that weight were in the Martin Pipe).

It is worth noting that Nicholls has won the County Hurdle and the Grand Annual Chase four times apiece – both are over 2m, and that is another factor to take into account.

# 43
CHELTENHAM FESTIVAL
WINNERS

# 16
DIFFERENT RACES WON

# 17
YEARS SINCE
FESTIVAL BLANK

# 1999
YEAR OF FIRST WINNER AT
CHELTENHAM

*13 of his last 18 festival winners have been over hurdles*

*Eight of his last 11 successes were achieved in handicaps*

*Does well with young, unexposed horses in handicaps*

## PAUL NICHOLLS FESTIVAL WINNERS BY RACE TYPE

- G1 chases **15**
- G1 hurdles **9**
- Non G1 chases **9**
- Non G1 hurdles **10**

# Golden stable on the up

TIZZARD took the biggest prize at the 2018 festival with Native River's epic triumph over Might Bite in the Cheltenham Gold Cup, which underlined the Dorset trainer's emergence as a powerful force in jump racing's major contests.

He has a relatively small total of seven festival winners but last year's brace came in Grade 1 contests (his other winner was Kilbricken Storm in the Albert Bartlett Novices' Hurdle) and put him alongside Nicky Henderson and Paul Nicholls as the best-performing British trainers.

Four of his seven festival winners have been big prices (40-1 twice, 33-1 and 28-1) but it is worth noting that Tizzard's fancied runners generally show up well. He has had 15 runners priced under 10-1 at the past seven festivals and nine have finished in the first three (201521F23F335P1).

The big-priced winners are harder to spot but a couple of possible pointers are that two of the quartet at 28-1 plus had run in Grade 1 or 2 company last time out and the two handicap winners were ridden by claimers.

Native River remains the stable star as he gets ready for his bid to become the first to retain the Gold Cup crown since Best Mate's hat-trick in 2002-04 and

*Fancied horses usually perform well*

*But don't rule out a surprise. Four of his seven festival winners were returned at huge prices*

there is a sprinkling of other Grade 1 hopefuls including Lostintranslation (JLT Novices' Chase), Elixir De Nutz (Supreme Novices' Hurdle), Fox Norton (Ryanair Chase, or Queen Mother Champion Chase) and Kilbricken Storm (Stayers' Hurdle).

Mister Malarky is a useful staying novice chaser who could go for the National Hunt Chase or the Ultima Handicap Chase, having

already proved himself in Graded and open handicap company.

Tizzard's strength in depth with staying chasers should mean he becomes more of a force in handicaps, with more options to choose from, and another to watch is Robinsfirth, a Grade 3 handicap chase winner at Cheltenham in December 2017 and again in the Grand National Trial at Haydock in February.

# Defi back with big chance

THE Somerset trainer has been on the scoresheet only once at the past four festivals, courtesy of 2017 Triumph Hurdle winner Defi Du Seuil. He had a poor season overall in 2017-18 and mustered only nine festival runners, with just one going off shorter than 20-1 (that was National Hunt Chase sixth No Comment at 9-1).

The stable has recovered well from that low, having already gone well past last season's figures for winners and prize-money, and could be more of a threat this time.

Defi Du Seuil looks to be the big hope again, in the Arkle or more likely the JLT Novices' Chase. The six-year-old has thrived at around 2m4f over fences and won at

Grade 1 level in the Scilly Isles Novices' Chase at Sandown – a race in which Captain Chris was a close second for Hobbs before his Arkle success in 2011. Hobbs's 19 festival wins have come in 14 different races but four of the last seven were gained over fences.

The stable regularly delivers with fancied runners like Defi Du Seuil – five of the last six winners were sent off no bigger than 6-1 – and can also turn up rewarding each-way odds in handicap hurdles. Several of Hobbs's early festival winners came in that sphere (two wins in both the County and the Coral Cup) and he often threatens another – in 2017 Verni finished second in the Martin

*Watch the market closely*

*Each-way prospects in big handicap hurdles*

Pipe at 25-1 and Ozzie The Oscar (50-1) was third in the County, and in 2016 Hobbs had the third in the Pertemps Final and the third and fourth in the County Hurdle.

Crooks Peak is an interesting prospect for the County this year, while other decent hopes lie with Jerrysback in the Close Brothers Novices' Handicap Chase and For Good Measure in the Cross Country Chase (Hobbs has won both races before).

# Check out novice chasers

THE Barbury Castle trainer had a golden period with 11 festival winners from 2004 to 2009 but has scored only in singles since then (in 2011, 2013, 2014 and 2015) and his score is stuck on 15 after three consecutive blank festivals.

King remains a competitive force, however, with seven runners finishing in the first four at the past three festivals – all seven were over hurdles, suggesting those races may be his best route to success.

He is also a good trainer of mares, making Mia's Storm (Mares' Hurdle) and Alsa Mix (Mares' Novices' Hurdle) worthy of each-way consideration. None of his nine runners in those two contests at the past five festivals started shorter than 16-1 and yet he had two seconds, two thirds and a fourth.

Most of King's chase wins at the festival have been with novices, not only in Grade 1s and the National Hunt Chase but also in handicaps. It will be interesting if RSA Chase hope Talkischeap is diverted to the Ultima Handicap Chase (Yanworth also a possible runner) and likewise Arkle outsider Ballywood could be aimed at the Grand Annual Handicap Chase. Another to note is Azzerti, who looks bound for the Close Brothers Novices' Handicap Chase.

The classiest horse in the yard is Sceau Royal, who won the Grade 2 Shloer Chase at the course in November but will have a much tougher task against Altior in the Queen Mother Champion Chase.

*Back novice chasers in handicaps*

*Consider backing runners in mares' races each-way*

 Facebook.com/racingpost      Twitter @RacingPost   **105**

*Excellent record with runners at 10-1 or lower*

*Eight of her 11 wins have been at around 2m*

# Top record with big fancies

HARRINGTON is the most successful female trainer in festival history with 11 winners and her record is outstanding as she has never sent a team of more than eight runners in 22 festivals, yet has achieved much more than most of her rival trainers.

Her big hope this year is Supasundae in his bid to go one better than last year's second in the Stayers' Hurdle and add to his 2017 Coral Cup success. Jezki, the 2014 Champion Hurdle winner, has dropped into handicap company this season and could go for the County Hurdle or Coral Cup (Jetez

another with those options). Magic Of Light is a handicap chaser to note in the Kim Muir and Got Trumped looks interesting in the Boodles Juvenile Handicap Hurdle.

Harrington's select approach and winning habit mean her followers would be in profit if they had backed every festival runner (11-80, +16.75pts), although like her they would have had to sit through several blank festivals to reap the rewards in the long term.

One thing punters can rely on is that Harrington doesn't have festival runners for the sake of it. As well as her 11 winners, she has also had 13

others in the first four, which means 30 per cent of her runners have made the first four.

Her record with fancied runners is also worth noting, with nine of her 11 winners priced at 10-1 or lower.

Punters who restricted their bets to Harrington runners in that price bracket would have had nine winners from 34 (26%) for a level-stakes profit of 28.75pts.

Nine of the other 13 who made the first four were also 10-1 or lower, which emphasises it is the fancied runners that should be the main focus.

# Stayers offer best chances

O'NEILL has long been a consistent trainer of winners at the festival and stands fourth among current trainers but he has had three blanks in the past four years as the superpowers have exerted a strong grip. Prior to the recent period he had been on the scoreboard at 13 of the 14 festivals up to 2014.

His last winner was Minella Rocco in the 2016 National Hunt Chase, his sixth success in that race. His first five came in 12 runnings from 1995 to 2007 but the recent changes in the race conditions (which made it a higher-class contest) appeared to have

taken away his edge until Minella Rocco's victory.

It is worth taking note of any fancied runners and staying races are clearly where O'Neill does best, with 21 of his 26 festival wins coming in races over 3m-plus, and he also has a good record in the Pertemps Final (four wins) and the Ultima Handicap Chase (three).

Last year he had only three festival runners and numbers might be on the low side again but he has reasonable hopes with staying handicap hurdlers Ready And Able and Dream Berry, both Pertemps possibles.

*Best in races over 3m-plus*

*Eleven of his last 13 winners came over fences*

*Don't ignore the stable second string – two of his recent handicap winners beat a better-fancied stablemate*

# Focus on handicap chases

LAST year was only the third festival blank for Pipe since he landed the 2007 Fred Winter Juvenile Handicap Hurdle with Gaspara in his first season and it was probably his most disappointing showing with an unusually small team yielding nothing better than a fifth place.

Overall last season was poor by the high standards of the Pipe stable, with the number of runners and winners well down, and his figures are well down again this season compared with the years when a century of winners was the norm.

He should not be discounted at the festival, however, especially in the three handicap chases (the Ultima, Kim Muir and Stable Plate) over 2m5f-plus. In the past five years he has won four of those contests – more than any other trainer – from a total of 15 runnings for a strike-rate of 15 per cent and a level-stake profit of +18pts.

Eleven of his 15 festival wins have been in chases and he has won the Ultima, Kim Muir and Stable Plate on three occasions apiece. Watch the market closely: from 27 runners priced at 12-1 or below in those three handicap chases, he has had seven winners (26%, +36.83pts), two seconds and a third.

Strong contenders are thin on the ground but possibles

*Eleven of his 15 festival victories have come over fences*

*Note his fancied runners in staying handicap chases*

for the handicap chases include Welsh Grand National runner-up Ramses De Teillee and Un Temps Pour Tout, who won the Ultima in 2016 and 2017 but has been hit by injury.

Two of Pipe's four wins over hurdles have been in the Pertemps Final, although both came early in his career with course specialist Buena Vista. He has yet to win a Grade 1 over hurdles at the festival and is short of that kind of quality this season.

# Watch out for fancied runners

*Novice chasers and fancied runners are a traditional strength*

*The New One is the yard's only festival winner over hurdles since 2008*

TWISTON-DAVIES'S festival record comes in fits and starts. He had two winners in 2009, three in 2010 (including the Gold Cup with Imperial Commander), two in 2013 and two again in 2016, but he drew blanks in the other six years in the past decade, including the last two.

His two most recent winners in 2016 both came in Grade 1 races – the RSA Chase with Blaklion and the Champion Bumper with Ballyandy – and his overall total stands at 17.

He has done best with fancied runners in the past decade, with six of his nine winners priced under 10-1 (another was 11-1). At the past three festivals

he has continued to do well with runners well signalled in the market with his ten priced at under 10-1 finishing 411224F634.

He had only one runner in that bracket last season but has a leading fancy this time in Betfair Hurdle

winner Al Dancer, who is set to go for the Supreme Novices'. The trainer has won that race before, although his stable is more noted for stayers and nine of his 17 festival winners have been at 3m-plus (and three more in the 2m5f Ballymore Novices' Hurdle).

Among his handicap hopes are Go Conquer (*above*, Ultima) and Calett Mad (Kim Muir) over fences and Ballyandy (Coral Cup) and Ballymoy (County) over hurdles.

**HENRY DE BROMHEAD** had his fifth festival success last year – and his fourth in a Grade 1 – when Balko Des Flos took the Ryanair Chase.

He usually does best with runners at 10-1 or lower – Balko Des Flos (8-1) was his fourth winner in that category (and Special Tiara was only just outside at 11-1 in the 2017 Queen Mother Champion Chase). Overall, at 10-1 or lower, he has had four winners, six seconds and three thirds from 20 runners in the past decade (4-20, +14.5pts).

**Joseph O'Brien** has technically had a festival winner already, having overseen Ivanovich Gorbatov's preparation for the 2016 Triumph Hurdle, but the horse ran in father Aidan's name and thus the fast-rising trainer is still seeking his first official success.

It is surely only a matter of time and, having had 14 festival runners so far, he has such a powerful team that he might well double that tally this year. He is particularly strong in juvenile hurdles – Sir Erec and Fakir D'Oudairies lead the ante-post market for the Triumph and Gardens Of Babylon, Konitho and Band Of Outlaws are among the possibles for the Fred Winter – but also has Arkle favourite Le Richebourg and Bumper fancy Dlauro.

**Dan Skelton** has had two festival winners and both in the County Hurdle (Superb Story at 8-1 in 2016 and Mohaayed at 33-1 last year). His record is sure to improve and perhaps handicap success is more likely for now. Superb Story is one of just six handicap runners he has had under 10-1 and two of the others were third at 7-1 and 15-2.

**Tom George**, who had his first festival winner in 2002 with Galileo (Ballymore Novices' Hurdle), bridged a 16-year gap when Summerville Boy became his second with last year's victory in the Supreme Novices' Hurdle.

George had been knocking on the door and, as well as Summerville Boy's win, he has had four seconds and five thirds from 30 runners at the past five festivals. In that period his runners at 10-1 or lower have finished 03265F152.

Summerville Boy sustained a leg fracture this season but George still has bright hopes with Singlefarmpayment (Ultima Handicap Chase), Black Op (Stayers' Hurdle) and Clondaw Castle (Close Brothers Novices' Handicap Chase).

**Enda Bolger** has had eight festival winners – five in the Cross Country and three in the Foxhunter – and has several leading chances again.

His Cross Country team includes 2016 winner Josies Orders, Auvergnat and My Hometown, while Stand Up And Fight and Gilgamboa give him a strong hand in the Foxhunter.

The market is a good guide. Four of his winners started favourite and none of the eight was bigger than 6-1 (8-24, +10.51pts with all runners at 6-1 or lower).

■ **Emma Lavelle**, whose two festival wins were in handicap hurdles in 2008 and 2010, has a big shot at Grade 1 success with Paisley Park, who jumped to Stayers' Hurdle favouritism after victory in the Grade 1 Long Walk at Ascot and the Grade 2 Cleeve at Cheltenham.

Officially the seven-year-old, who was 13th in last year's Albert Bartlett Novices' Hurdle, has improved 2st this season from a 140-rated handicap prospect to a mark of 168, which puts him 3lb ahead of last year's Stayers' Hurdle winner Penhill.

Lavelle, based near Marlborough in Wiltshire, was confident after Paisley Park's 12-length victory in the Cleeve. "How could he not be made favourite? I don't think there's anyone this side of the water who wasn't in the Cleeve, and with Penhill not having run this season he would have to come over in tip-top shape."

■ **Ruth Jefferson** took over the family stables in Malton on the death of her father Malcolm in February last year and quickly made her mark with Waiting Patiently's Grade 1 Ascot Chase win later that month.

Quick ground was blamed for Waiting Patiently's defeat behind Cyrname last time when he went for an Ascot Chase repeat, but he will be a leading contender if the going allows him to take his chance in the Ryanair Chase.

Jefferson sent out Cloudy Dream to finish third in last year's Ryanair but will have a much better shot with Waiting Patiently, who is officially rated nearly a stone better than his former stablemate and beat other British hopefuls Frodon and Top Notch in last year's Ascot Chase.

■ **Kayley Woollacott** also became a trainer in sad circumstances following the death of her husband Richard in January last year and she has a leading Arkle contender in Lalor, who made a good start over fences with

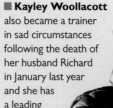

victory against Dynamite Dollars in the Racing Post Arkle Trophy Trial at Cheltenham.

Although that rival had Lalor back in third the following month in the Grade 1 Henry VIII Novices' Chase at Sandown, Woollacott *(left)* is hopeful of a strong showing in the Arkle.

"All of his best runs have come off the back of a long break," the Devon trainer said. "He was so good at Cheltenham in November and that's how we hope to get him back there in March. It was very soft at Sandown and he still ran creditably. He'd want, good, good to soft."

*The Presenting Percy team in the winner's enclosure after last year's RSA Chase*

methods and is looking forward to the festival again.

"To have a horse like Presenting Percy is incredible," he said. "Pat Kelly has only one day in mind for him, so there is bound to be some improvement there."

■ **Olly Murphy** has made rapid strides in the training ranks since his first winner in July 2017 and looks set to have around half a dozen runners in his bid for a festival breakthrough.

The Warwickshire trainer ranks in the top six for winners in Britain this season and his team includes novice hurdlers Thomas Darby and Itchy Feet in the Supreme, Brewin'upastorm in the Ballymore and Finawn Bawn in the Albert Bartlett.

Shortest-priced in the ante-post betting is Brewin'upastorm, who was in front when falling at the last in a Grade 2 at Cheltenham's January meeting.

"He went up 6lb, so the handicapper obviously thought it was a good run, and he was halved in price by most bookmakers," he said. "The fall was one of those things – he's a forward-going type and it won't have knocked his confidence. He came away from Cheltenham with a lot of credit and roll on March."

■ **Amy Murphy**, who became Britain's youngest trainer when she had her first runner in September 2016 at the age of 24, went close to festival success with Kalashnikov's neck second in last year's Supreme Novices' Hurdle and has faith in her stable star despite a shock defeat in the Kingmaker Novices' Chase at Sandown in February.

Kalashnikov is still being aimed at the Racing Post Arkle (or the JLT Novices' Chase) and Murphy is confident he can get back to the form he showed in a pair of easy wins in minor events before he was second to high-class rival Dynamite Dollars in the Grade 2 Wayward Lad Novices' Chase at Kempton.

"Hopefully we'll be able to look back on Sandown and say it's just one of those runs you can put a line through," she said. "The plan is still the Arkle. I went back and

watched every race he's ever run and whether it's his Betfair Hurdle win, his second in the Supreme, either of his two novice chase wins, or his second at Kempton, he doesn't lack for speed."

■ **Pat Kelly** has become a respected and feared trainer with a winner at each of the past three festivals from just a handful of runners – Mall Dini and Presenting Percy in the Pertemps Final in 2016 and 2017 and then Presenting Percy again in last year's RSA Chase.

This time he will be fully in the spotlight as he chases the biggest prize of all with Presenting Percy in the Cheltenham Gold Cup, having bypassed the traditional big races in favour of an unconventional build-up.

Philip Reynolds, owner of Presenting Percy and Mall Dini (who could go for one of the handicap chases), has complete faith in the trainer's

## 1.30 Sky Bet Supreme Novices' Hurdle  ITV/RTV
### 2m½f  Grade 1  £125,000

It was still 5-1 the field for the traditional curtain-raiser after the main trials and this looks the most open year since 2012, when Galileo's Choice was the unplaced 6-1 favourite and Cinders And Ashes won at 10-1. One of the complicating factors is that leading fancy Fakir D'Oudairies is a four-year-old and would be expected to go for the Triumph Hurdle but for the fact that trainer Joseph O'Brien is so well stocked with juveniles he could send him here instead to take advantage of a hefty age allowance. Fakir D'Oudairies could end up favourite if he comes here but there is a strong British defence headed by Nicky Henderson's Angels Breath, a Grade 2 winner on his debut in December, and the more battle-hardened Betfair Hurdle winner Al Dancer from the Nigel Twiston-Davies stable. As well as Fakir D'Oudairies, Ireland's customary strong hand includes Klassical Dream and Aramon for Willie Mullins.

### AL DANCER
**6 gr g; Trainer** Nigel Twiston-Davies
**Hurdles form** 1111, best RPR 152
**Left-handed** 11, best RPR 142
**Right-handed** 11, best RPR 152
**Cheltenham form** 1, best RPR 142

Progressive form in bumpers last season and has continued to improve and develop into a top-class novice hurdler. Barely off the bridle in first two novice hurdles and then, handed a handicap mark of 129, he made a laughing stock of the assessor's initial effort when trotting up by 11 lengths at Cheltenham in December. That form had worked out well even before he went to the rescheduled Betfair Hurdle at Ascot in February and ran out a commanding winner by three and three-quarter lengths despite racing with the choke out nearly all the way round. That was off a mark of 141 and when the handicapper reassesses him he'll almost certainly head to the Supreme as the highest-rated horse in the race. Three Betfair Hurdle winners in recent seasons – Get Me Out Of Here, My Tent Or Yours and Kalashnikov – went on to finish second in the Supreme and the novice Make A Stand went on to win the Champion Hurdle after his Newbury success in 1997, so it's not a bad race to have on his CV. Jumping is fast and accurate and he certainly has far more solid claims than ownermate Angels Breath.

*Going preference* Seems to handle anything
*Star rating* ✪✪✪✪✪

### ANGELS BREATH
**5 gr g; Trainer** Nicky Henderson
**Hurdles form** (right-handed) 1, best RPR 144

Cost €85,000 as an unraced store at Goffs in June 2017 and that is already starting to look a bargain after he won his point by 12 lengths the following April and, on being sent to Nicky Henderson, made a sparkling hurdles debut in a Grade 2 at Ascot in December, beating the well-regarded Danny Kirwan by four and a half lengths. That race was in some ways unsatisfactory as there were only four hurdles due to high winds and none was jumped in the straight, which meant the last was a long way from home and it was more like a Flat race. Still, he seemed to show a smart turn of foot to win with a deal in hand and a Racing Post Rating of 144 is unusually high for a hurdling debutant. Not many will have been asked to debut in a Grade 2 in the first place and the fact he was up to it has to bode well, even if he looks sure to head to the festival with less match practice than is ideal. Trainer sees him as a two-miler based on homework despite his 3m point win, but he was due to run in the Sidney Banks at Huntingdon over 2m3½f in early February until the equine flu outbreak intervened and racing was postponed. That would have opened the possibility of squeezing in another run before the festival but he'll surely only get one more now. On pedigree he'll get further than 2m (sire's best Cheltenham performers have come beyond the minimum trip) and horses with a point-to-point background tend to do better in the Ballymore or Albert Bartlett. Only two winners of this race in the past 20 years had run in points and by the time they turned up here they were having their ninth starts under rules. Still, he's been near the head of the market since his debut and despite his owner having another likely sort in Al Dancer, the chances are he'll go here to avoid stablemate Champ.

*Going preference* Too early to say
*Star rating* ✪✪

## FAKIR D'OUDAIRIES
**4 b g; Trainer** Joseph O'Brien
**Hurdles form** 2611, best RPR 147
**Left-handed** 261, best RPR 147
**Right-handed** 1, best RPR 116
**Cheltenham form** 1, best RPR 147

Four-year-old who was 0-5 in bumpers, over hurdles and fences in France, but is 2-2 since joining Joseph O'Brien and put up one of the best performances by a novice hurdler of any age this term when destroying arguably the best Britain had to offer for the Triumph Hurdle on trials day at Cheltenham. Won by 13 lengths from stablemate Fine Brunello there and was quickly made favourite for the Triumph, but O'Brien then had the 1-2 in the big juvenile hurdle at Leopardstown and he was superseded by winner Sir Erec. JP McManus, owner of the front two at Leopardstown, then purchased Fakir D'Oudairies, which surely increases the likelihood of his participation here. The last four-year-old winner of the Supreme was Hors La Loi in 1999 but only 13 have tried since and, according to the Racing Post Rating earned by Fakir D'Oudairies at Cheltenham, he is considerably better going into the race than any other horse since, including the owner's Binocular (RPR 138), who was second to Captain Cee Bee. McManus won the Supreme anyway that year, but not the Triumph when his short-priced favourite Franchoek was turned over, so the switch doesn't always work, but the rest of his Supreme challengers don't look up to it and running Fakir D'Oudairies here would make

sense. The 8lb weight-for-age allowance given to four-year-olds in this race must surely make him a big player.

*Going preference* Handles good to soft and soft
*Star rating* ✪✪✪✪

## KLASSICAL DREAM
**5 b g; Trainer** Willie Mullins
**Hurdles form** P324P11, best RPR 144
**Left-handed** 324P11, best RPR 144
**Right-handed** P

Failed to score in five outings over hurdles in France, being pulled up twice, but also showed some useful form and was beaten under five lengths when fourth to Guillaume Macaire's unfortunately injured winning machine Master Dino in an Auteuil Grade 1 in November 2017. A year off and switch to Willie Mullins certainly hasn't done him any harm and he's 2-2 for his new yard, having won his maiden at Leopardstown over Christmas and then scored a battling win from stablemate Aramon in the Grade 1 Chanelle Pharma Novice Hurdle at the Dublin Racing Festival. Certainly had to work hard but, having been up with the pace throughout and headed after the last by the more patiently ridden runner-up, he really put his head down to get back up by a head, the pair six lengths clear. Hard to argue that form is outstanding but the same is true of pretty much all the 2m novice hurdle form, so his willingness in a fight is not a bad weapon to have.

*Going preference* Best form on decent surface so far
*Star rating* ✪✪✪

## MISTER FISHER
**5 b g; Trainer** Nicky Henderson
**Hurdles form** 211, best RPR 142
**Left-handed** 21, best RPR 142
**Right-handed** 1, best RPR 135

Bumper winner last season who has improved with every run over hurdles, winning the last two of his three starts while still looking as though he has plenty to learn. Certainly found plenty when asked at Kempton over Christmas in race Nicky Henderson won with Altior in 2015 and both second and third have won since, albeit at long odds-on without needing to improve. Stepped up for the Grade 2 Rossington Main Novices' Hurdle at Haydock in January, he again answered every call and was well on top at the end, beating Bright Forecast by two and a half lengths. Once again the form doesn't look brilliant – third hardly upheld it when only third in ordinary novice at Market Rasen next time – but it puts him in the mix in a wide-open year and he certainly shapes as though there is more to come.

*Going preference* Handles good to soft and soft

*Star rating* ✪✪✪

## ARAMON

**6 b g; Trainer** Willie Mullins
**Hurdles form** 121312, best RPR 146
**Left-handed** 2112, best RPR 146
**Right-handed** 13, best RPR 140

German-bred who won two his 11 Flat starts in nation of his birth, albeit for small money at a low level. Has looked a bargain at €40,000 since, winning three of his six hurdles starts for Willie Mullins, including the Grade 1 Future Champions Novice Hurdle at Leopardstown by ten lengths from shorter-priced stablemate Sancta Simona. Surprised

his rider Ruby Walsh there and those behind have not done much for the form, while Walsh was on board head winner Klassical Dream when the pair clashed in the Grade 1 Chanelle Pharma Novice Hurdle in February. There is quite obviously very little between the pair at the moment, but the winner has run only twice since missing a season and is a year younger, so you'd have to think he has more scope to improve than a six-year-old veteran of 17 races. Still, Aramon is one of the best on the figures going into the race.

*Going preference* Best form on good
*Star rating* ✪✪✪

## ELIXIR DE NUTZ

**5 gr g; Trainer** Colin Tizzard
**Hurdles form** 6F2111, best RPR 141
**Left-handed** 6F211, best RPR 139
**Right-handed** 1, best RPR 141
**Cheltenham form** 6211, best RPR 139

Second-season hurdler, but first 'campaign' should not be held against him as he was rather highly tried in the Triumph Hurdle Trial of January 2018 just three months after a winning bumper debut in France. Never competitive there, finishing a distant last, and then fell at the last when holding every chance at Uttoxeter in May. Has switched

*Aramon: one of the best in the race on the figures*

from Philip Hobbs to Colin Tizzard since and improved with every start, winning his last three, culminating in the Grade 1 Tolworth Hurdle at Sandown, a race that has seen five winners go on to festival success later that season since 1998. All three wins have come in five-runner races and his trademark has been his willingness to pull out more when challenged, but it's hard not to think that was one of the weakest renewals of the Tolworth with short-priced favourite Rathhill not coming up to scratch and third-placed Southfield Stone getting turned over at odds-on at Taunton next time. Will have more than four rivals to fend off at Cheltenham and probably only has outside chance at best.

*Going preference* Seems to handle any
*Star rating* ✪✪

## CHAMPAGNE PLATINUM
**5 gr g; Trainer** Nicky Henderson
**Hurdles form** (left-handed) 11, best RPR 134

Point winner (sold to JP McManus for £250,000 afterwards) who is almost as unexposed as Nicky Henderson's first string Angels Breath after just two starts over hurdles in ordinary company. Has won both with ease, but hard to put a big figure on him as he beat some fairly average horses. Still, he was entered in a race at Exeter the trainer used for his 2011 Supreme runner-up Spirit Son until equine flu intervened. You'd imagine they will find something else for him in the meantime and, while he has stuck to 2m for the time being, there is little doubt he will get further in time, hence the entry in the Ballymore. Trainer says he is good and "will be very good", so interesting to see what happens with him.

*Going preference* Handles soft, untried on good
*Star rating* ✪✪

## GETAWAY TRUMP
**6 b g; Trainer** Paul Nicholls
**Hurdles form** 41124, best RPR 144
**Left-handed** 412, best RPR 142
**Right-handed** 14, best RPR 144

Point winner who showed only fair form in two bumpers last season but has taken off

over hurdles since a somewhat lacklustre debut when a distant fourth at Chepstow in October. Won his next two starts, on the first occasion over 2m4½f at Plumpton and then dropped to 2m1f at Exeter, where he toyed with Tedham, giving him 6lb and a five-length beating with a smart turn of foot. The runner-up is now rated 131 after being a well-backed handicap winner next time, so the form looks solid, and Getaway Trump stepped up again when second to Champ in the Grade 1 Challow Hurdle at Newbury, even though he was no match for the two-and-a-half-length winner. Steady gallop in Betfair Hurdle at Ascot didn't play to his strengths, but he stayed on strongly for fourth and can improve on that in a stronger-run race.

*Going preference* Early days but doesn't seem to have any issues
*Star rating* ✪✪

## FELIX DESJY
**6 ch g; Trainer** Gordon Elliott
**Hurdles form** 17521, best RPR 147
**Right-handed** 121, best RPR 147
**Left-handed** 75, best RPR 131
**Cheltenham form** 6 (bumper), best RPR 135
**At the festival** 14 Mar 2018 Unfurnished, looked well, in touch racing keenly, tracked leaders going well 3f out, went 2nd 2f out, ridden when lost 2nd and not quicken over 1f out, no extra final 100yds, finished sixth, beaten seven and a half lengths by Relegate in Champion Bumper

Had big reputation as a bumper horse and went off 8-1 for the Champion Bumper at the festival, finishing a creditable sixth before a lesser effort in the Punchestown version a month later. Started hurdles campaign well enough with a ten-length maiden win at Galway at odds of 2-7, but seemingly found out on next two starts when last of seven to Aramon and fifth of eight to East Game in a pair of Navan Grade 3s. Was switched to a front-running role next time at Limerick and showed improved form to be second to highly-thought-of mare Salsaretta and progressed again when five-length winner from Jetez in Punchestown Grade 2 in January. Suspicion he was given too much of an easy time in front, but an RPR of 147 is one of the best

## SUPREME NOVICES' HURDLE RESULTS AND TRENDS

| | FORM | WINNER | AGE & WGT | Adj RPR | SP | TRAINER | BEST RPR LAST 12 MONTHS (RUNS SINCE) |
|---|---|---|---|---|---|---|---|
| 18 | 12231 | **Summerville Boy** D | 6 11-7 | 157·3 | 9-1 | T George | won Gd1 Tolworth Hurdle (2m) **(0)** |
| 17 | 11RR6 | **Labaik** D | 6 11-7 | 150·8 | 25-1 | G Elliott (IRE) | won Navan Gd3 nov hdl (2m) **(3)** |
| 16 | 61111 | **Altior** CD | 6 11-7 | 163ᵀ | 4-1 | N Henderson | won Kempton class 2 nov hdl (2m) **(0)** |
| 15 | 2111 | **Douvan** D | 5 11-7 | 160·3 | 2-1f | W Mullins (IRE) | won Punchestown Gd2 nov hdl (2m) **(0)** |
| 14 | 2-111 | **Vautour** D | 5 11-7 | 157ᵀ | 7-2j | W Mullins (IRE) | won Gd1 Deloitte Hurdle (2m2f) **(0)** |
| 13 | -1231 | **Champagne Fever** C,D | 6 11-7 | 157·13 | 5-1 | W Mullins (IRE) | won Gd1 Deloitte Hurdle (2m2f) **(0)** |
| 12 | -2111 | **Cinders And Ashes** D | 5 11-7 | 152·6 | 10-1 | D McCain | won Aintree class 4 mdn hdl (2m1f) **(2)** |
| 11 | -F311 | **Al Ferof** D | 6 11-7 | 146·17 | 10-1 | P Nicholls | won Newbury class 3 nov hdl (2m½f) **(0)** |
| 10 | 11212 | **Menorah** D, BF | 5 11-7 | 160·3 | 12-1 | P Hobbs | won Kempton class 2 nov hdl (2m) **(1)** |
| 09 | 12121 | **Go Native** D | 6 11-7 | 153·8 | 12-1 | N Meade (IRE) | won Punchestown Listed nov hdl (2m) **(2)** |

**WINS-RUNS:** 4yo 0-3, 5yo 4-79, 6yo 6-61, 7yo 0-13, 8yo 0-4, 9yo 0-1 **FAVOURITES:** -£4.75

**TRAINERS IN THIS RACE (w-pl-r):** Willie Mullins 3-3-27, Nicky Henderson 1-8-18, Paul Nicholls 1-0-5, Philip Hobbs 1-0-6, Gordon Elliott 1-1-4, Noel Meade 1-0-2, Donald McCain 1-0-2, Alan King 0-1-5, David Pipe 0-0-6, Dan Skelton 0-0-2, Harry Fry 0-0-1, Henry de Bromhead 0-1-4, Colin Tizzard 0-0-5, Nigel Twiston-Davies 0-0-4

**FATE OF FAVOURITES:** 5340211220 **POSITION OF WINNER IN MARKET:** 6436211203

in the field and he's clearly going the right way now. One possible question mark is his form on left-handed tracks, as along with his bumper sixth his figures read 675. That's compared to 115121 right-handed and his best over hurdles is a full 16lb better than his left-handed form.

*Going preference* Handles everything
*Star rating* ✪✪

## OTHERS TO CONSIDER

There's room for any number of horses to make an impact, although time is running out for **Annamix**, ante-post favourite this year and last, to show he's up to it. One of interest at a massive price could be **Sams Profile**, who raced keenly and jumped badly early on at Navan last time but took the final three flights well when the pace quickened. He's 50-1 for this and 16-1 for the Ballymore (winner is fav) but a strongly run 2m might just suit. **Grand Sancy** may have won a weak Kingwell Hurdle but that entitles him to respect back in novice companyy.

## VERDICT

*I've been a big fan of **AL DANCER** all season and can't see any reason to desert him after his Betfair Hurdle success. The one I'd be most wary of is **Fakir D'Oudairies**.*

### Key trends

☞ Adjusted RPR of at least 150, nine winners in last ten runnings

☞ Ran within the last 59 days, 9/10

☞ Previously contested a Graded race, 9/10 (eight won)

☞ Won at least 50 per cent of hurdle starts, 8/10

☞ Won last time out, 8/10

☞ Rated within 8lb of RPR top-rated, 8/10 (only two were top-rated)

### Other factors

☞ Only one winner had come via the Flat. Seven of the other nine started their careers in bumpers, where they had earned an RPR of at least 110. The other two started over hurdles in France

☞ Three winners had previously run in the Champion Bumper (Al Ferof second in 2010, Cinders And Ashes fifth in 2011 and Champagne Fever won in 2012)

☞ For many years, the shortest-priced Irish runner was often beaten by a compatriot. However, of the last ten to win, seven were the most fancied

## 2.10 Racing Post Arkle Chase
### 2m · Grade 1 · £175,000
**ITV/RTV**

JP McManus, who is way out in front as the leading owner at the festival with 54 winners, has never won the Arkle but has a big chance this year with Le Richebourg. Trained by Joseph O'Brien, who could be a major player at this year's festival, the six-year-old has won Ireland's top two Grade 1 novice chases over 2m1f in decisive style. The British defence is led by Lalor, a Grade 2 winner at the course on his chasing bow before disappointing at Sandown, and surprise package Glen Forsa, who has come out of left-field but is firmly in the reckoning for Mick Channon after his victory in the Grade 2 Kingmaker at Sandown. The other leading fancy in the ante-post market is Cilaos Emery, whose trainer Willie Mullins is going for his fourth Arkle success in five years.

## LE RICHEBOURG
**6 b g; Trainer** Joseph O'Brien
**Chase form** 11211, best RPR 160
**Left-handed** 1111, best RPR 160
**Right-handed** 2, best RPR 154
**Cheltenham form** (hurdles) 0, best RPR 129
**At the festival** 16 Mar 2018 Held up towards rear, headway after 3 out, in touch when mistake next, soon ridden, weakened before last, finished 15th, beaten 22 and a quarter lengths by Mohaayed in County Hurdle

Fair novice over hurdles last season but not up to Graded company and ran in the County Hurdle at the festival, finishing well down the field. We perhaps shouldn't hold that against him, as he was faced with deep ground for most of last season, having done his early winning on a quicker surface. The chances are he would have proved more competitive on a decent surface, but a drier winter and fences have been the making of him and he is a natural at his obstacles. He has won four of his five starts, going down by only half a length to leading RSA fancy Delta Work in the 2m4f Grade 1 Drinmore at Fairyhouse. His two subsequent wins have been in the two best 2m1f trials in Ireland, the Racing Post Novice Chase and Frank Ward Solicitors Arkle, and he won both Grade 1s with plenty in hand. That arguably entitles him to his place at the head of the market and as long as we don't get a heavy-ground festival he should be a major player.

*Going preference* Suspicion he wants a decent surface
*Star rating* ✪✪✪✪✪

## LALOR
**7 b g; Trainer** Kayley Woollacott
**Chase form** 13, best RPR 160
**Left-handed** 1, best RPR 160
**Right-handed** 3, best RPR 147
**Cheltenham form** (all) 21, best RPR 160

Winner at the last two Aintree festivals, in a bumper and then the Grade 1 Top Novices' Hurdle last season, and made a scintillating start to chase career when slamming Dynamite Dollars by seven lengths in a Grade 2 at Cheltenham in November. After travelling strongly and jumping superbly, he took it up after three out and fairly sauntered clear, earning a Racing Post Rating of 160. That's exceptionally high for a horse having his first run over fences and it has been bettered only a couple of times in the last 12 years, but all did not go to plan when he ran in the Grade 1 Henry VIII Novices' Chase at Sandown next time as he was beaten just under 12 lengths into third by Dynamite Dollars, reversing the Cheltenham form. Trainer was inclined to blame the ground there, as she did when he made no impact in last season's Betfair Hurdle, but his Grade 1 hurdle win came on soft ground and there's surely just as strong an argument for suggesting he is not at his best going right-handed. Although he has two bumper wins to his name at Wincanton, one of those came after the winner was subsequently disqualified and he has since proved in a different class to the horses he raced against then. He has run over obstacles three times right-handed and tasted defeat at odds of 10-11, 7-4 and 8-11. His best form left-handed according to RPRs is 12lb better in bumpers, 24lb better over hurdles and 13lb better over fences than the other way around. He missed a possible engagement at Doncaster because the ground was too quick, but he goes well fresh and, his inexperienced trainer notwithstanding, it's not easy to banish from the memory just how good he looked over the Arkle course and distance on his debut.

*Going preference* Acts on good and soft
*Star rating* ✪✪✪✪

## CILAOS EMERY

**7 b g; Trainer** Willie Mullins
**Chase form** (right-handed) 1, best RPR 143
**Cheltenham form** (hurdles) 5, best RPR 142
**At the festival** 14 Mar 2017 Led, not fluent 5th, ridden and headed after 2 out, weakened last, finished fifth, beaten 16 and a half lengths by Labaik in Supreme Novices' Hurdle

Fair novice hurdler a couple of seasons ago who finished fifth in what was admittedly a far from vintage Supreme Novices' Hurdle, but then won the equivalent Grade 1 at Punchestown from stablemate Melon, who went on to finish second in last year's Champion Hurdle. Obviously he's been difficult to train since as he managed only two starts in the early part of last season, although his second to Mick Jazz in the Grade 1 Ryanair Hurdle earned him a rating of 159 in that sphere. That confirms he has the latent talent to take high rank over fences and he certainly took to them well enough on his chase debut after 391 days off when winning at Gowran Park in January. He won comfortably enough in the end but did have to be pushed out to make sure and the runner-up carried a rating of just 131, so he's going to head into the

Arkle with a huge amount to find on that form if he doesn't gain more experience in the meantime. Hardly an ante-post proposition anyway given he has managed just eight starts across four seasons.

*Going preference* Seems versatile
*Star rating* ✪✪✪

## GLEN FORSA

**7 b g; Trainer** Mick Channon
**Chase form** 111, best RPR 155
**Left-handed** 1, best RPR 128
**Right-handed** 11, best RPR 155

Showed promise a couple of seasons ago but missed 21 months due to injury and started this campaign running, and getting beaten, in a lowly novice hurdle at Newton Abbot. To say his progress has been remarkable since would be some understatement and he's certainly gone about becoming a serious Arkle contender via a circuitous route as he made his chase debut in November in a Chepstow novice handicap (mark of 114) over nearly 3m. He didn't have much trouble with the trip there, winning by a couple of lengths, but he still made big improvement dropped to 2m4½f at Kempton over Christmas when defying an 11lb higher mark in good style in a race that worked out remarkably well. Was made favourite for the Close Brothers Novices' Handicap Chase on the strength of that, but after giving long-time ante-post favourite Kalashnikov a jumping lesson over 2m at Sandown in February he now looks certain to be appearing much earlier on the Tuesday card. If he jumps that well at Cheltenham not many will get past him.

*Going preference* Handles soft and good to soft
*Star rating* ✪✪✪✪✪

## TRAINER'S VIEW

**Joseph O'Brien on Le Richebourg** "I think nice ground is important to him. He's a very quick and accurate jumper. The strong pace suited him and it was good to see him jump the last so well [in the Irish Arkle] as he'd made a mistake there when winning at Christmas. The Arkle is the plan – they'll probably go even quicker there" *Has improved with every chase run to an RPR of 160*

## PALOMA BLUE

**7 br g; Trainer** Henry de Bromhead
**Chase form** (left-handed) 41, best RPR 144
**Cheltenham form** (hurdles) 4, best RPR 150
**At the festival** 13 Mar 2018 Tracked leader, ridden after 2 out, kept on but not quite pace to mount challenge, finished fourth, beaten three lengths by Summerville Boy in Supreme Novices' Hurdle

Decent novice hurdler who improved with almost every start last season, finishing third in a Grade 1 at Leopardstown in February and then a three-length fourth to Summerville Boy in the Supreme. Jumping fell apart when he was tailed off as an 11-2 shot for Punchestown Grade 1 in April, but it subsequently emerged he had pulled a left-fore shoe and that was clearly not his form. Hardly made the perfect start to his chase career when only fourth at odds-on at Navan in November and, while he improved to get off the mark at Leopardstown over Christmas, an RPR of 144 is as much as 20lb shy of what is going to be required. No doubt he is capable of much better, however, and trainer says he jumps better at home than he has so far on the track. In fairness, when asked to put in a big one at Leopardstown he did, but he seemed to guess if left to his own devices and it would take a brave ride to fire him into every fence at Cheltenham.

*Going preference* Seems versatile enough
*Star rating* ✪✪

## KNOCKNANUSS

**9 b g; Trainer** Gary Moore
**Chase form** (left-handed) F112F, best RPR 158

Lightly raced for his age, but has finished in the first two on nine of 11 completed starts and has developed into a surprisingly classy novice chaser despite falls on his first and latest start. A horse who races enthusiastically if a little too keenly, he only got as far as the fifth on his Plumpton debut in October, but then racked up two wide-margin wins when never seeing a rival at Fakenham and Newbury. In the latter event he had his rivals toiling a long way from home and beat the 133-rated Kupatana by 17 lengths in a time that suggested the form was as good as it looked. Next time he was up against it when

taking on French winning machine Master Dino, who had a BHA rating of 157 and was receiving 5lb, but he still led until after the second-last and was beaten only seven lengths over a trip that may have stretched him. Sent to Leopardstown for the Frank Ward Solicitors Arkle, he was the only horse seriously backed against Le Richebourg, but unfortunately came down at the second. His jumping can be breathtaking, but going off at the rate he does leaves little margin for error, and that can only be a worry in what might prove a decent-sized field this year. He is also a nine-year-old and the last horse to win this race at such an advanced age was Danish Flight in 1988.

*Going preference* Best form on good to soft or quicker
*Star rating* ✪

## ORNUA

**8 ch g; Trainer** Henry de Bromhead
**Chase form** 3112122, best RPR 157
**Left-handed** 311, best RPR 152
**Right-handed** 2122, best RPR 157

Useful performer who has earned plenty of experience since making his chase debut in May and is beginning to look a ready-made replacement for the stable's 2017 Champion Chase winner Special Tiara, who sadly lost his life at the Dublin Racing Festival in February. Whether he can ever match that one is another matter, but he usually adopts a catch-me-if-you-can style while putting in some lightning-fast and sometimes breathtaking leaps. The best of his three wins in seven starts came, surprisingly, when he was held up at Roscommon in October, but his best on RPRs was at Sandown in the Henry VIII Novices' Chase when he went off at a blistering pace and treated jumps fans to an exemplary round apart from one minor error at the water. The 153-rated Diakali was the only one to try to go with him from the off and he was a spent force before the Pond fence and was pulled up at the next, so it was to Ornua's credit he was still in front jumping the last and went down by less than two lengths to Dynamite Dollars. That was on soft ground and now represents his best form, but all five career

*Knocknanuss: Flamboyant jumper who leaves little margin for error*

wins have been on good, so no surprise if there is more to come with a dry festival. Making all in an Arkle, especially with fellow tearaway Knocknanuss a possible rival, would not be easy but there is an argument that he shouldn't be quite as big in the betting as he is.

*Going preference* Handles everything
*Star rating* ✪✪✪

## US AND THEM
**6 b g; Trainer** Joseph O'Brien
**Chase form** (left-handed) 41222, best RPR 152
**Cheltenham form** (hurdles) 0, best RPR 91
**At the festival** 16 Mar 2018 Mid-division, headway approaching 3 out, weakening when mistake 2 out, tailed off, finished 12th, beaten 62 and a quarter lengths by Summerville Boy in Supreme Novices' Hurdle

Slow-burner who was a 28-1 chance when sinking without trace in the Supreme Novices' Hurdle last season, but otherwise has a profile of a horse making steady and consistent progress. Has won only one of his five chases, a beginners' event at Navan in November, but has since been runner-up three times, the last two at the top level to stablemate Le Richebourg. Was outspeeded by the winner both times and, although he has raced keenly in the past, he is arguably bred for more of a test. That said, the Arkle is his only entry unless handicaps are being considered. Big horse and sound jumper who ought to continue progressing and may be one to keep an eye on beyond this season.

*Going preference* Won on good and heavy
*Star rating* ✪✪

## VOIX DU REVE
**7 b g; Trainer** Willie Mullins
**Chase form** 113F, best RPR 151
**Left-handed** 3F, best RPR 150
**Right-handed** 11, best RPR 151
**Cheltenham form** (hurdles) F0, best RPR 143
**At the festival** 16 Mar 2016 Held up towards rear, headway from 3 out, good run on inner final bend, travelling well and mounting strong challenge when fell last in Fred Winter Juvenile Handicap Hurdle won by Diego Du Charmil 14 Mar 2018 Looked well, raced keenly, in touch, closed approaching 3 out where not fluent, every chance 2 out, weakened before last, finished 14th, beaten 20 and three-quarter lengths by Bleu Berry in Coral Cup

Fair hurdler without any pretensions to Grade 1 class and was well beaten in last year's Coral Cup, although might have won the previous season's Fred Winter had he not fallen at the last. Started well over fences, winning first two easily, including Grade 2 at Punchestown, but limitations seemingly exposed when third to Le Richebourg in the Racing Post Novice Chase at Leopardstown over Chrismas and was being swamped by that one and Us And Them when falling at the last in the Frank Ward Solicitors Arkle in February. Also in the JLT, but surely no more than an outside contender for either.

*Going preference* Handles quick ground well
*Star rating* ✪✪

## MENGLI KHAN
**6 b g; Trainer** Gordon Elliott
**Chase form** 143, best RPR 149
**Left-handed** 43, best RPR 149
**Right-handed** 1, best RPR 144
**Cheltenham form** (hurdles) 3, best RPR 151
**At the festival** 13 Mar 2018 Tall, in touch, took closer order 3 out, ridden to chase leader after next, kept on but no extra from last, finished third, beaten two lengths by Summerville Boy in Supreme Novices' Hurdle

Talented if mercurial six-year-old who was a Grade 1 winner as a novice over hurdles at Fairyhouse in December 2017 but then ran out when even-money favourite for another at Leopardstown later that month. Finished third in the Supreme in a first-time tongue-tie, though, and while a bit below that form when third in the Punchestown equivalent next time, it wasn't a bad run. Made an impressive debut over fences in November, winning by ten lengths from the 145-rated mare Forge Meadow, and was briefly as short as 7-1 for this. There was always a chance he was flattered, though, as the runner-up had not performed well on her chase debut and ran worse next time and is back over hurdles now. Still, Mengli Khan was originally made odds-on for the Racing Post Novice Chase at Leopardstown over Christmas, only to drift right out to 7-4 before finishing fourth to Le Richebourg. Beaten by a much greater margin back there in February, so has plenty to prove

## ARKLE CHASE RESULTS AND TRENDS

| | FORM WINNER | AGE & WGT | Adj RPR | SP | TRAINER | BEST RPR LAST 12 MONTHS (RUNS SINCE) |
|---|---|---|---|---|---|---|
| 18 | 3-111 **Footpad** D | 6 11-4 | 178ᵀ | 5-6f | W Mullins (IRE) | won Leopardstown Gd1 nov ch (2m1f) (0) |
| 17 | -1111 **Altior** C, D | 7 11-4 | 185ᵀ | 1-4f | N Henderson | won Newbury Gd2 ch (2m½f) (0) |
| 16 | -1111 **Douvan** C, D | 6 11-4 | 180ᵀ | 1-4f | W Mullins (IRE) | won Leopardstown Gd1 nov ch (2m1f) (1) |
| 15 | 1-F11 **Un De Sceaux** D | 7 11-4 | 181ᵀ | 4-6f | W Mullins (IRE) | won Leopardstown Gd1 nov ch (2m1f) (0) |
| 14 | 1-261 **Western Warhorse** | 6 11-4 | 148⁻²³ | 33-1 | D Pipe | won Doncaster class 3 nov ch (2m3f) (0) |
| 13 | 11-11 **Simonsig** C, D | 7 11-7 | 174ᵀ | 8-15f | N Henderson | won Kempton Gd2 nov ch (2m) (0) |
| 12 | 3-111 **Sprinter Sacre** D | 6 11-7 | 179ᵀ | 8-11f | N Henderson | won Newbury Gd2 ch (2m½f) (0) |
| 11 | 22221 **Captain Chris** C, D | 7 11-7 | 163⁻⁴ | 6-1 | P Hobbs | 2nd Sandown Gd1 nov ch (2m4½f) (1) |
| 10 | 41111 **Sizing Europe** C, D | 8 11-7 | 170ᵀ | 6-1 | H de Bromhead (IRE) | won Leopardstown Gd1 nov ch (2m1f) (0) |
| 09 | -1222 **Forpadydeplasterer** D | 7 11-7 | 160⁻⁶ | 8-1 | T Cooper (IRE) | 2nd Gd1 nov ch (2m5f) (0) |

**WINS-RUNS:** 5yo 0-4, 6yo 4-28, 7yo 5-42, 8yo 1-12, 9yo 0-6, 10yo 0-1 **FAVOURITES:** -£0.74

**TRAINERS IN THIS RACE (w-pl-r):** Nicky Henderson 3-3-11, Willie Mullins 3-1-10, Henry de Bromhead 1-2-7, Philip Hobbs 1-1-4, Colin Tizzard 0-1-1, Gordon Elliott 0-0-2, Paul Nicholls 0-0-7, Kim Bailey 0-0-1, Gary Moore 0-0-1, Harry Fry 0-0-1, Tom George 0-1-3

**FATE OF FAVOURITES:** F041121111 **POSITION OF WINNER IN MARKET:** 3341181111

now, but at least we know he acts well at Cheltenham and he probably has the talent to be involved if he fancies it. Also in the JLT but yet to race beyond 2m1f.

*Going preference* Not much between his best form on all surfaces
*Star rating* ✪✪

## OTHERS TO CONSIDER

This looks wide open but there probably aren't too many more to consider as **Winter Escape** and **Defi Du Seuil** look sure to go for the JLT as does the mare **Camelia De Cotte**, and **Kalashnikov** is hard to fancy now as he can't jump. **Hardline** is talented enough and is the shortest-priced of Gordon Elliott's contenders. He didn't seem to stay 2m5f behind La Bague Au Roi last time but might just be in his element over a strongly run 2m.

## VERDICT

*GLEN FORSA wasn't even on my radar for this race until the middle of February but his win over Kalashnikov was stunning and he could be the one to beat. Yes, Kalashnikov didn't jump well and is a busted flush now, but the winner was superb and I'm not sure the market has reacted enough. I'm still a fan of **Lalor**, while **Le Richebourg** has to be feared if the ground stays on the quick side.*

### Key trends

🏇 Finished in the first two on all completed chase starts, 10/10

🏇 RPR hurdle rating of at least 153, 10/10

🏇 SP no bigger than 8-1, 9/10

🏇 Aged six or seven, 9/10

🏇 Rated within 6lb of RPR top-rated, 9/10 (seven were top-rated)

🏇 Adjusted RPR of at least 160, 9/10

🏇 Three to five chase runs, 8/10 (both exceptions had fewer)

### Other factors

🏇 Eight winners had previously won a 2m-2m1f Graded chase

🏇 Seven winners had previously run at the festival, showing mixed form in a variety of hurdle races

🏇 A French-bred has finished in the first three on seven occasions (four won)

NOTES

## 2.50 Ultima Handicap Chase
### 3m1f — Grade 3 — £110,000
**ITV/RTV**

Last year Coo Star Sivola became just the third winning favourite of this prestigious handicap chase since 1977 (the others were Antonin at 4-1 in 1994 and Wichita Lineman at 5-1 in 2009) when scoring at 5-1 for Nick Williams and Lizzie Kelly. However, shock results have been fairly rare in this 3m1f contest with 14 of the past 20 winners returned at 10-1 or lower. Un Temps Pour Tout, 9-1 when he won the race for the second year in a row in 2017, was the first back-to-back winner since Scot Lane in 1983, with Sentina (1957-1958) the only other to achieve the feat. Coo Star Sivola might be back for another try, while Un Temps Pour Tout – whose trainer David Pipe has an excellent record in festival handicap chases – could bid for an unprecedented third victory.

With his first victory, Un Temps Pour Tout became the first horse since Dixton House in 1989 to land the prize having not won a race over fences before, although he did continue the recent trend of inexperienced chasers taking this competitive handicap. In the last ten years only two horses, Golden Chieftain (2013) and The Druids Nephew (2015), had run more than ten times over fences before landing the prize. Coo Star Sivola was having his sixth chase run when he won last year.

While second-season chasers have traditionally done well, Coo Star Sivola's win last March meant a raw novice has landed the race six times in the last 15 runnings.

Eight-year-olds have won the race eight times since the turn of the millennium, along with five seven year-olds. Together they account for 72 per cent of winners (13-18) in that period.

An official rating of 137 was required to get into last year's race and in the last 12 seasons no horse rated under 129 has qualified. In 2017 Un Temps Pour Tout (off 155) became the first winner since 1983 with a mark higher than 150. He carried 11st 12lb, the highest winning weight since Different Class with 11st 13lb in 1967.

The only winner in the past 14 years without any previous course form was the Irish-trained Dun Doire, who completed a six-timer over fences in this race for Tony Martin in 2006. While Irish-bred horses account for ten of the last 12 winners, those trained across the Irish Sea have not done so well, having been successful only twice since 1966 with Youlneverwalkalone (2003) and Dun Doire.

■ **ONES TO WATCH Singlefarmpayment** – second and fifth in the last two runnings – could return with a leading chance again, while **Beware The Bear**, a good winner in first-time blinkers at Cheltenham on New Year's Day, was keeping on strongly when fourth in this race last year. **Give Me A Copper**, who returned from a 15-month layoff with a good fourth at Sandown in February, looks on the right sort of mark for Paul Nicholls.

*Give Me A Copper: could make up for lost time with big win*

## ULTIMA HANDICAP CHASE RESULTS AND TRENDS

| | FORM WINNER | AGE & WGT | OR | SP | TRAINER | BEST RPR LAST 12 MONTHS (RUNS SINCE) |
|---|---|---|---|---|---|---|
| 18 | 53421 **Coo Star Sivola** C, D | 6 10-10 | 142-2 | 5-1f | N Williams | won Exeter class 3 nov hcap ch (3m) (0) |
| 17 | -1036 **Un Temps Pour Tout** CD | 8 11-12 | 155-10 | 9-1 | D Pipe | won Ultima Handicap Chase (3m1f) (5) |
| 16 | -1224 **Un Temps Pour Tout** D, BF | 7 11-7 | 148-15 | 11-1 | D Pipe | 2nd Newbury Gd2 nov ch (2m7½f) (1) |
| 15 | -1275 **The Druids Nephew** | 8 11-3 | 146T | 8-1 | N Mulholland | 2nd Cheltenham Gd3 hcap ch (3m3½f) (1) |
| 14 | 32U11 **Holywell** C, D | 7 11-6 | 145-9 | 10-1 | J O'Neill | won Doncaster class 4 nov ch (3m) (0) |
| 13 | P3633 **Golden Chieftain** D | 8 10-2 | 132-1 | 28-1 | C Tizzard | won Worcester class 3 hcap ch (2m4f) (5) |
| 12 | -PF75 **Alfie Sherrin** (1oh) D | 9 10-0 | 129-5 | 14-1 | J O'Neill | 7th Kempton class 3 hcap ch (2m4½f) (0) |
| 11 | F2-52 **Bensalem** C, BF | 8 11-2 | 143T | 5-1 | A King | fell Ultima Handicap Chase (3m½f) (3) |
| 10 | -3701 **Chief Dan George** D | 10 10-10 | 142-6 | 33-1 | J Moffatt | won Doncaster class 2 hcap ch (3m) (0) |
| 09 | 9-121 **Wichita Lineman** C, D | 8 10-9 | 142T | 5-1f | J O'Neill | won Chepstow class 3 nov ch (3m) (0) |

**WINS-RUNS:** 6yo 1-16, 7yo 2-41, 8yo 5-59, 9yo 1-53, 10yo 1-28, 11yo 0-16, 12yo 0-4, 13yo 0-1 **FAVOURITES:** +£2.00

**FATE OF FAVOURITES:** 12F0200021 **POSITION OF WINNER IN MARKET:** 1027032531

**OR 121-133** 2-2-26, **134-148** 7-21-151, **149-161** 1-7-41

### Key trends

- Ran no more than five times that season, 9/10
- Ran at a previous festival, 9/10
- Aged seven to nine, 8/10
- Officially rated 132-148, 8/10
- Won over at least 3m, 8/10
- No more than nine runs over fences, 8/10
- Top-three finish on either or both of last two starts, 8/10
- Carried no more than 11st 3lb, 7/10

### Other factors

- Five had recorded a top-four finish at a previous festival
- Five winners had run well in a handicap at Cheltenham earlier in the season (three placed and two fourth). 2011 winner Bensalem and Un Temps Pour Tout in 2017 had run well in a Grade 2 hurdle at the course
- This was once seemingly an impossible task for novices, but five of the past ten winners have been first-season chasers

NOTES

## 3.30 Unibet Champion Hurdle ITV/RTV
2m½f   Grade 1   £450,000

Buveur D'Air will bid to become the sixth to complete a Champion Hurdle hat-trick – and the second for trainer Nicky Henderson after See You Then in the mid-1980s – but it looks a more difficult task now that he has lost his air of invincibility and has a serious rival in Apple's Jade. Defeat in the Christmas Hurdle by stablemate Verdana Blue was only the second over jumps for Buveur D'Air, the first having been in the 2016 Supreme Novices' Hurdle behind Altior, but it was a jolt to the Buveur believers, swiftly followed by another when Apple's Jade landed the Irish Champion Hurdle in such dominant style that her connections were quick to target this race rather than the Mares' Hurdle. Gordon Elliott's challenger will attempt to emulate the great Dawn Run and Annie Power – the two Irish-trained mares to land the Champion – and there are other mares high up the betting in Verdana Blue and the Willie Mullins-trained Laurina. Mullins also has Sharjah and last year's runner-up Melon in the reckoning as he attempts to land the prize for the fifth time in nine years.

### APPLE'S JADE
**7 b m; Trainer** Gordon Elliott
**Hurdles form** 11211221211111331111, best RPR 168
**Left-handed** 12121113111, best RPR 168
**Right-handed** 112121131, best RPR 163
**Cheltenham form** 213, best RPR 150
**At the festival** 18 Mar 2016 Close up, went 2nd 5th, led before 2 out, ridden when pressed and went slightly left last, headed final 110yds, soon outpaced by winner, finished second, beaten one and a quarter lengths by Ivanovich Gorbatov in Triumph Hurdle
14 Mar 2017 Tracked leaders, led 5th, ridden when strongly pressed after 2 out, headed last, rallied gamely to lead run-in, ran on well to assert final 100yds, driven out, won OLBG Mares' Hurdle by a length and a half from Vroum Vroum Mag
13 Mar 2018 Led until 6th, tracked leader, challenged after 3 out, ridden turning in, every chance last, stayed on same pace from last, finished third, beaten one and a half lengths by Benie Des Dieux in OLBG Mares' Hurdle

Top-class mare even before this season and boasts Cheltenham Festival form figures of 213 but was beaten at odds-on (1-2) in the Mares' Hurdle last season and again at Punchestown in April (5-6), so began this campaign with something to prove. She has done that in spades, though, winning all four starts, the last three in Grades 1, by an aggregate of 73 lengths. The fact she has been able to win at the top level at 2m, 2m4f and 3m this term is testament to her remarkable versatility and she seems to be getting better with every run, which is frightening given the level she has now reached. After sauntering home by 26 lengths in the 3m Christmas Hurdle at Leopardstown, she dropped down a mile in trip for the Irish Champion Hurdle in February for her first run over 2m since being beaten by Irving in the Fighting Fifth at Newcastle in November 2016. Any concerns she might not have the pace for 2m were soon dispelled, though, as she made all at a solid

### OWNER'S VIEW

**Michael O'Leary on Apple's Jade** "If you're going to lose, I'd rather lose trying to win a Champion Hurdle than a Mares' Hurdle, now that we know she can run a fast two miles. We won't make a decision until Cheltenham week and we'll see how she is, how everyone else is and what else we have going, but if she's all right and the ground is okay, it's probably 75-25 she'd run in the Champion Hurdle. Would she beat Buveur D'Air? Probably not, but she's entitled to try now" *Recorded 168 on RPR in the Irish Champion Hurdle, a career-best by 5lb and making her top-rated for the Champion Hurdle taking into account her 7lb mares' allowance*

pace and came home in splendid isolation in a time more than four seconds faster than the top handicap on the card. Given her 7lb sex allowance, the Racing Post Rating of 168 she earned there would, theoretically at least, have been good enough to win any Champion Hurdle you could care to mention, including all three won by Istabraq (his best was 174 at Cheltenham, although he ran bigger figures elsewhere). It's ludicrous to think connections were still contemplating the mares' race after this, but it seems now the Champion is the plan and she goes there with rock-solid claims. There is one slight question mark, though, and that's her suitability to Cheltenham. That might sound daft given her festival form of 213, but she has run to much bigger figures elsewhere each season and, on Racing Post Ratings, her three runs at the track represent the joint 14th and 17th best of her 20-race career. We'll find out for sure soon enough.

*Going preference* No major issues
*Star rating* ✪✪✪✪✪

## BUVEUR D'AIR

**8 b g; Trainer** Nicky Henderson
**Hurdles form** 11311111111121, best RPR 173
**Left-handed** 13111111, best RPR 173
**Right-handed** 111121, best RPR 164
**Cheltenham form** 311, best RPR 170
**At the festival** 15 Mar 2016 Held up in rear, headway from 3 out, not fluent 2 out, soon ridden, went 3rd at the last, kept on but not pace to get on terms, finished third, beaten eight and a half lengths by Altior in Supreme Novices' Hurdle
14 Mar 2017 Held up in midfield, hit 4 out, headway soon after, ridden to lead approaching last, ran on run-in, edged right final 75yds when drawing clear, won Champion Hurdle by four and a half lengths from My Tent Or Yours
13 Mar 2018 Tracked leaders, leant on rival when going well after 3 out, led just before 2 out, pressed with rival upsides approaching last, hard ridden run-in, gamely found extra and edged right towards finish, won Champion Hurdle by a neck from Melon

Dual Champion Hurdle winner who seems to have gone from being considered unbeatable

*Apple's Jade: question mark over her suitability to Cheltenham*

to the horse everyone wants to take on in the space of a couple of months. After finishing third to Altior in the 2016 Supreme Novices' Hurdle he went on a ten-race winning spree that included his two Champion Hurdle successes and, after extending that run to 11 when he toyed with last season's sensational novice Samcro in the Fighting Fifth at Newcastle on his return, he was made odds-on across the board to become the sixth three-time winner after Hatton's Grace, Sir Ken, Persian War, See You Then and Istabraq. Few could see anything beating him but at that point Apple's Jade was still a 16-1 shot and an unlikely runner and Buveur D'Air had gone more than two and a half years without defeat. Soon it was all change, though, as a day after the Fighting Fifth Apple's Jade thumped Supasundae by 20 lengths and, a few weeks later, Buveur D'Air's aura of invincibility was banished forever when he had his pocket picked by stablemate Verdana Blue in the Christmas Hurdle at Kempton. Everything was going swimmingly there until he kicked the third-last out of the ground, but it wasn't so much the mistake as Barry Geraghty's reaction to it that might have got him beat as he seemed too keen to shut down the pace-setting Global Citizen and he asked for everything from the second-last. Buveur D'Air's trademark change of gear took him a few lengths clear between the final two flights rather than after the last, but he then had no answer to Verdana Blue, who had stalked him all the way. The Kempton crowd may have been stunned into silence but nobody seemed more shocked than Verdana Blue's rider Nico de Boinville, who looked rather embarrassed and, some would say, disappointed, to have

just won a Grade 1. Buveur D'Air has hit the front at similar points of races before but not when being asked for everything and surely he will be better played late. That said, it is easy enough to pick holes in a lot of his form as you just have to look at some of the names of those who have finished second to him (Rayvin Black, Irving, John Constable, Melon, Vision Des Flos) to realise he hasn't been dominating a vintage division. He'll certainly have to be better than when scrambling home by a neck from Melon last year.

*Going preference* Handles everything
*Star rating* ✪✪✪✪

## LAURINA
**6 b m; Trainer** Willie Mullins
**Hurdles form** F211111, best RPR 160
**Left-handed** F21, best RPR 154
**Right-handed** 1111, best RPR 160
**Cheltenham form** 1, best RPR 154
**At the festival** 15 Mar 2018 Strong, lengthy, looked well, midfield, smooth headway 3 out, cruised into lead between last 2, effortlessly going clear when not fluent last, very easily, won Trull House Stud Mares' Novices' Hurdle by 18 lengths from Cap Soleil

Young mare who is unbeaten in five starts since joining Willie Mullins from France and had everyone salivating when cantering home by 18 lengths in the mares' novice hurdle at the festival on the third of them last season. Won the Fairyhouse equivalent on her final start of the season in similar fashion, but so far restricted to just one run this term. That came in a 2m4f soft-ground match at Sandown, where she started at odds of 1-8 and cruised round to win as she liked by 48 lengths. A provisional Racing Post Rating of 160 for that effort put her in the right

ballpark as a Champion Hurdle contender, but how accurately you can handicap horses in races like that is hard to tell, especially as she returned the worst Topspeed figure on the card. No doubt she is hugely exciting, but surely there are too many negatives for her to be considered at around 7-2 for a race like the Champion Hurdle. For a start, she has never run outside her own sex, while none of the mares she has beaten would be any shorter than 1,000-1 even for an average Champion Hurdle. Add the fact she shapes like a stayer and has a really high knee action, which suggests soft ground is a must (and she has never raced on anything quicker), and it's hard not to think people are getting carried away. Also in the 2m4f Mares' Hurdle and it would be no surprise if she went down that route.

*Going preference* Soft/heavy looks a must
*Star rating* ✪

## VERDANA BLUE

**7 b m; Trainer** Nicky Henderson
**Hurdles form** U1143513001141, best RPR 156
**Left-handed** 43004, best RPR 156
**Right-handed** U11513111, best RPR 156
**Cheltenham form** 434, best RPR 156
**At the festival** 16 Mar 2017 Tracked leaders, led before last where headed, edged right under pressure run-in and outpaced by winner, lost 2nd final 100yds, no extra near finish, finished fourth, beaten three and a quarter lengths by Let's Dance in Trull House Stud Mares' Novices' Hurdle

Fine mare who has shown fairly dramatic improvement this season given the good ground that is considered necessary. Started this term with a three-race winning spree, which included an all-weather contest. While that run came to an end when she was only fourth when favourite for the Greatwood Handicap Hurdle at Cheltenham, she didn't really get the rub of the green and finished strongly. Improvement continued when she was second in a 1m4f Listed contest at Kempton on the Flat in early December and then she really put the cat among the Champion Hurdle pigeons when mugging Buveur D'Air close home in the Christmas Hurdle at Kempton to inflict his first defeat since the 2016 Supreme. Quite possible she took advantage of her stablemate being sent for home too soon, but she is improving and Nicky Henderson would have run her in last season's Champion Hurdle if the ground hadn't been so soft. That's the big problem for her, though, as Cheltenham won't let it be any faster than good to soft on day one and might even have it on the easier side of that. She has run on genuinely soft ground only twice, finishing a tailed-off last on her debut and being beaten 30 lengths in last season's Betfair Hurdle. Her form figures tell you she is 0-5 over hurdles racing left-handed and 6-9 going the other way, but she has finished fourth in the mares' novice at the festival and she ran right up to her best in the Greatwood, so it's probably not wise to read too much into it. The ground, however, is another matter.

*Going preference* Faster the better
*Star rating* ✪✪✪

*Buveur D'Air (second right): bids to become the sixth to complete a Champion Hurdle hat-trick*

## SHARJAH

**6 b g; Trainer** Willie Mullins
**Hurdles form** 11F784631311, best RPR 168
**Left-handed** F7831, best RPR 159
**Right-handed** 1146131, best RPR 168
**Cheltenham form** 8, best RPR 144
**At the festival** 13 Mar 2018 Mid-division, headway after 3 out, soon ridden, held 5th jumping last, faded, finished eighth, beaten ten and a half lengths by Summerville Boy in Supreme Novices' Hurdle

In-and-out performer as a novice but looked very good at times, particularly when sweeping through with what looked like a winning run in the Future Champions Novice Hurdle at Leopardstown only to fall at the last. After that race his rider Patrick Mullins said no horse, "not even Samcro", should be odds-on to beat him in a novice hurdle. Samcro was, and did just that, though, when Sharjah trailed home only seventh behind him in the Deloitte Novice Hurdle back at Leopardstown next time out. After that there were further disappointments when he was a well-beaten fourth at Fairyhouse and an even more distant sixth at Punchestown, but all season he was faced with soft and heavy ground and he has been a different proposition on a better surface this term. Although it was officially soft when he won the Galway Hurdle in August, it wasn't winter soft by any stretch of the imagination and, following a disappointing third to Bedrock in a muddling race at Down Royal, he has won back-to-back Grade 1s at Punchestown and Leopardstown. He was impressive when slamming stablemate Faugheen in the Morgiana in November and, while it is easy to put that down to the 2015 Champion Hurdle winner being a fading light, Sharjah at least backed it up when coming from the back off a steady pace to land the Ryanair Hurdle by three and three-quarter lengths from Supasundae. That's not quite the margin of defeat dished out to Supasundae by Apple's Jade, but hold-up horses rarely win by a long way and he is at least coming into the race in pretty good heart.

*Going preference* Soft would be bad news
*Star rating* ✪✪✪

## MELON

**7 ch g; Trainer** Willie Mullins
**Hurdles form** 1221352F44, best RPR 166
**Left-handed** 1235244, best RPR 166
**Right-handed** 21F, best RPR 162
**Cheltenham form** 232, best RPR 166
**At the festival** 14 Mar 2017 Travelled strongly, tracked leaders, every chance after turning in, ridden when not fluent last, kept on until no extra final 100yds, finished second, beaten two and a quarter lengths by Labaik in Supreme Novices' Hurdle
13 Mar 2018 Midfield, headway 4 out, checked when not much room on inner after 3 out, challenging from 2 out, ridden and upsides approaching last, edged right and held towards finish, finished second, beaten a neck by Buveur D'Air in Champion Hurdle

Has been runner-up at the last two festivals, first when joint-favourite for the Supreme won by outsider Labaik and then when nearly causing an upset as he headed Buveur D'Air after the last in the Champion Hurdle but was ultimately battled out of it. Such festival form makes it hard to write him off but his overall profile is questionable as he has been successful on only two of his ten starts over hurdles, both in 2017 when long odds-on. He has been below form in both outings this season, finishing fourth to Sharjah in the Ryanair Hurdle and occupying the same spot in the Irish Champion when 22 lengths behind Apple's Jade. Always a chance the return to Cheltenham and a strongly run race will see him recapture his form, but not hard to have reservations.

*Going preference* Best on soft or worse
*Star rating* ✪✪

## ESPOIR D'ALLEN

**5 b g; Trainer** Gavin Cromwell
**Hurdles form** 11114111, best RPR 158
**Left-handed** 1411, best RPR 155
**Right-handed** 1111, best RPR 158

Five-year-old who has won eight of his nine career starts but, a bit like a young untried boxer being primed for a big payday, has compiled his record against opposition of questionable merit. Won four of his five starts as a juvenile hurdler but started favourite for every one and was beaten 23 lengths into fourth of five when upped to Grade 1

## CHAMPION HURDLE RESULTS AND TRENDS

| FORM WINNER | AGE & WGT | Adj RPR | SP | TRAINER | BEST RPR LAST 12 MONTHS (RUNS SINCE) |
|---|---|---|---|---|---|
| 18 1-111 **Buveur D'Air** CD | 7 11-10 | 175ᵀ | 4-6f | N Henderson | Won Gd1 Aintree Hurdle (2m4f) (3) |
| 17 1-111 **Buveur D'Air** D | 6 11-10 | 163⁷ | 5-1 | N Henderson | Won Gd1 Aintree nov hdl (2m½f) (1) |
| 16 1F-11 **Annie Power** C, D | 8 11-3 | 173ᵀ | 5-2f | W Mullins (IRE) | Won Gd1 Punchestown Mares Hurdle (2m2f) (1) |
| 15 1-111 **Faugheen** C, D | 7 11-10 | 173⁴ | 4-5f | W Mullins (IRE) | Won Gd1 Christmas Hurdle (2m) (0) |
| 14 -1124 **Jezki** D | 6 11-10 | 169⁸ | 9-1 | J Harrington (IRE) | 2nd Gd1 Ryanair Hurdle (2m) (1) |
| 13 1-111 **Hurricane Fly** CD | 9 11-10 | 177ᵀ | 13-8f | W Mullins (IRE) | won Gd1 Irish Champion Hurdle (2m) (0) |
| 12 23-12 **Rock On Ruby** C, D | 7 11-10 | 170⁷ | 11-1 | P Nicholls | 2nd Gd1 Christmas Hurdle (2m) (0) |
| 11 1-111 **Hurricane Fly** D | 7 11-10 | 172² | 11-4f | W Mullins (IRE) | won Gd1 Irish Champion Hurdle (2m) (0) |
| 10 3-531 **Binocular** D | 6 11-10 | 171² | 9-1 | N Henderson | won Sandown Listed hdl (2m½f) (0) |
| 09 1-1F3 **Punjabi** D, BF | 6 11-10 | 168⁸ | 22-1 | N Henderson | won Gd1 Punchestown Champ Hurdle (2m) (3) |

**WINS-RUNS:** 5yo 0-28, 6yo 4-30, 7yo 4-23, 8yo 1-17, 9yo 1-7, 10yo 0-4, 11yo 0-4, 12yo 0-2, 13yo 0-1 **FAVOURITES:** £3.34

**TRAINERS IN THIS RACE (w-pl-r):** Willie Mullins 4-5-19, Nicky Henderson 4-6-23, Paul Nicholls 1-1-8, Jessica Harrington 1-0-3, Gordon Elliott 0-1-1, Harry Fry 0-1-1, Henry de Bromhead 0-1-3, Dan Skelton 0-0-2, Charles Byrnes 0-0-1, Tom George 0-0-1

**FATE OF FAVOURITES:** 3013141101 **POSITION OF WINNER IN MARKET:** 9714151121

company for the first time in the Spring Juvenile Hurdle. Still, he beat the winner of that race (Triumph second Mr Adjudicator) on his return this season in a Grade 3 at Naas in November and has added another couple of Grade 3 wins since. For the last of those successes he took on horses who weren't last season's juveniles for the first time and ran out a fairly comfortable two-and-a-half-length winner from Wicklow Brave. That horse is a ten-year-old who has been on the decline for a while, though, and it's a long way off Champion Hurdle form.

*Going preference* Seems versatile
*Star rating* ✪✪

### SAMCRO
**7 ch g; Trainer** Gordon Elliott
**Hurdles form** 1111F225, best RPR 163
**Left-handed** 11125, best RPR 163
**Right-handed** 1F2, best RPR 161
**Cheltenham form** 1, best RPR 160
**At the festival** 14 Mar 2018 Held up in midfield, headway 4 out, travelling strongly to lead on bend between last 2, asserted and edged right after last, driven out and ran on, won Ballymore Novices' Hurdle by two and three-quarter lengths from Black Op

Looked a potential superstar on first four starts last season, the last two of them being easy Grade 1 wins in the Deloitte Novice Hurdle and Ballymore Novices' Hurdle. However, he fell when odds-on in open

### Key trends
🏇Adjusted RPR of at least 163, 10/10
🏇Rated within 8lb of RPR top-rated, 10/10
🏇No more than 12 hurdle runs, 9/10
🏇Won a Grade 1 hurdle, 9/10
🏇Aged between six and eight, 9/10
🏇Ran within the past 51 days, 8/10
🏇Won last time out, 7/10

### Other factors
🏇Katchit (2008) broke a longstanding trend when he became the first five-year-old to win since See You Then in 1985. In the intervening years 73 had failed, while 28 have come up short since

🏇Only two winners had not run since the turn of the year (Rock On Ruby and Faugheen)

NOTES

company on his final start last term in the Punchestown Champion Hurdle and hasn't gone on as expected this season. Such is his fanbase that even after being beaten by the 149-rated Bedrock on his return at Down Royal in November, he was backed down to favouritism to beat the 169-rated Buveur D'Air in the Fighting Fifth at Newcastle the following month. There his devotees had to accept a dose of reality as the reigning champion toyed with him, winning by eight lengths, but even Samcro's critics have to concede there must have been something wrong with him when he was only fifth of six behind Sharjah next time. A lung infection has since been diagnosed, but while Samcro was declared unlikely to run for the rest of the season, his name still appeared among the entries for this and the Stayers' Hurdle. Just how good last season's novices were is open to question now, as by the beginning of February just one of the first nine in the Ballymore had won a race this season. Masses to prove if and when he returns to racing.

*Going preference* Handles all sorts
*Star rating* ✪✪

## GLOBAL CITIZEN
**7 b g; Trainer** Ben Pauling
**Hurdles form** 521162141, best RPR 160
**Left-handed** 51611, best RPR 160
**Right-handed** 2124, best RPR 154

Free-going front-runner who went too fast for his own good when a 13-length fourth to Verdana Blue in the Christmas Hurdle but has otherwise progressed well this season. Confirmed soft ground wasn't such a major problem when making all in the Gerry Feilden at Newbury and, following his Kempton blowout, he improved again to beat Silver Streak by three lengths in the Haydock trial in January. It would have been closer had the runner-up not made a mess of three out, but it was a step forward all the same and entitles him to take his chance. Will ensure there is no hanging around and that Apple's Jade doesn't have to do all the donkey work, but hard to see him hanging on.

*Going preference* Good ground suits best
*Star rating* ✪✪

## SILVER STREAK
**6 gr g; Trainer** Evan Williams
**Hurdles form** 43211412U611222, best RPR 159
**Left-handed** 421U11222, best RPR 159
**Right-handed** 311426, best RPR 137
**Cheltenham form** 22, best RPR 159

Has this term confirmed himself a classy performer when the ground isn't too deep by winning the Welsh Champion Hurdle (a handicap, off just 10st 4lb) and then running second in good-quality races on his next three starts. Got closer than looked likely when second to Brain Power in the International at Cheltenham in December (didn't get clearest passage but winner stopped in front) and it would have been close between him and Global Citizen at Haydock had he not made a mistake three out. Is going to appreciate a strongly run race and, if the going isn't too soft, is not beyond picking up a bit of place money late on, but a chunk of improvement is needed for him to trouble the front two.

*Going preference* Quicker the better
*Star rating* ✪✪

## OTHERS TO CONSIDER
It will be a major surprise if the winner hasn't been mentioned as **Supasundae** no longer looks fast enough to be taken seriously and I'm not buying **Brain Power's** rebirth as a hurdler. He may have won the International at Cheltenham, but it was a weak renewal that he had the run of and he still doesn't like the place. The rest would be making up the numbers.

## VERDICT
*It's hard to build up any enthusiasm for taking on the big two as the pair most likely to threaten them – Verdana Blue and Sharjah – probably want the ground quicker than Cheltenham will allow on the day, whether it rains or not. Laurina, on the other hand, is going to need it soft. If Apple's Jade can reproduce her best form at Cheltenham the race is hers for the taking based on her scintillating efforts this term, but I'm far from convinced she can, so it's BUVEUR D'AIR for me in the hope his challenge is delayed for longer than it was at Kempton.*

## 4.10 OLBG Mares' Hurdle ITV/RTV
### 2m4f · Grade 1 · £120,000

Willie Mullins' eight-year winning streak in this contest was brought to an end in 2017 when Apple's Jade scored for Gordon Elliott but Ireland's champion trainer was back on top last year when Benie Des Dieux took the prize with odds-on Apple's Jade back in third, giving Mullins his ninth victory in 11 runnings. Benie Des Dieux followed up her festival win with another Grade 1 success in the Mares Champion Hurdle at Punchestown but has not raced since, although that is nothing unusual for a Mullins-trained mare as Quevega often made her seasonal debut at the festival in the later years of her six-timer. If Apple's Jade goes for the Champion Hurdle as expected, Mullins will hold a dominant hand that also includes Laurina, Limini and Stormy Island. British trainers have not had a look-in since Donald McCain won the inaugural running in 2008 with Whiteoak but home challengers could include Philip Kirby's prolific winner Lady Buttons, Roksana (Dan Skelton), Apple's Shakira (Nicky Henderson) and Mia's Storm (Alan King).

## OLBG MARES' HURDLE RESULTS AND TRENDS

| | FORM WINNER | AGE & WGT | Adj RPR | SP | TRAINER | BEST RPR LAST 12 MONTHS (RUNS SINCE) |
|---|---|---|---|---|---|---|
| 18 | /1-11 **Benie Des Dieux** D | 7 11-5 | 156$^{-13}$ | 9-2 | W Mullins (IRE) | Seasonal debutante (0) |
| 17 | 12212 **Apple's Jade** D, BF | 5 11-5 | 171$^{T}$ | 7-2 | G Elliott (IRE) | won Aintree Gd1 juv hdl (2m1f) (5) |
| 16 | 1-111 **Vroum Vroum Mag** D | 7 11-5 | 160$^{T}$ | 4-6f | W Mullins (IRE) | won Ascot Gd2 hdl (2m7½f) (0) |
| 15 | 7521 **Glens Melody** D | 7 11-5 | 162$^{-11}$ | 6-1 | W Mullins (IRE) | won Warwick Listed hdl (2m5f) (0) |
| 14 | 1/11- **Quevega** CD | 10 11-5 | 171$^{T}$ | 8-11f | W Mullins (IRE) | won Gd1 Punchestown World Hurdle (3m) (0) |
| 13 | /111- **Quevega** CD | 9 11-5 | 168$^{T}$ | 8-11f | W Mullins (IRE) | won Gd1 Punchestown World Hurdle (3m) (0) |
| 12 | 1/1-1 **Quevega** CD | 8 11-5 | 168$^{T}$ | 4-7f | W Mullins (IRE) | won Gd1 Punchestown World Hurdle (3m) (0) |
| 11 | 3911- **Quevega** CD | 7 11-5 | 166$^{T}$ | 5-6f | W Mullins (IRE) | won Gd2 Mares' Hurdle (2m4f) (1) |
| 10 | 11-39 **Quevega** CD | 6 11-5 | 168$^{T}$ | 6-4f | W Mullins (IRE) | 3rd Gd1 Punchestown Champ Hurdle (2m) (1) |
| 09 | 19-31 **Quevega** D | 5 11-3 | 156$^{-4}$ | 2-1f | W Mullins (IRE) | won Punchestown hdl (2m4f) (0) |

**WINS-RUNS:** 4yo 0-2, 5yo 2-22, 6yo 1-50, 7yo 4-45, 8yo 1-35, 9yo 1-8, 10yo 1-3, 11yo 0-1 **FAVOURITES:** £4.03

**TRAINERS IN THIS RACE (w-pl-r):** Willie Mullins 9-3-16, Gordon Elliott 1-1-3, Alan King 0-2-7, Harry Fry 0-1-4, Fergal O'Brien 0-0-1, Nicky Henderson 0-2-9, Warren Greatrex 0-0-2

**FATE OF FAVOURITES:** 111111F133 **POSITION OF WINNER IN MARKET:** 1111112132

### Key trends

- At least nine career starts, 10/10
- Adjusted RPR of at least 156, 10/10
- Top-three finish in a Grade 1 or 2 hurdle, 9/10
- Trained by Willie Mullins, 9/10
- Won last time out, 8/10

### Other factors

- A runner priced 16-1 or bigger has finished in the first three in nine of the ten renewals
- Quevega used to come here fresh when defending her crown but the other four winners had between two and five outings that season

## 4.50 **Close Brothers Novices' Handicap Chase**　　　RTV
*2m4f　Listed　£70,000*

The first six runnings of this race were on the New course over 2m5f but it was then moved to the Old course over half a furlong less and there has been a growing accent on quality. The ceiling rating is now 145, raised from 140 in 2017, and in the last two years a rating of 137 has been the minimum requirement to get in. Hunt Ball achieved the best weight-carrying performance in the race's history when securing the 2012 edition off a mark of 142 under 12st.

Strong recent form is important, with 11 of the 14 winners having secured a top-two finish last time out, seven of them winning. Seven-year-olds have the best record, winning seven out of 14, although six-year-olds have been successful in four of the last six renewals. The 2016 scorer Ballyalton (aged nine) was the oldest winner.

Winners have been prominent in the betting, with 12 sent off at odds between 9-2 and 12-1. The biggest-priced winner was 20-1 scorer L'Antartique in 2007.

■ **ONES TO WATCH** Tom George described **Clondaw Castle** as "tailor-made" for this race after a Leicester novice chase success over 2m in January. Higher up the ratings is **Secret Investor**, runner-up to National Hunt Chase fancy Ok Corral in a Warwick Listed contest over 3m. The Terence O'Brien-trained **Articulum** could be interesting if he doesn't go for one of the Grade 1s.

### CLOSE BROTHERS NOVICES' HANDICAP CHASE RESULTS AND TRENDS

| | FORM WINNER | AGE & WGT | OR | SP | TRAINER | BEST RPR LAST 12 MONTHS (RUNS SINCE) |
|---|---|---|---|---|---|---|
| 18 | -3121 **Mister Whitaker** C, D | 6 11-2 | 137-2 | 13-2 | M Channon | won Cheltenham class 2 nov hcap ch (2m5f) (0) |
| 17 | 4-162 **Tully East** | 7 11-8 | 138-10 | 8-1 | A Fleming (IRE) | 2nd Navan Gd3 nov ch (2m1f) (0) |
| 16 | /U62F **Ballyalton** C | 9 11-10 | 140-6 | 12-1 | I Williams | 2nd Market Rasen class 2 ch (2m5½f) (1) |
| 15 | 7-323 **Irish Cavalier** | 6 11-7 | 137-4 | 11-1 | R Curtis | 3rd Cheltenham class 2 nov hcap ch (2m5f) (0) |
| 14 | 32121 **Present View** D | 6 11-7 | 137-1 | 8-1 | J Snowden | won Kempton class 3 hcap ch (2m4½f) (0) |
| 13 | -2F17 **Rajdhani Express** D | 6 11-7 | 140T | 16-1 | N Henderson | won Kempton class 3 hcap ch (2m4½f) (1) |
| 12 | 12111 **Hunt Ball** D | 7 12-0 | 142-4 | 13-2f | K Burke | won Kempton class 3 hcap ch (2m4½f) (0) |
| 11 | 31591 **Divers** D | 7 11-4 | 132-6 | 10-1 | F Murphy | won Musselburgh class 3 nov ch (2m4f) (0) |
| 10 | -1321 **Copper Bleu** | 8 11-1 | 139-3 | 12-1 | P Hobbs | won Exeter class 4 ch (2m1½f) (0) |
| 09 | 9-F21 **Chapoturgeon** | 5 10-11 | 135-2 | 8-1 | P Nicholls | won Doncaster class 2 nov ch (2m½f) (0) |

**WINS-RUNS:** 5yo 1-12, 6yo 4-43, 7yo 3-75, 8yo 1-49, 9yo 1-17, 10yo 0-2 **FAVOURITES:** £-2.50

**FATE OF FAVOURITES:** 00515026F8 **POSITION OF WINNER IN MARKET:** 2541836533

**OR 123-130** 0-1-4, **131-140** 9-24-171, **141-148** 1-5-23

#### Key trends
- Officially rated 132-142, 10/10
- Top-three finish on last completed start, 9/10
- Won over at least 2m2f, 8/10
- Carried no more than 11st 8lb, 8/10
- Aged six or seven, 7/10
- Finished in the first four in all completed starts over fences, 6/10

#### Other factors
- Three winners had fallen at least once over fences
- Three winners ran over hurdles at a previous festival
- Two winners had hurdle RPRs of at least 140, three in the 130s and three in the 120s
- Only one winner started bigger than 12-1

# 5.30 National Hunt Chase — RTV

*4m — Grade 2 — Amateur riders' novice chase — £125,000*

This is the longest and oldest race at the festival, although the structure has changed over the years and it has gradually lost its reputation for producing shocks. Last year's winner Rathvinden (9-2) was the seventh to score at 8-1 or lower in the last eight runnings (Tiger Roll at 16-1 in 2017 being the only winner to buck that trend). The race was awarded Listed status in 2014, and raised to Grade 2 in 2017, and is now more of a four-mile RSA Chase in quality.

Rathvinden was the fourth winner in the past eight runnings to have the highest official rating, while Shotgun Paddy (top-rated in 2014) was beaten only a neck and, despite his odds, Tiger Roll was second-highest in 2017.

■ **ONES TO WATCH Ok Corral** (Nicky Henderson) and **Champagne Classic** (Gordon Elliott) are rated 150-plus and look set to head here. Ok Corral appeared to be primed for this race with a Listed victory at Warwick in January when top Irish amateur Derek O'Connor travelled over to ride him, while Champagne Classic is a previous festival winner in the 2017 Martin Pipe Handicap Hurdle. **Ballyward**, a Grade 3 winner over 3m with Champagne Classic back in third, looks a live challenger for Willie Mullins.

## NATIONAL HUNT CHASE RESULTS AND TRENDS

| FORM | WINNER | AGE & WGT | Adj RPR | SP | TRAINER | BEST RPR LAST 12 MONTHS (RUNS SINCE) |
|---|---|---|---|---|---|---|
| 18 | 112BU Rathvinden | 10 11-6 | 167ᵀ | 9-2 | W Mullins (IRE) | 2nd Fairyhouse Gd1 nov ch (2m4f) (2) |
| 17 | 22133 Tiger Roll C | 7 11-6 | 159⁻⁶ | 16-1 | G Elliott (IRE) | won Limerick hcap ch (3m) (2) |
| 16 | -3P62 Minella Rocco | 6 11-6 | 159⁻⁷ | 8-1 | J O'Neill | 2nd Ascot Gd2 nov ch (3m) (0) |
| 15 | 20-75 Cause Of Causes | 7 11-6 | 159⁻² | 8-1 | G Elliott (IRE) | 2nd Kim Muir hcap ch (3m1½f) (3) |
| 14 | 61U21 Midnight Prayer | 9 11-6 | 154⁻¹² | 8-1 | A King | won Warwick class 3 nov ch (3m2f) (0) |
| 13 | /2111 Back In Focus | 8 11-6 | 161ᵀ | 9-4F | W Mullins (IRE) | won Leopardstown Gd1 nov ch (3m) (0) |
| 12 | 321P1 Teaforthree | 8 11-6 | 161ᵀ | 5-1F | R Curtis | won Chepstow class 3 nov ch (3m) (2) |
| 11 | 11F25 Chicago Grey C | 8 11-6 | 163ᵀ | 5-1F | G Elliott (IRE) | 2nd Cheltenham class 2 nov ch (3m1½f) (1) |
| 10 | -2951 Poker De Sivola | 7 11-6 | 145⁻⁸ | 14-1 | F Murphy | 2nd Kelso class 3 hcap ch (3m1f) (3) |
| 09 | 42212 Tricky Trickster | 6 11-11 | 140⁻¹⁸ | 11-1 | N Twiston-Davies | 2nd Cheltenham class 2 nov hcap ch (2m5f) (0) |

**WINS-RUNS:** 5yo 0-1, 6yo 2-21, 7yo 3-73, 8yo 3-54, 9yo 1-16, 10yo 1-8, 12yo 0-1 **FAVOURITES:** £5.25

**TRAINERS IN THIS RACE (w-pl-r):** Gordon Elliott 3-0-7, Willie Mullins 2-3-13, Alan King 1-1-9, Nigel Twiston-Davies 1-0-8, Rebecca Curtis 1-0-5, Jonjo O'Neill 1-0-5, Colin Tizzard 0-2-2, David Pipe 0-1-7, Nicky Henderson 0-1-4, Paul Nicholls 0-1-6, Warren Greatrex 0-1-4, Neil Mulholland 0-0-2, Philip Hobbs 0-0-3, Kim Bailey 0-0-1, Tom George 0-0-1, Joseph O'Brien 0-0-1

**FATE OF FAVOURITES:** 451110045U **POSITION OF WINNER IN MARKET:** 5711143592

### Key trends

🐎 Ran at least three times over fences, 10/10

🐎 Hurdles RPR of at least 118, 10/10

🐎 Finished first or second in a chase over at least 3m, 10/10

🐎 Top-five finish last time out, 9/10 (exception unseated)

🐎 Top-three finish on either or both of last two starts, 8/10

🐎 Had won over at least 3m (hurdles or chases), 8/10

🐎 Aged six to eight, 8/10

### Other factors

🐎 The last eight winners had adjusted RPRs of 154-167

🐎 The 2011, 2012 and 2013 winners were outright favourites – the last to oblige before them was Keep Talking in 1992

# WEDNESDAY, MARCH 13 (OLD COURSE)

## PAUL KEALY
## ON THE KEY
## CONTENDERS

## 1.30 Ballymore Novices' Hurdle — ITV/RTV
### 2m5f — Grade 1 — £125,000

JP McManus's Champ, who is named in honour of legendary jockey AP McCoy, has the opportunity to live up to his name in a typically intriguing renewal. The Nicky Henderson-trained seven-year-old has notched a four-race winning streak this season, culminating in an impressive success in the Grade 1 Challow at Newbury last time out. His main rival in the ante-post market is Gordon Elliott's Battleoverdoyen, who is less experienced with only three outings under rules but was also a Grade 1 winner at Naas in early January. Henderson and Elliott have other good options in Birchdale and Commander Of Fleet respectively, while a couple of trainers looking for a first festival winner have live hopes – Martin Brassil sends the improving City Island from his County Kildare yard and Warwickshire-based Olly Murphy will be hoping for better luck with Brewin'upastorm, a final-flight faller at Cheltenham in January when looking set to beat Birchdale.

## CHAMP
**7 b g; Trainer** Nicky Henderson
**Hurdles form** 21111, best RPR 150
**Left-handed** 111, best RPR 150
**Right-handed** 21, best RPR 138

Slow-burner who raced only once as a novice last season, going down by a neck to the now highly promising novice chaser Vinndication, but has made up for lost time by winning all four starts this term. Was awarded a handicap mark of 139 following a pair of ten-length novice wins at odds-on and then made a mockery of that by cruising home at Newbury by four and a half lengths from Le Musee at the Ladbrokes Trophy meeting. The next four home were all well beaten on their next starts, but the second has subsequently won and so has the sixth, although that doesn't really matter given Champ boosted the form himself when a commanding winner of the Grade 1 Challow Hurdle back at Newbury just before the turn of the year. There he beat Getaway Trump by two and a half lengths and the runner-up went on to finish fourth to another crack novice, Al Dancer, when well backed for the Betfair Hurdle, while fourth-placed Brewin'upastorm would have gone very close on trials day at Cheltenham if he hadn't fallen and 30-length last Nestor Park won his novice next time. A peak Racing Post Rating of 150 is still around 6lb shy of what an average winner needs to produce at Cheltenham, but he's still at the head of the

pack in form terms of those likely to run and he jumps and travels well, so could easily have more to come. There are historical negatives, as no Challow winner has ever won this race and only two Ballymore winners (Brown Lad in 1974 and French Holly in 1998) have scored aged seven or older.
*Going preference* Seems to go on any
*Star rating* ✪✪✪✪

## BATTLEOVERDOYEN
**6 b g; Trainer** Gordon Elliott
**Hurdles form** (left-handed) 11, best RPR 144

Went to Gordon Elliott for £235,000 following win in sole point (runner-up won first four starts for Harry Whittington) at Loughanmore and remains unbeaten in three further outings. Had no trouble winning his bumper at Punchestown in November and looked potentially very smart when landing 21-runner Navan maiden hurdle by 13 lengths the following month from a horse who had already shown a decent level of form. Put straight into Grade 1 company afterwards, he went off favourite for the Lawlor's of Naas Novice Hurdle in January and stayed on strongly for a two-and-three-quarter-length victory from Sams Profile. There is a bit of a question mark over the form as his two main market rivals were pulled up and finished last, the runner-up made plenty of mistakes and was also hampered, and the third and fourth were well beaten by Commander Of

Fleet next time. Still, he's uncomplicated and seems to have a good attitude and there should be plenty more to come from a big horse who looks certain to make into a better chaser. Trainer looking to get another run into him before any Cheltenham decisions are Zmade and most winners of this will have raced more than twice over hurdles.

*Going preference* Only raced on good/yielding; expected to appreciate more ease
*Star rating* ✪✪✪

## CITY ISLAND
**6 b g; Trainer** Martin Brassil
**Hurdles form** 1d11, best RPR 145
**Left-handed** 11, best RPR 145
**Right-handed** 1d, best RPR 132

Bumper winner who has the dubious honour of having won two maiden hurdles. That's because he was disqualified due to a positive sample after the first of them at Galway in August, although it's worth recalling he rather comfortably took care of the now 135-rated Getareason there. Was a similarly easy winner of his next maiden at Leopardstown, this time dishing out a three-length beating to Dallas Des Pictons, who two starts later won a valuable Leopardstown handicap off a mark of 130. Completed preparation with comfortable seven-length win in ordinary Naas novice at odds of 1-5 in February and will head to Cheltenham untried in any Graded company. Still, his early form has obviously worked out very well and there is plenty to like about him. This is his only entry, which is not surprising as he is owned by the race sponsors.

*Going preference* Seems versatile
*Star rating* ✪✪✪

## BREWIN'UPASTORM
**6 b g; Trainer** Olly Murphy
**Hurdles form** 14F, best RPR 147
**Left-handed** 4F, best RPR 147
**Right-handed** 1, best RPR 134
**Cheltenham form** F, best RPR 147

Decent form in bumpers last season and made perfect start to novice hurdle career when a four-length winner at Huntingdon in December. Was set a pretty stiff task going in against some more battle-hardened rivals in the Grade 1 Challow Hurdle at Newbury only three weeks later but acquitted himself with credit to be beaten only four lengths into fourth by Champ, giving the impression he'd have been better suited by a much stronger gallop. He was in the process of putting up an improved display again in the Grade 2 trial at Cheltenham in January only to fall at the last. It's hard to be sure what would have happened as winner Birchdale was only half a length down and staying on at the time, but Richard Johnson certainly hadn't asked Brewin'upastorm for everything. Would be good to see him given a confidence-booster before the festival if time allows.

*Going preference* Seems versatile
*Star rating* ✪✪

## BIRCHDALE
**5 b g; Trainer** Nicky Henderson
**Hurdles form** (left-handed) 11, best RPR 147
**Cheltenham form** 1, best RPR 147

Big, raw five-year-old who is unbeaten in a point and two hurdles. Started rules career well despite running green with four-length success at Warwick in a race that worked out well and was closing on leader Brewin'upastorm in Grade 2 trial at

---

## TRAINER'S VIEW

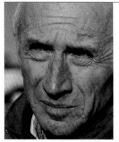

**Martin Brassil on City Island** "[Owners and race sponsors Sean and Bernadine Mulryan] are mad keen to have a horse to run in their own race at Cheltenham and thankfully we might have fallen on one. It's been the plan since Galway and we just picked out a couple of races to fit in. He jumps very well and Mark [Walsh, jockey] said he'll probably get three miles in time, so the trip of the Cheltenham race won't be an inconvenience" *By same sire as 2017 Ballymore winner Willoughby Court and only 5lb behind him on RPR at same stage without having been tested in Graded company*

Cheltenham when that one fell, leaving him to come home alone 18 lengths clear. That's pretty decent form and he still has plenty to learn, so there's every chance he will do better still, but he does look a shade inexperienced for the festival. Owner/trainer combination have favourite Champ for this and Birchdale is also in the Albert Bartlett, for which he's shorter in the betting, although that race normally turns into a war of attrition and tends to be won by horses with plenty of experience.

*Going preference* Has raced only on good/good to soft
*Star rating* ✪✪

## COMMANDER OF FLEET
**5 b g; Trainer** Gordon Elliott
**Hurdles form** 141, best RPR 145
**Left-handed** 1, best RPR 145
**Right-handed** 14, best RPR 136

Won a good-quality bumper in fine style last season and successful in two of three starts over hurdles, the only failure coming when he was last of four dropped to 2m at Fairyhouse in December. Looked an out-and-out stayer when landing a 2m6f Grade 1 at Leopardstown's Dublin Racing Festival and favourite for the Albert Bartlett.

*Going preference* Seems versatile
*Star rating* ✪✪✪✪

## BEAKSTOWN
**6 b g; Trainer** Dan Skelton
**Hurdles form** (left-handed) 121, best RPR 141

Point winner who was favourite for first three starts under rules, but won only the second of them, his 2m4f hurdles debut at Uttoxeter. Was surprisingly beaten in a three-way photo by a 50-1 shot on next start at Newcastle (2m6f, soft) but the winner won unchallenged next time and is clearly useful enough, while Beakstown obviously learned from the experience as he was impressive next time when winning the Grade 2 Leamington Novices' Hurdle at Warwick by three and three-quarter lengths from Stoney Mountain. That race has a rich recent history having been won by subsequent Ballymore scorers The New One and Willoughby Court and, while Beakstown was a 6-1 chance, he had been a much bigger price in the morning. Form is somewhat suspect with short-priced favourite Tidal Flow finishing stone last and

*City Island: heading to Cheltenham untried in any Graded company*

Birchdale a non-runner, but there was a lot to like about the way he travelled and, while he looks certain to appreciate 3m in time, he hasn't even been put in the Albert Bartlett.

*Going preference* Bit early to say, but both wins on good and both defeats on soft
*Star rating* ✪✪✪

## HONEYSUCKLE
**5 b m; Trainer** Henry de Bromhead
**Hurdles form** (right-handed) 111, best RPR 137

Mare who has the option of the mares' novice, for which she is ante-post favourite. However, after the third of her three hurdles successes, over 2m2f at Fairyhouse in January, Henry de Bromhead said nothing was set in stone as he was of the opinion she might be better over further than 2m. It would be a real sign of confidence from the trainer to run her against the boys when she has a favourite's chance in another race, but she does look a very useful recruit and would be worth considering. She pretty much laughed at rivals rated in the 130s at Fairyhouse and her sex allowance might just make her competitive.

*Going preference* Has raced only on good/yielding over hurdles but won point on soft
*Star rating* ✪✪

## RHINESTONE
**6 b g; Trainer** Joseph O'Brien
**Hurdles form** (left-handed) 142, best RPR 146
**Cheltenham form** (bumper) 9, best RPR 132
**At the festival** 14 Mar 2018 In touch, ridden and not quicken over 1f out, weakened inside final furlong, finished ninth, beaten ten and three-quarter lengths by Relegate in Champion Bumper

Another JP McManus-owned contender who has the option of the Albert Bartlett. However, he looked to be just outstayed by Commander Of Fleet in a 2m6f Grade 1 at Leopardstown in February, having travelled well and looked the winner entering the straight. The pair did pull nicely clear, though, and he was well ahead of fifth-placed Relegate, who beat him into ninth in last season's Champion Bumper. Rhinestone jumped a lot better there than he had on his debut at Naas or when he disappointed in a Grade 2 at Navan, so he's clearly learning as he goes along.

*Going preference* Hurdles form on good/yielding, but bumper winner on heavy
*Star rating* ✪✪✪

## SAMS PROFILE
**5 b g; Trainer** Mouse Morris
**Hurdles form** 122, best RPR 136
**Left-handed** 2, best RPR 136
**Right-handed** 12, best RPR 136

Comfortably accounted for the now 132-rated Eclair De Beaufeu in 20-runner four-year-old maiden hurdle at Cork on debut and has not been without serious promise in two subsequent starts, the first when second upped to 3m in Grade 3 back at Cork and then when taking the runner-up spot to Battleoverdoyen in the 2m4f Grade 1 Lawlor's of Naas Novice Hurdle. A couple of the main market protagonists didn't run their races, but the winner is second favourite for this and may not have had it all his own way if Sams Profile had not jumped so poorly and been hampered. He was beaten only two and three-quarter lengths and connections will have every right to think they can get closer when they meet again.

*Going preference* Seems versatile
*Star rating* ✪✪✪

## OTHERS TO CONSIDER
As usual there are plenty of horses with entries in more than one novice hurdle and those left out here include the likes of **Aramon**, **Angels Breath**, **Al Dancer** and **Getaway Trump**, who are all dealt with in the Supreme section. Nicky Henderson would really cause a ripple if one-time Supreme favourite Angels Breath ran here, but that must have become a shade more likely given how well Al Dancer won the Betfair Hurdle and it's worth noting Angels Breath is a 3m point winner who was due to run over nearly 2m4f in the Sidney Banks at Huntingdon before equine flu intervened. The unbeaten **Emitom** was going to take on Angels Breath at Huntingdon and remains a horse of serious promise, while **Thomas Darby** looks as though he is crying out for a step up in trip, having been campaigned up to now at 2m. Another potential fly in the

## BALLYMORE NOVICES' HURDLE RESULTS AND TRENDS

| | FORM | WINNER | AGE & WGT | Adj RPR | SP | TRAINER | BEST RPR LAST 12 MONTHS (RUNS SINCE) |
|---|---|---|---|---|---|---|---|
| 18 | 1-111 | **Samcro** | 6 11-7 | 161ᵀ | 8-11f | G Elliott (IRE) | won Navan Gd3 nov hdl (2m4f) (1) |
| 17 | 5-211 | **Willoughby Court** D | 6 11-7 | 154-5 | 14-1 | B Pauling | won Warwick Gd2 nov hdl (2m5f) (0) |
| 16 | 1-111 | **Yorkhill** | 6 11-7 | 159-8 | 3-1 | W Mullins (IRE) | won Sandown Gd1 nov hdl (2m) (0) |
| 15 | -1142 | **Windsor Park** | 6 11-7 | 154-3 | 9-2 | D Weld (IRE) | 2nd Leopardstown Gd1 nov hdl (2m2f) (0) |
| 14 | 1111 | **Faugheen** | 6 11-7 | 156ᵀ | 6-4f | W Mullins (IRE) | won Limerick Gd3 nov hdl (3m) (0) |
| 13 | -1112 | **The New One** CD, BF | 5 11-7 | 162-1 | 7-2 | N Twiston-Davies | 2nd Cheltenham Gd2 nov hdl (2m4½f) (0) |
| 12 | 1121 | **Simonsig** | 6 11-7 | 160ᵀ | 2-1f | N Henderson | 2nd Sandown Gd2 nov hdl (2m4f) (1) |
| 11 | -4131 | **First Lieutenant** | 6 11-7 | 152-8 | 7-1 | M Morris (IRE) | won Leopardstown Gd1 nov hdl (2m) (0) |
| 10 | 111 | **Peddlers Cross** | 5 11-7 | 155-1 | 7-1 | D McCain | won Haydock Gd2 nov hdl (2m½f) (0) |
| 09 | 21111 | **Mikael D'Haguenet** | 5 11-7 | 160-4 | 5-2f | W Mullins (IRE) | won Punchestown Gd2 nov hdl (2m) (0) |

**WINS-RUNS:** 4yo 0-2, 5yo 3-46, 6yo 7-65, 7yo 0-20 **FAVOURITES:** +£0.73

**TRAINERS IN THIS RACE (w-pl-r):** Willie Mullins 3-6-23, Gordon Elliott 1-0-3, Ben Pauling 1-0-2, Nicky Henderson 1-0-12, Nigel Twiston-Davies 1-0-2, Mouse Morris 1-1-4, Alan King 0-3-9, Noel Meade 0-1-4, Dan Skelton 0-1-3, Paul Nicholls 0-1-3, Tom George 0-1-1, Colin Tizzard 0-0-3, Harry Fry 0-1-1, Henry de Bromhead 0-0-2, Jessica Harrington 0-0-2, Kim Bailey 0-0-1

**FATE OF FAVOURITES:** 1331313221 **POSITION OF WINNER IN MARKET:** 1441213251

ointment is last year's Champion Bumper runner-up **Carefully Selected**, who has been quoted fairly short in the market for both this and the Albert Bartlett. Wherever he goes, though, he will be short on experience as by the middle of February we were still waiting for his debut over hurdles. He had been appearing among the entries for a few maiden hurdles, though, so we must assume it remains the plan, although he could always have another crack at the Champion Bumper if they can't get a run into him.

## VERDICT

*I wouldn't really argue with* **Champ** *being favourite but wouldn't have him or* **Battleoverdoyen** *as far ahead of the rest of the field in what looks an open race.* **SAMS PROFILE** *is entered in all three novice hurdles and has form over all trips, but wherever he runs I'm going to end up backing him as I'm sure there's a big run in him when he brushes up his jumping. I certainly wouldn't be afraid to take on* **Battleoverdoyen** *again and can't see why Sams Profile is more than three times the price.*

### Key trends

- Aged five or six, ten winners in last ten runnings
- Rated within 8lb of RPR top-rated, 10/10
- Adjusted RPR of at least 152, 10/10
- Started career in Irish points or bumpers, 9/10
- Won at least 50 per cent of hurdle runs, 9/10
- Scored over at least 2m4f, 9/10
- Won a Graded hurdle, 9/10
- Finished first or second on all completed starts over hurdles, 8/10
- At least three runs over hurdles, 8/10

### Other factors

- Four of the last ten favourites have obliged (Mikael D'Haguenet 2009, Simonsig 2012, Faugheen 2014, Samcro 2018) and in that period only Willoughby Court's SP (14-1 in 2017) was bigger than 7-1

NOTES

## 2.10 RSA Insurance Novices' Chase    ITV/RTV
### 3m½f    Grade 1    £175,000

Nicky Henderson's two recent winners of this race, Bobs Worth in 2012 and Might Bite in 2017, went on to land the Cheltenham Gold Cup and King George VI Chase respectively and there are similarly lofty ambitions for Santini, but first he must overcome his inexperience to follow their example with victory here. A Grade 1 winner as a novice hurdler last season, he started his chasing career in great style with a Grade 2 victory at Newbury in December but then was third behind La Bague Au Roi in a Grade 1 at Kempton's Christmas meeting. Ireland's chief hope is Gordon Elliott's Delta Work, a festival winner last year in the Pertemps Final who is three from three over fences, including two Grade 1s. Topofthegame, narrowly denied at the festival in the Coral Cup a year ago, has strong claims for Paul Nicholls, having been second to La Bague Au Roi at Kempton. La Bague Au Roi herself would have a good shout but Warren Greatrex's mare is considered an unlikely runner.

## SANTINI
**7 b g; Trainer** Nicky Henderson
**Chase form** 13, best RPR 157
**Left-handed** 1, best RPR 157
**Right-handed** 3, best RPR 157
**Cheltenham form** (hurdles) 13, best RPR 153
**At the festival** 16 Mar 2018 Held up, headway on outer approaching 2 out, edged left between last 2, stayed on under pressure to chase leaders last, kept on but held final 75yds, finished third, beaten four and a half lengths by Kilbricken Storm in Albert Bartlett Novices' Hurdle

Was on everyone's lips for this even before last year's festival, where he finished third to Kilbricken Storm when favourite for the Albert Bartlett. That still wasn't a bad run given he had much less experience than a normal winner of that sometimes brutal race and he showed no ill effects afterwards as he went on to win the 3m Grade 1 novice hurdle at Aintree. Made quite a sparkling debut over fences at Newbury's Ladbrokes Trophy meeting in December, landing a Grade 2 against more experienced rivals, and that only served to see him shorten as favourite for this. He was also a warm favourite for the Kauto Star Novices' Chase at Kempton but never really travelled as well as front pair La Bague Au Roi and Topofthegame and finished third, although he came home best of all after the last, indicating he would appreciate the extra distance at Cheltenham. That was also his first start on a right-handed track and he is

expected to prove better suited to racing the other way round. That said, he is priced as though that is certain and he is one of those who heads a Cheltenham market without boasting the best form. Still, he is not exactly a mile off the best and clearly remains a horse of immense potential. He has not had the best of preparations, though, as his intended run in the Reynoldstown Novices' Chase at Ascot in February had to be cancelled because he had to have a flu jab.

*Going preference* Can't say he didn't act on good to soft at Kempton but obviously handles deep ground well
*Star rating* ✪✪✪

## DELTA WORK
**6 br g; Trainer** Gordon Elliott
**Chase form** 111, best RPR 160
**Left-handed** 1, best RPR 160
**Right-handed** 11, best RPR 156
**Cheltenham form** (hurdles) 1, best RPR 147
**At the festival** 15 Mar 2018 Midfield, headway 2 out, not clear run and switched right approaching last, hit and led last, strongly pressed after, gamely prevailed in driving finish, won Pertemps Final by a nose from Glenloe

Already a Cheltenham Festival winner having scrambled home by a nose off a mark of 139 in the Pertemps Final and trying to follow in the footsteps of Gold Cup favourite Presenting Percy, who won that race in 2017 before following up in the RSA last year. Has certainly improved again for fences this term and, following a workmanlike debut success at Down Royal in November, he won back-to-back Grade 1s over 2m4f at Fairyhouse and 3m at Leopardstown in December. Neither was entirely straightforward, especially at Fairyhouse where he made a mistake at the last and had to rally to get back up past Le Richebourg on the run-in. That form looks pretty strong now, given the runner-up has bagged his own brace of Grade 1s dropped in trip and is now favourite for the Racing Post Arkle. Next time in the 3m Neville Hotels Novice Chase, Delta Work won by eight lengths from Joseph O'Brien's Mortal but not before the latter had traded at odds-on in running (1.6) going to the last before making a mistake. Given how strong he was at the end, Delta Work would probably have won anyway and he does keep putting his head in front, so he has to be considered Ireland's leading hope, especially given his previous festival form. Mortal could have done more to boost the form than finish last to La Bague Au Roi next time, but he probably didn't run his race and probably wants further than 2m5f.

*Going preference* Seems versatile
*Star rating* ✪✪✪✪

## TOPOFTHEGAME

**7 ch g; Trainer** Paul Nicholls
**Chase form** (right-handed) 22, best RPR 160
**Cheltenham form** (hurdles) 42, best RPR 155
**At the festival** 14 Mar 2018 Tracked leaders, upsides when bunny-hopped 2 out, led last, headed narrowly final 100yds, kept on near finish, just held, finished second, beaten a neck by Bleu Berry in Coral Cup

Big horse who has shown immense promise in both chase starts without winning either. On his Exeter debut in December he whipped around at the start and lost 20 lengths, but slowly worked his way into contention and looked a serious threat three out before finishing second to Defi Du Seuil, who had race fitness and previous experience on his side (and has subsequently won a Grade 1 and is favourite for the JLT). Just 19 days later Topofthegame went sent straight into Grade 1 battle in the Kauto Star Novices' Chase, in which he travelled best and looked

the likely winner until his jumping got a bit ragged at the final two (not helped by being given a slap as he was about to take off two out and subsequently jumping too high) and La Bague Au Roi rallied and battled past him. Still, he gave Warren Greatrex's mare, another subsequent Grade 1 winner next time, more of a fight than any other horse has over fences this season and, while many are expecting Santini to prove better suited to Cheltenham, it's worth remembering Topofthegame was the biggest horse in the Kempton field and is hardly likely to be inconvenienced by a more galloping track. It's also worth remembering that, while Delta Work won his festival handicap hurdle off a mark of 139, Topofthegame was only just denied in the Coral Cup off an 11lb higher rating. Despite his waywardness at Exeter, he had shown a really good attitude in a finish over hurdles and it's hard not to see him being a player. Was due to complete his preparation in the Reynoldstown at Ascot but trainer Paul Nicholls had a change of heart, saying he wants him to go there fresh.

*Going preference* Acts on good to soft and soft
*Star rating* ✪✪✪✪✪

## OK CORRAL

**9 b g; Trainer** Nicky Henderson
**Chase form** (left-handed) 11, best RPR 156
**Cheltenham form** (hurdles) 2, best RPR 151
**At the festival** 16 Mar 2018 Midfield, headway between last 2, hung left when chasing leaders and mistake last, continued to hang left run-in, went 2nd final 100yds, stayed on, not reach winner,

## TRAINER'S VIEW

**Gordon Elliott on Delta Work** "He's a good horse – he was a 150-rated hurdler – and he loves a battle as well. Davy [Russell, jockey] said the [good] ground was as quick as he'd want it now as he was just a little bit careful early [in the Grade 1 Neville Hotels Novice Chase at Leopardstown]. He's a lovely horse. I put a hood on him and he's actually gone very relaxed, which is great, so I'll leave it on" *Delta Work will attempt to follow Presenting Percy by landing the RSA after victory in the Pertemps Final the previous year*

finished second, beaten three lengths by Kilbricken Storm in Albert Bartlett Novices' Hurdle

Fragile horse who has run only nine times since his racecourse debut at Kempton in 2015 and didn't run over hurdles until he was seven. He has always looked potentially smart, though, and he finished ahead of stablemate Santini when second in the Albert Bartlett last term. He didn't run his race when well behind Santini at Aintree but has looked fairly natural over fences in two outings this term. It was hard to put a big figure on his two-and-a-quarter-length win from Impulsive Star at Plumpton in December, but the form took on a much better look when the runner-up won the Warwick Classic Handicap Chase next time and, on the same card, Ok Corral was a deeply impressive winner of a Listed chase. It's quite possible short-priced favourite Rocky's Treasure didn't run his race, but the 143-rated Secret Investor sure did and Ok Corral beat him fairly handily by six lengths That entitles him to serious consideration if he comes here, but his owner has an affinity

with the four-mile National Hunt Chase and Derek O'Connor was on board at Warwick, which suggests that amateur riders' race is where he will go.

*Going preference* Seems versatile
*Star rating* ✪✪✪✪

## ON THE BLIND SIDE
**7 b g; Trainer** Nicky Henderson
**Chase form** 41, best RPR 149
**Left-handed** 4, best RPR 68
**Right-handed** 1, best RPR 149
**Cheltenham form** (all) 14, best RPR 150

Useful novice hurdler in the first part of last season, winning his first three starts, the last two in Grade 2s at Cheltenham and Sandown. However, he missed the festival with a "small muscle issue" and was then well beaten when a short-priced favourite behind Black Op at Aintree. Things did not go as planned on his return to action after a wind op this season

*Vinndication: all seven of his runs have been on right-handed tracks*

either, as he seemed to lose confidence after a minor error at the first fence and trailed in 85 lengths last of four behind Lostintranslation. Given time to get over that, he returned just under four weeks later over 3m and this time jumped and travelled very well and found plenty when challenged to see off Talkischeap by just over three lengths. He needs to improve again but that is entirely possible and at least he seems to be back on the right track now. Trainer Nicky Henderson, responsible for favourite Santini, says he will need to get another run into him before thinking about festivals.

*Going preference* Best form on good to soft
*Star rating* ✪✪

## VINNDICATION

**6 b g; Trainer** Kim Bailey
**Chase form** (right-handed) 113, best RPR 154

Promising youngster who is said to be "bone idle" but that didn't stop him winning his first six races. Showed a decent level of form to win all four outings over hurdles last season (only horse to beat current Ballymore Novices' Hurdle favourite Champ) but missed all the spring festivals as he was always viewed as a long-term chase prospect. He hasn't disappointed on that score either, winning his first two and jumping particularly well in a Grade 2 success at Ascot but, reading between the lines, his trainer knew he was pushing it keeping him at 2m4f for the Grade 1 Scilly Isles Novices' Chase at Sandown in February. That didn't stop him from being sent off 11-8 favourite, but they always seemed to be going a shade fast for him and it wasn't until after the last that he started to make serious inroads on winner Defi Du Seuil and runner-up Lostintranslation. There's no doubt he's going to be a stayer, and a strong one at that, but while trainer says the fact all seven of his runs have been on right-handed tracks is no more than coincidence, he did jump to his right occasionally at Sandown and he'll have that to prove if lining up at Cheltenham.

*Going preference* Almost certainly wants soft ground
*Star rating* ✪✪✪

## CHAMPAGNE CLASSIC

**8 b g; Trainer** Gordon Elliott
**Chase form** (left-handed) 3, best RPR 140
**Cheltenham form** (hurdles) 1, best RPR 145
**At the festival** 17 Mar 2017 Mid-division, headway 6th, led after 2 out, stayed on strongly, ridden out, won Martin Pipe Conditional Jockeys' Handicap Hurdle by two and a quarter lengths from Verni

Called "just about the worst horse we have" by owner Michael O'Leary in the aftermath of his Martin Pipe Handicap Hurdle victory in 2017, but suggested otherwise when he beat Albert Bartlett and subsequent Stayers' Hurdle winner Penhill in a Punchestown Grade 1 on his next start. Unfortunately he was off for 641 days after that, not reappearing until this January, when he was a perfectly respectable third in a Grade 3 novice chase at Naas. You would want to see him get more experience before taking on the big guns in a race like this, but he will be worthy of respect as a past festival winner wherever he goes. There was some money for him for the JLT in February, but his trainer has since said the National Hunt Chase is more likely, so it's all up in the air.

*Going preference* Acts on any, probably doesn't want it too soft
*Star rating* ✪✪

## DROVERS LANE

**7 b g; Trainer** Rebecca Curtis
**Chase form** 1711, best RPR 154
**Left-handed** 71, best RPR 154
**Right-handed** 11, best RPR 149
**Cheltenham form** 1, best RPR 154

Spent two seasons as a novice hurdler and was rated only 127 at the end of the second of them, but form has taken off over fences this term. Started off in October on good to firm ground at Hereford, where he stayed on strongly for a nine-length win, and while he couldn't defy an 8lb higher mark next time at Aintree, he had the stuffing knocked out of him by a mistake three out. He soon recovered dropped in trip to 2m5½f at Market Rasen, bolting up by 11 lengths, and then went to Cheltenham in Class 2 novice company, giving the 144-rated Le Breuil 3lb and a one-and-a-half-length beating. Although getting tired in the closing stages, he was always in

control and it was a fair effort. Trainer has won this race before and said she'll try to find something for him at the festival, but handicaps are probably out as he is now rated 150. The JLT might be a better fit, but he does stay.

*Going preference* Looks a case of the quicker the better
*Star rating* ✪✪

## MORTAL
**7 b g; Trainer** Joseph O'Brien
**Chase form** 126, best RPR 152
**Left-handed** 26, best RPR 152
**Right-handed** 1, best RPR 135

Rated only 127 over hurdles but quickly developed into a much better chaser, starting with a debut success over 2m5f when just getting the better of the 143-rated Any Second Now at odds of 10-1 at Fairyhouse in early December. Proved that was no fluke when an eight-length second to Delta Work in the 3m Grade 1 Neville Hotels Novice Chase at Leopardstown next time and he wouldn't have been beaten anywhere near as far had he not made a mistake at the last. Indeed, he was trading at odds-on in running heading to the last and that is obviously form that ties him in closely to the favourite. Not so good at the Dublin Racing Festival back at Leopardstown when last of six to La Bague Au Roi, but he seemed to get outpaced when it mattered back at 2m5f and trainer has always seen him as a stayer, saying: "He could be quite an exciting horse when he goes over a trip." Entered in the National Hunt Chase and the JLT and owners Gigginstown have a wide range of options for the novice chases, but he's one who has the talent to go well at a decent price wherever he ends up.

*Going preference* Improvement over fences has been on decent ground
*Star rating* ✪✪✪

## TALKISCHEAP
**7 b g; Trainer** Alan King
**Chase form** 3212, best RPR 153
**Left-handed** 321, best RPR 151
**Right-handed** 2, best RPR 153
**Cheltenham form** (hurdles) P
**At the festival** 16 Mar 2018 Midfield, lost place

before 3 out, behind 2 out, pulled up soon after last in Albert Bartlett Novices' Hurdle won by Kilbricken Storm

Three-time winner as a novice over hurdles last season, including on soft ground, but said to want a better surface and was pulled up in the Albert Bartlett. Has won only one of his four chases and that was a match at Doncaster, but has been highly tried as he was twice placed behind La Bague Au Roi at Newbury, beaten no more than seven lengths each time, before his success. Was no match for On The Blind Side last time at Kempton but was conceding the winner 6lb, so it's not bad form. Would be entitled to take his chance but has been left on a mark of 145 and, knowing Alan King, he must be considering the Ultima Handicap Chase on the opening day of the festival. King won that race with the novice Fork Lightning in 2004, while in 2010 his novice Bensalem was cruising when coming down two out in the same race (he won it the following year).

*Going preference* Said to want decent ground
*Star rating* ✪✪

## THE WORLDS END
**8 b g; Trainer** Tom George
**Chase form** 1316, best RPR 159
**Left-handed** 131, best RPR 159
**Right-handed** 6, best RPR 130
**Cheltenham form** (all) F4731, best RPR 159
**At the festival** 17 Mar 2017 Held up, rapid headway after 3 out, upsides when fell 2 out in Albert Bartlett Novices' Hurdle won by Penhill 15 Mar 2018 Looked well, held up, headway approaching 2 out, every chance between last 2, ridden and outpaced before last, kept on one pace run-in, finished seventh, beaten seven and a half lengths by Penhill in Stayers' Hurdle

Has become a bit of a Jekyll and Hyde character but very capable of going well at his best and jumped like a stag when winning by 26 lengths at Cheltenham in December. Also won by a wide margin on his chase debut at Chepstow but has thrown in a couple of poor runs, too, particularly when tailed off in the Kauto Star at Kempton. His best form is certainly not far off what the market principals have shown themselves capable off and much

## RSA CHASE RESULTS AND TRENDS

| | FORM WINNER | AGE & WGT | Adj RPR | SP | TRAINER | BEST RPR LAST 12 MONTHS (RUNS SINCE) |
|---|---|---|---|---|---|---|
| 18 | 13112 **Presenting Percy** C, D, BF | 7 11-4 | 171-1 | 5-2f | P Kelly (IRE) | won Fairyhouse hcap ch (3m5f) **(1)** |
| 17 | -21F1 **Might Bite** C, D | 8 11-4 | 175T | 7-2f | N Henderson | Fell Kempton Gd 1 nov ch (3m) **(1)** |
| 16 | 4F121 **Blaklion** C, D | 7 11-4 | 172-1 | 8-1 | N Twiston-Davies | won Wetherby Gd 2 nov ch (3m) **(0)** |
| 15 | 1-211 **Don Poli** C, D | 6 11-4 | 165-2 | 13-8f | W Mullins (IRE) | won Leopardstown Gd1 nov ch (3m) **(0)** |
| 14 | 4-2P1 **O'Faolains Boy** D | 7 11-4 | 160-9 | 12-1 | R Curtis | won Gd2 Reynoldstown Nov Ch (3m) **(0)** |
| 13 | 22123 **Lord Windermere** | 7 11-4 | 155-10 | 8-1 | J Culloty (IRE) | 3rd Gd1 Dr PJ Moriarty Nov Ch (2m5f) **(0)** |
| 12 | 1-132 **Bobs Worth** C, D | 7 11-4 | 172-6 | 9-2 | N Henderson | 3rd Gd1 Feltham Nov Ch (3m) **(1)** |
| 11 | 21411 **Bostons Angel** D | 7 11-4 | 160-13 | 16-1 | J Harrington (IRE) | won Gd1 Dr PJ Moriarty Nov Ch (2m5f) **(0)** |
| 10 | 3F122 **Weapon's Amnesty** C, D | 7 11-4 | 160-15 | 10-1 | C Byrnes (IRE) | 2nd Leopardstown Gd1 nov ch (3m) **(1)** |
| 09 | -8131 **Cooldine** | 7 11-4 | 166-3 | 9-4f | W Mullins (IRE) | won Gd1 Dr PJ Moriarty Nov Ch (2m5f) **(0)** |

**WINS-RUNS:** 5yo 0-3, 6yo 1-19, 7yo 8-61, 8yo 1-21, 9yo 0-5 **FAVOURITES:** £3.88

**TRAINERS IN THIS RACE (w-pl-r):** Willie Mullins 2-3-16, Nicky Henderson 2-4-11, Nigel Twiston-Davies 1-0-4, Jessica Harrington 1-1-3, Rebecca Curtis 1-0-2, Paul Nicholls 0-1-10, Colin Tizzard 0-1-4, Gordon Elliott 0-1-4, Henry de Bromhead 0-1-3, Philip Hobbs 0-1-2, David Pipe 0-0-4

**FATE OF FAVOURITES:** 1554421311 **POSITION OF WINNER IN MARKET:** 1572481311

depends on what sort of mood he is in, but on a going day he would look a very big price.

*Going preference* Prefers better ground
*Star rating* ✪✪

## OTHERS TO CONSIDER

Connections have ruled **La Bague Au Roi** out of the festival, which was always on the cards given how poorly she has run at Cheltenham in the past. She'd obviously have had a fine form chance and there aren't too many more you can say that about. The Reynoldstown Novices' Chase at Ascot often produces a strong RSA contender but this year's renewal had a weak look and Colin Tizzard, trainer of winner **Mister Malarky**, reckoned it would be the four-miler for him.

## VERDICT

*I have a feeling this is going to attract a small field and will come down to **Santini**, **Delta Work** and **TOPOFTHEGAME**. Of that trio, I don't see why Topofthegame should be the outsider. He may still be a maiden over fences but he finished ahead of Santini in the Kauto Star and we know he handles Cheltenham because of his hurdles form. He nearly won the Coral Cup, traditionally a better handicap than the Pertemps Final, off an 11lb higher mark than Delta Work defied in the latter, and he has to go well.*

*Key trends*

🐎Did not run on the Flat, 10/10

🐎Top-three finish last time out, 10/10

🐎Contested a Graded chase, 10/10 (six won)

🐎Adjusted RPR of at least 160, 9/10

🐎Last ran between 24 and 53 days ago, 9/10

🐎Ran at least three times over fences, 9/10

🐎Six to 12 hurdles and chase runs, 8/10

🐎Aged seven, 8/10

🐎Rated within 10lb of RPR top-rated, 8/10 (only one was top-rated)

*Other factors*

🐎Of the combined 46 chase starts of winners, only 2016 scorer Blaklion had finished outside the first three (four had fallen)

🐎Eight winners had previously run at the festival – five ran in the Albert Bartlett (1P14P), one in the Martin Pipe (1), one in the Pertemps Final (1) and one in the Bumper two years earlier (7)

## 2.50 **Coral Cup Handicap Hurdle**  ITV/RTV
🐎 *2m5f*  🐎 *Grade 3*  🐎 *£100,000*

Only one outright and one joint-favourite have won this tricky handicap hurdle in its 25-year history and there have been just two winners at single-figure odds since 2004. Eleven of the past 13 winners were in the first seven in the betting, however, so the market is not such a bad guide.

The race has tended to suit younger, less exposed types, with ten of the past 18 winners aged five or six and just three winners in the last 19 renewals aged eight or older. Ten of the last 11 victors arrived at Cheltenham with single figures of runs over hurdles, including last year's winner Bleu Berry, who had run just six times over hurdles and was competing in a handicap for only the second time in his career.

Ireland has had ten winners, including the last three, and only Xenophon, 4-1 favourite in 2003, was heavily fancied. The other nine Irish winners were returned at between 11-1 and 20-1.

■**ONES TO WATCH** Willie Mullins' **Uradel** was second in the Cesarewitch last autumn and a fine fifth to Off You Go in the big 2m handicap hurdle on his return to jumps at the Dublin Racing Festival in February. **Off You Go** is trained by the shrewd Charles Byrnes and could bid to follow up, while stablemate **Wonder Laish** should not be written off despite finishing well down the field in that race.

### CORAL CUP RESULTS AND TRENDS

| | FORM WINNER | AGE & WGT | OR | SP | TRAINER | BEST RPR LAST 12 MONTHS (RUNS SINCE) |
|---|---|---|---|---|---|---|
| 18 | 115-0 **Bleu Berry** | 7 11-2 | 143-5 | 20-1 | W Mullins (IRE) | won Fairyhouse Gd2 nov hdl (2m) (2) |
| 17 | 48124 **Supasundae** | 7 11-4 | 148-2 | 16-1 | J Harrington (IRE) | won Punchestown hdl (2m4f) (2) |
| 16 | P-421 **Diamond King** | 8 11-3 | 149-5 | 12-1 | G Elliott (IRE) | won Punchestown hdl (2m4f) (0) |
| 15 | 1-31 **Aux Ptits Soins** | 5 10-7 | 139-4 | 9-1 | P Nicholls | won Auteuil hdl (2m1½f) (0) |
| 14 | -3312 **Whisper** C, D, BF | 6 11-6 | 153-4 | 14-1 | N Henderson | 2nd Ffos Las class 2 hcap hdl (2m4f) (0) |
| 13 | -2241 **Medinas** | 6 11-10 | 148-3 | 33-1 | A King | won Ffos Las class 2 hcap hdl (2m4f) (0) |
| 12 | -9090 **Son Of Flicka** | 8 10-6 | 135T | 16-1 | D McCain | 2nd Martin Pipe Cond Hcp Hdl (2m4½f) (5) |
| 11 | 2-102 **Carlito Brigante** (2ow) | 5 11-0 | 142-10 | 16-1 | G Elliott (IRE) | 2nd Fairyhouse hdl (2m) (0) |
| 10 | 1-510 **Spirit River** C | 5 11-2 | 141-1 | 14-1 | N Henderson | won Cheltenham class 3 hcap hdl (2m1f) (1) |
| 09 | -4511 **Ninetieth Minute** | 6 10-3 | 140T | 14-1 | T Taaffe (IRE) | won Thurles Listed hdl (2m) (0) |

**WINS-RUNS:** 5yo 3-50, 6yo 3-81, 7yo 2-63, 8yo 2-37, 9yo 0-16, 10yo 0-12, 11yo 0-3, 12yo 0-1 **FAVOURITES:** -£10

**FATE OF FAVOURITES:** 0002053004 **POSITION OF WINNER IN MARKET:** 6677052660

*Key trends*

🐎 Officially rated 135 to 149, 9/10

🐎 Not run for at least 32 days, 9/10

🐎 No more than four runs that season, 9/10

🐎 No more than nine hurdle runs, 9/10

🐎 Won a race earlier in the season, 8/10 (four won last time out)

🐎 Aged five to seven, 8/10

🐎 Won between 2m2f and 2m6f over hurdles, 7/10

🐎 Carried no more than 11st 3lb, 7/10

*Other factors*

🐎 The only winner to have had more than nine hurdle runs had 22 starts (Son Of Flicka in 2012)

## 3.30 Betway Queen Mother Champion Chase ITV/RTV
### 2m  Grade 1  £400,000

Altior was ranked eighth in the recent Racing Post series on the top 50 two-mile chasers and at the age of nine Nicky Henderson's superstar still has time to move further up the list of all-time greats, starting here with his fourth consecutive victory at the festival and his second in this championship contest. His three festival wins have been by seven lengths, six lengths and seven lengths, and the closest any rival has got to him this season was the four-length margin of victory over Un De Sceaux in the Tingle Creek. Having effortlessly stretched his 100 per cent record over jumps to 17 races with two more wins since then, few expect him to be given a serious race here and several potential rivals look likely to head for the Ryanair Chase instead. Min, runner-up last year and in Altior's Supreme Novices' Hurdle in 2016, is one who could stand his ground but Altior would have to underperform for the gap to close. It has been Min's misfortune to come along in the same era as a champion of rare quality and the same goes for Footpad, Un De Sceaux, Sceau Royal and Fox Norton – as long as Altior is performing at his peak, they're all running for the places.

### ALTIOR
**9 b g; Trainer** Nicky Henderson
**Chase form** 111111111111, best RPR 183
**Left-handed** 1111, best RPR 183
**Right-handed** 11111111, best RPR 180
**Cheltenham form** (all) 1111, best RPR 183
**At the festival** 15 Mar 2016 Travelled and jumped well, mid-division, headway after 5th, challenged after 2 out, ridden to lead before last, quickened clear, impressive, won Supreme Novices' Hurdle by seven lengths from Min
14 Mar 2017 Tracked leaders, went 2nd before 5th, ½ length down and pressing leader when left in lead 2 out, ridden out after last, ran on to draw clear inside final 100yds, won Racing Post Arkle Chase by six lengths from Cloudy Dream
14 Mar 2018 Looked well, in touch, disputed 4th after 7th, niggled along approaching 3 out, switched right approaching 2 out, challenged between last 2, led soon after last, soon ridden, forged clear, impressive, won Champion Chase by seven lengths from Min

Simply brilliant two-miler who has now won all 17 starts over jumps, the last 12 of them chases. Did not have a clear run last season, needing a wind operation in November, but it didn't affect him one bit as he toyed with Politologue in the Game Spirit and then rocked up at Cheltenham to power to his third straight festival win and dish out his second seven-length drubbing to the high-class Min, having done the same to him in the Supreme Novices' Hurdle two years earlier. In doing so he was awarded a career-best Racing Post Rating of 183 and this term he hasn't been far off that while winning comfortably each time. Un De Sceaux looked like he might make a race of it with him in the Tingle Creek at Sandown in December on his favoured soft ground, but ultimately Altior needed only one crack with the whip to assert and after that was only nudged out for a four-length win. Sauntered home by 19 lengths at odds of 1-8 from Diego Du Charmil in the Desert Orchid next time at Kempton and was sent off even shorter in the Clarence House at Ascot

## TRAINER'S VIEW
**Nicky Henderson on Altior** "When they're as good as he is they're put under such scrutiny. Yes, he did drift to his left a couple of times [at Ascot last time] but it's not his natural trait to do that and it'll be left-handed next time anyway" *Altior is 4-4 at Cheltenham and recorded his best RPR of 183 in last year's race*

(1-10). There he gave fans a few moments of concern as he continually jumped to the left, sometimes markedly so, but he was so good he was still able to win eased down by seven lengths from the long-absent Fox Norton. Trainer didn't seem too concerned by his jumping antics, reasoning that he was probably bored with having to make his own running, and Altior has often edged to his left during other races on right-handed tracks. Unless there is an issue, and it's hard to believe there is, he'll win again.

*Going preference* Handles everything
*Star rating* ⭕⭕⭕⭕⭕

## MIN

**8 b g; Trainer** Willie Mullins
**Chase form** 1112122411, best RPR 176
**Left-handed** 1121221, best RPR 176
**Right-handed** 141, best RPR 167
**Cheltenham form** (all) 22, best RPR 176
**At the festival** 15 Mar 2016 Tracked leader, mistake 3rd, challenged after 2 out, soon ridden, kept on but readily outpaced by winner, finished second, beaten seven lengths by Altior in Supreme Novices' Hurdle
14 Mar 2018 Looked well, travelled well, held up, hit 8th, headway when hampered 4 out, led approaching 2 out, ridden when joined last, headed soon after, kept on but outpaced final 120yds, finished second, beaten seven lengths by Altior in Champion Chase

Top-class operator who has won eight of his 15 starts and six of his ten chases but has simply been unlucky enough to be around at the same time as Altior. A three-time Grade 1 winner in his own right but best performances, over hurdles and fences, have come while watching Altior's backside disappear into the distance. The Racing Post Rating he earned for finishing second in last season's Champion Chase (176) would be good enough to win a lot of runnings and he hasn't needed to match that to win the John Durkan Memorial (2m4f) and Dublin Chase (2m1f) on his two starts this season. He did it particularly easily at Leopardstown and is probably more of a two-miler than anything else, but you wouldn't blame connections for having a crack at the Ryanair instead. That said, Willie Mullins looks sure to run something against Altior and there's still a lot of money for second.

*Going preference* Handles everything
*Star rating* ⭕⭕⭕

## FOOTPAD

**7 b g; Trainer** Willie Mullins
**Chase form** 11111F2, best RPR 172
**Left-handed** 11111F2, best RPR 172
**Right-handed** 1, best RPR 164
**Cheltenham form** (all) 341, best RPR 172
**At the festival** 18 Mar 2016 Behind, ridden after 2 out to go pace, headway soon after, switched left slightly between last 2, went 3rd approaching last, stayed on, not pace to trouble front pair, finished third, beaten seven and a quarter lengths by Ivanovich Gorbatov in Triumph Hurdle
14 Mar 2017 Held up, headway approaching last, soon chasing leaders and ridden, not quicken, kept on under pressure run-in but not pace of leaders, finished fourth, beaten ten and a half lengths by Buveur D'Air in Champion Hurdle
14 Mar 2018 Raced in 3rd place, chased clear leaders approaching 5th, blundered 6th, headway before 4 out, went 2nd before 3 out where upsides, led on bend before 2 out, drew clear from last, stayed on strongly and well in command after, won Racing Post Arkle Chase by 14 lengths from Brain Power

Decent hurdler who was fourth in the 2017 Champion Hurdle and looked like turning into a superstar over fences following an unbeaten first season which included four Grade 1 wins in five starts. Earned a peak RPR of 172 when trouncing Brain Power by 14 lengths in the Racing Post Arkle and then cruised to a 12-length success at Punchestown, but it is beginning to look like last season's two-mile novices were not a great bunch and he hasn't done much to dispel that notion with defeats on his two starts this term. Looked beaten when falling two out in the Grade 3 Poplar Square Chase at Naas (won by Arkle distant fourth Saint Calvados) and, while he was said to have suffered an overreach, it was

*Altior: bidding to stretch his winning run over jumps to 18*

disappointing he couldn't see off the near 12-year-old Simply Ned in a Leopardstown Grade 1 over Christmas. It looks like last year's Arkle form was overrated (it's far from the only race at the festival that hasn't worked out) as the second and third have given up the ghost and gone back over hurdles and Saint Calvados beat only second-season novices on his return and has been well and truly found out in open company since. Footpad may well do better then the ground eases as he's 8-13 on soft ground or worse but only 2-9 when it's quicker, but it takes a leap of faith to think he can trouble Min, let alone Altior. Stays further and could be Ryanair-bound anyway.

*Going preference* Softer the better
*Star rating* ✪

## SCEAU ROYAL

**7 b g; Trainer** Alan King
**Chase form** 1211114, best RPR 166
**Left-handed** 12111, best RPR 164
**Right-handed** 14, best RPR 166
**Cheltenham form** (all) 101621, best RPR 164
**At the festival** 18 Mar 2016 In touch, effort to chase leading bunch after 2 out, no impression, weakened before last, finished 12th, beaten 25 lengths by Ivanovich Gorbatov in Triumph Hurdle
14 Mar 2017 Held up, headway after 3 out, chasing leaders after 2 out, ridden before last, soon weakened, finished sixth, beaten 13 and a half lengths by Buveur D'Air in Champion Hurdle

Two places and three lengths behind ownermate Footpad when sixth in the 2017 Champion Hurdle and would have been one of his bigger dangers for last year's Arkle had he not missed out through injury. Returned to action in fine fettle when winning the Shloer Chase at Cheltenham in November, finishing just over two lengths in front of the veteran Simply Ned, albeit in receipt of 3lb. May not have wanted the ground so sticky or could have bounced when 24-length last of four to Altior in the Tingle Creek three weeks later, but that couldn't have been his form considering how impressive he had looked when winning a Grade 1 on the track as a novice. Ran okay when second in the Kingwell Hurdle in February, and better can be expected, although he has disappointed

on his two previous runs at the festival. That said, his other form figures at the track read 1121 and he should do a lot better than his previous festival finishing figures given there will be only a handful of runners.

*Going preference* Handles soft but better ground suits
*Star rating* ✪✪

## FOX NORTON

**9 b g; Trainer** Colin Tizzard
**Chase form** 1123333111221112P23, best RPR 174
**Left-handed** 233331112211, best RPR 174
**Right-handed** 1112P23, best RPR 169
**Cheltenham form** 2311121, best RPR 172
**At the festival** 15 Mar 2016 Tracked leaders, pushed along and lost place after 3 out, outpaced after, slightly hampered 2 out, kept on to take 3rd final 75yds, no chance, finished third, beaten ten and three-quarter lengths by Douvan in Racing Post Arkle Chase
15 Mar 2017 Tracked leaders, slightly outpaced after 3 out, headway between last 2, strong run from last to press winner close home, just held, finished second, beaten a head by Special Tiara in Champion Chase

High-quality performer with an excellent record at Cheltenham who has the back form to be in the fight for the places. Was second in a substandard Champion Chase in 2017, but missed just over a year after being pulled up in the King George later that year and didn't reappear until the Clarence House Chase in January. His seven-length second to Altior was a perfectly respectable effort but it highlighted the gulf in class between them and he's another who could easily head to the Ryanair as he's a Grade 1 winner over 2m4f. Will have to do better than his distant third to Cyrname in the Ascot Chase, though.

*Going preference* Handles good and soft
*Star rating* ✪✪

## SIMPLY NED

**12 ch g; Trainer** Nicky Richards
**Chase form** F1221321235614253P223972412421, best RPR 164
**Left-handed** 122132123561423P2239724124 21, best RPR 164
**Right-handed** F5, best RPR 158
**Cheltenham form** 2542942, best RPR 164
**At the festival** 11 Mar 2015 Held up, mistake

## CHAMPION CHASE RESULTS AND TRENDS

| | FORM WINNER | AGE & WGT | Adj RPR | SP | TRAINER | BEST RPR LAST 12 MONTHS (RUNS SINCE) |
|---|---|---|---|---|---|---|
| 18 | 111-1 **Altior** CD | 8 11-10 | 181ᵀ | Evensf | N Henderson | won Gd 1 Celebration Chase (1m7½f) **(1)** |
| 17 | -6315 **Special Tiara** D | 10 11-10 | 174⁻⁸ | 11-1 | H de Bromhead (IRE) | 3rd Gd 1 Champion Chase (2m) **(4)** |
| 16 | P2-11 **Sprinter Sacre** CD | 10 11-10 | 177⁻¹ | 5-1 | N Henderson | won Kempton Gd2 ch (2m) **(0)** |
| 15 | 5-311 **Dodging Bullets** CD | 7 11-10 | 178⁻⁶ | 9-2 | P Nicholls | won Gd1 Clarence House Ch (2m1f) **(0)** |
| 14 | 12111 **Sire De Grugy** D | 8 11-10 | 178ᵀ | 11-4f | G Moore | won Gd1 Clarence House Ch (2m1f) **(0)** |
| 13 | 11-11 **Sprinter Sacre** CD | 7 11-10 | 182ᵀ | 1-4f | N Henderson | won Gd1 Victor Chandler Ch (2m1f) **(0)** |
| 12 | 21-12 **Finian's Rainbow** D, BF | 9 11-10 | 171⁻⁹ | 4-1 | N Henderson | 2nd Gd1 Victor Chandler Ch (2m1f) **(0)** |
| 11 | 3-223 **Sizing Europe** CD | 9 11-10 | 170⁻⁹ | 10-1 | H de Bromhead (IRE) | 3rd Punchestown Gd2 ch (2m) **(0)** |
| 10 | -2141 **Big Zeb** D | 9 11-10 | 171⁻¹⁹ | 10-1 | C Murphy (IRE) | won Navan Gd2 ch (2m) **(2)** |
| 09 | 12-11 **Master Minded** CD | 6 11-10 | 191ᵀ | 4-11f | P Nicholls | won Gd1 Champion Chase (2m) **(3)** |

**WINS-RUNS:** 6yo 1-5, 7yo 2-18, 8yo 2-26, 9yo 3-22, 10yo 2-14, 11yo 0-7, 12yo 0-2, 13yo 0-1 **FAVOURITES:** -£1.64

**TRAINERS IN THIS RACE (w-pl-r):** Nicky Henderson 4-1-10, Paul Nicholls 2-0-13, Henry de Bromhead 2-4-11, Tom George 0-3-6, Alan King 0-0-1, Willie Mullins 0-2-9, Colin Tizzard 0-1-2, Nicky Richards 0-0-2

**FATE OF FAVOURITES:** 140211P201 **POSITION OF WINNER IN MARKET:** 1452113241

4 out, soon ridden, stayed on from 2 out but never finding pace to get involved, finished fifth, beaten 17 lengths in Champion Chase won by Dodging Bullets

15 Mar 2017 In touch, took closer order 4 out, ridden after 3 out, soon weakened, finished ninth, beaten 41 and three-quarter lengths in Champion Chase won by Special Tiara

Admirable veteran who has been superbly campaigned by Nicky Richards and has taken a real shine to Leopardstown at Christmas, where his form figures read 32311. In the last two runnings of the Grade 1 over 2m1f at that meeting he has lowered the colours of Min and Footpad and if this race was at Leopardstown you'd give him half a chance of reaching the frame at the age of 12. It isn't, however, and Simply Ned, who missed another Leopardstown engagement on veterinary advice in February, does not have such a strong record here. He is said to be a near certain runner, though, and you can't say that about many.

*Going preference* Has won on ground ranging from good to firm to soft
*Star rating* ✪

### VERDICT

*This race revolves around the one and only **ALTIOR**. The Cheltenham crowd will be stunned into silence if he doesn't make it 18 out of 18. Should **Min** run, it will be almost as much of a surprise if he doesn't finish second.*

### Key trends

🏇 Won over at least 2m1f, 10/10

🏇 At least seven runs over fences, 10/10

🏇 Adjusted RPR of at least 170, 10/10

🏇 No more than 9lb off RPR top-rated, 9/10

🏇 Grade 1 chase winner, 9/10

🏇 No older than nine, 8/10

🏇 Won Graded chase last time out, 7/10

### Other factors

🏇 Five winners had previously won at the festival

🏇 In the past ten years 33 French-breds have run, yielding four wins, four seconds and four thirds

NOTES

## 4.10 Glenfarclas Cross Country Chase

**ITV/RTV**

🐎 3m6f   🐎 £65,000

This unusual event is in its fourth year as a conditions race, having previously been a handicap, and that may have been a factor in bringing Gordon Elliott to the fore as the trainer to watch. In the three runnings as a conditions race, he had the runner-up in 2016, a one-two in 2017 and the winner again last year.

Ireland has won 12 of the 14 runnings, helped largely by the success in the early years of Enda Bolger, who is widely regarded as the cross-country master. He trained four of the first five winners and after a lengthy gap was on the mark again in 2016 when it changed to a conditions race. Philip Hobbs is the only trainer to have won for Britain, with Balthazar King in 2012 and 2014.

It has generally paid to back horses at the head of the market, with nine of the 13 winners returned at 11-2 or shorter, although Josies Orders in 2016 is the only successful favourite since 2007. The biggest-priced winner was A New Story at 25-1 in 2010.

■ **ONE TO WATCH** Grand National winner **Tiger Roll**, who has won at three of the last five festivals, including this race last season, has been campaigned with a repeat bid in mind. He would be the third horse to win the race for a second time.

## CROSS COUNTRY RESULTS AND TRENDS

| FORM | WINNER | AGE & WGT | OR | SP | TRAINER | BEST RPR LAST 12 MONTHS (RUNS SINCE) |
|---|---|---|---|---|---|---|
| 18 P-2P5 | Tiger Roll C | 8 11-4 | 150-8 | 7-1 | G Elliott (IRE) | won Cheltenham Gd2 NH Chase (4m) (4) |
| 17 -5P05 | Cause Of Causes C | 9 11-4 | 166-3 | 4-1 | G Elliott (IRE) | won Kim Muir Hcap Chase (3m2f) (5) |
| 16 18119 | Josies Orders CD | 8 11-4 | 148-7 | 15-8f | E Bolger (IRE) | won Cheltenham cross-country ch (3m6f) (1) |
| 15 4172F | Rivage D'Or | 10 10-10 | 134-4 | 16-1 | T Martin (IRE) | 2nd Kilbeggan hcp ch (3m1f) (2) |
| 14 P-111 | Balthazar King CD | 10 11-12 | 150-5 | 4-1 | P Hobbs | won Cheltenham cl 2 hcap ch (3m½f) (1) |
| 13 -F742 | Big Shu | 8 10-5 | 136-10 | 14-1 | P Maher (IRE) | 2nd Punchestown cross-country ch (3m) (0) |
| 12 15P00 | Balthazar King C | 8 10-9 | 139-3 | 11-2 | P Hobbs | won Cheltenham cl 2 hcap ch (3m½f) (4) |
| 11 4-138 | Sizing Australia | 9 10-9 | 140-7 | 13-2 | H de Bromhead (IRE) | 3rd Cheltenham cross-country ch (3m7f) (0) |
| 10 70454 | A New Story (4oh) | 12 9-7 | 135-3 | 25-1 | M Hourigan (IRE) | 3rd Cork National hcap ch (3m4f) (4) |
| 09 1-421 | Garde Champetre CD | 10 11-12 | 150-4 | 7-2 | E Bolger (IRE) | won Cheltenham cross-country ch (3m7f) (0) |

**WINS-RUNS:** 6yo 0-5, 7yo 0-10, 8yo 4-20, 9yo 2-29, 10yo 3-30, 11yo 0-25, 12yo 1-23, 13yo 0-12, 14yo 0-3, 15yo 0-2

**FAVOURITES:** -£7.13 **FATE OF FAVOURITES:** 254P030133 **POSITION OF WINNER IN MARKET:** 2933727123

### Key trends

🐎 Won over at least 3m, 10/10

🐎 Trained in Ireland, 8/10

🐎 At least 13 chase runs, 7/10

🐎 Top-five finish in last completed start, 7/10

🐎 Won or placed in a cross-country race at Cheltenham or Punchestown, 6/10 (one exception carried out when set to place)

### Other factors

🐎 The inaugural running was in 2005 and JP McManus and Enda Bolger teamed up for four of the first five winners. They also had 2016 winner Josies Orders following his promotion on the disqualification of Any Currency

🐎 Two winners since 2008 had landed the PP Hogan at Punchestown in February, while 2013 winner Big Shu was runner-up in that event

🐎 Only ten British-trained runners have made the first four, although in 2014 the home team had first, second and fourth

🐎 Ireland has had the first four on three occasions and in 2009 had the first nine

## 4.50 Boodles Juvenile Handicap Hurdle RTV
### 2m½f   Grade 3   £80,000

A fiercely competitive and often wide-open handicap hurdle that has gone to a 33-1 shot in the past two years.

The big stables are always worth noting. Paul Nicholls has been responsible for three winners, as well as several placed horses, and Nicky Henderson, David Pipe and Gordon Elliott have had a winner apiece.

Nicholls' three winners were French-breds, who have done extremely well in this juvenile contest with six wins in 14 runnings (a French-bred has finished first or second in the last seven renewals, with Henderson's Style De Garde chasing home Veneer Of Charm last year).

Nine of the 14 winners had won on one of their last two starts and four of the last five winners carried 11st or 11st 1lb to victory. Crack Away Jack (11st 10lb in 2008) is the only winner to carry more than 11st 4lb.

It is important to look for runners rated in a certain bracket – 13 of the 14 winners were rated between 124 and 134.

Claiming jockeys can be significant, with three of the 14 winners having been partnered by conditional or amateur riders, most recently Henderson's Une Artiste in 2012 by then 5lb claimer Jeremiah McGrath.

■ **ONES TO WATCH** Joseph O'Brien has a strong juvenile team and **Band Of Outlaws**, **Gardens Of Babylon** and **Fine Brunello** are possibles here. Nicky Henderson has a likely sort in **Style De Vole** and Jessica Harrington could have a decent shot with **Got Trumped**.

## BOODLES JUVENILE HANDICAP HURDLE RESULTS AND TRENDS

| | FORM | WINNER | AGE & WGT | OR | SP | TRAINER | BEST RPR LAST 12 MONTHS (RUNS SINCE) |
|---|---|---|---|---|---|---|---|
| 18 | 127 | Veneer Of Charm D | 4 11-0 | 129-14 | 33-1 | G Elliott (IRE) | 2nd Fairyhouse hdl (2mf) (1) |
| 17 | 2P614 | Flying Tiger D | 4 11-5 | 134-2 | 33-1 | N Williams | won Newbury class 4 hdl (2m½f) (1) |
| 16 | 322 | Diego Du Charmil BF | 4 11-1 | 133-17 | 13-2 | P Nicholls | 2nd Enghien hdl (2m½f) (0) |
| 15 | 3-421 | Qualando | 4 11-0 | 131-9 | 25-1 | P Nicholls | 4th Auteuil Listed hdl (2m1½f) (2) |
| 14 | 1216 | Hawk High D | 4 11-1 | 130-12 | 33-1 | T Easterby | won Warwick class 4 hdl (2m) (1) |
| 13 | 125 | Flaxen Flare D | 4 10-8 | 127-5 | 25-1 | G Elliott (IRE) | 5th Leopardstown Gd1 nov hdl (2m) (0) |
| 12 | 11114 | Une Artiste D | 4 10-8 | 127-6 | 40-1 | N Henderson | won Haydock class 2 hdl (2m) (1) |
| 11 | 757 | What A Charm | 4 10-6 | 115-3 | 9-1 | A Moore (IRE) | 7th Fairyhouse Gd2 nov hdl (2m) (0) |
| 10 | 531 | Sanctuaire D | 4 11-2 | 127-9 | 4-1f | P Nicholls | 3rd Auteuil hdl (2m2f) (1) |
| 09 | 52111 | Silk Affair (5x) | 4 10-4 | 125-12 | 11-1 | M Quinlan | won Sandown cl 3 nov hcap hdl (2m4f) (1) |

**FAVOURITES:** -£5.00 **FATE OF FAVOURITES:** 4143000023 **POSITION OF WINNER IN MARKET:** 4150000200

### Key trends
- Officially rated 125 to 134, 9/10
- Top-three finish in at least one of last two starts, 9/10
- Had lost maiden tag over hurdles, 8/10
- Won within last three starts, 8/10
- Sired by a Group 1 Flat winner, 6/10

### Other factors
- Four of the five winners who had run on the Flat had earned an RPR of at least 87; the other five were unraced on the Flat
- Four winners were French-bred
- Five winners were beaten on their first two starts over hurdles

## 5.30 Weatherbys Champion Bumper RTV
### 2m½f — Grade 1 — £75,000

The picture for this race never becomes clear until entries are confirmed in festival week and it can remain hazy even on raceday, with last year's winner Relegate sent off at 25-1 despite coming from the Willie Mullins stable. Ireland's champion trainer first made his name in this race and now has nine wins in 26 runnings, although he pops up with the winner less frequently than in his early days. His two main hopes judging by the ante-post betting are Blue Sari and Mt Leinster but there is still time for others to emerge and the pack reshuffled. Gordon Elliott won this race for the first time with Fayonagh two years ago and has a strong hand this time with leading fancies Envoi Allen, Malone Road and Andy Dufresne. Joseph O'Brien, who has assembled a powerful team of young horses for this year's festival, has several possibles in Sempo, Front View and Meticulous. British trainers hold their own in this race now and the home team may include Ask For Glory (Paul Nicholls), King Roland (Harry Fry) and Glory And Fortune (Tom Lacey).

### ENVOI ALLEN
**5 b g; Trainer** Gordon Elliott
**Bumper form** 111, best RPR 135
**Left-handed** 11, best RPR 135
**Right-handed** 1, best RPR 119

Point winner who has started odds-on for all three bumper starts and won the lot. Scored by a comfortable four lengths on Fairyhouse debut in December and, while none of his beaten rivals has won since, he went on to dish out a similarly easy beating to five previous winners in a Listed event at Navan two weeks later. Completed his preparation with Grade 2 victory at the Dublin Racing Festival when always travelling and finding plenty and holding off Meticulous (received 3lb) by a length and a quarter. A peak RPR of 135 puts him near the top of the tree heading into the race.

*Going preference* Has raced only on good/yielding in bumpers but point win came on easier ground
*Star rating* ✪✪✪✪

### MALONE ROAD
**5 b g; Trainer** Gordon Elliott
**Bumper form** (right-handed) 11, best RPR 135

Another point winner with a big reputation and was a 2-5 chance when making easy winning debut at Down Royal in November (runner-up won a bumper and maiden hurdle since). Looked really good when thrashing Mt Leinster at Punchestown a couple of weeks later but has since been said to have a minor injury (knee) and is not certain to make the line-up.

*Going preference* Has raced only on good/yielding in bumpers but point win came on easier ground
*Star rating* ✪✪

### ANDY DUFRESNE
**5 b g; Trainer** Gordon Elliott
**Bumper form** (right-handed) 1, best RPR 129

A third potential star for Gordon Elliott, this one won a point last March and was subsequently knocked down to JP McManus for £330,000. He made his bumper debut at the end of January at Down Royal, where he was backed down to 8-15 favourite and duly romped home by ten lengths from Golden Spread, who had been third in a bumper in the summer, showing reasonable form. Time was pretty dreadful given the ground conditions, though, so hard to weigh up.

*Going preference* Too early to say
*Star rating* ✪✪

### BLUE SARI
**4 b g; Trainer** Willie Mullins
**Bumper form** (right-handed) 1, best RPR 125

The shortest-priced of what will probably be

a strong contingent for Willie Mullins, who will be bidding for an amazing tenth victory in the race. This four-year-old wasn't favourite on his debut at Gowran in January but made short work of the one who was (Front View) and strode clear by 11 lengths. The form has barely been tested but Front View went off favourite next time at Naas and was moving well entering the straight when brought down. Only three four-year-olds have won this race and none was trained by Mullins.

*Going preference* Win came on soft
*Star rating* ✪✪

## BLACKBOW

**6 b g; Trainer** Willie Mullins
**Bumper form** 1152, best RPR 142
**Left-handed** 115, best RPR 142
**Right-handed** 2, best RPR 142
**Cheltenham form** 5, best RPR 137
**At the festival** 14 Mar 2018 Raced keenly, held up in midfield, headway 2f out, ridden and chased leaders over 1f out, kept on same pace final 100yds, finished fifth, beaten five and three-quarter lengths by Relegate in Champion Bumper.

Fifth when the shortest-priced of Willie Mulllins' five Champion Bumper runners last season and then finished second in the Grade 1 at Punchestown. Has not been seen since but does have entries in all three novice hurdles at the festival, so it seems trainer has not given up hope of getting a run into him over obstacles.

*Going preference* Seems to handle all ground
*Star rating* ✪✪

*Andy Dufresne: Down Royal winner is hard to weigh up*

## SEMPO

**5 b g; Trainer** Joseph O'Brien
**Bumper form** 431, best RPR 125
**Left-handed** 43, best RPR 108
**Right-handed** 1, best RPR 125

Regarded as an "exciting horse to go novice hurdling with next season" by Joseph O'Brien but threw his hat into the ring with a much-improved display to win third bumper start by 15 lengths in the first week of February at Thurles. Will almost certainly need to improve again.

*Going preference* Much the best effort on good last time out
*Star rating* ✪✪

## ASK FOR GLORY

**5 b g; Trainer** Paul Nicholls
**Bumper form** (left-handed) 1, best RPR 128

By Irish Derby and Ascot Gold Cup winner Fame And Glory and knocked down to Paul Nicholls for £280,000 after winning his point by ten lengths. Made mincemeat of his rivals when odds-on for his bumper debut at Chepstow over Christmas (form untested apart from well-beaten seventh who was thrashed again) and, like a lot of these, could be anything. That win came on soft ground but trainer's assistant Harry Derham says he's "not a plodder by any means" and may prefer it better. Seen as a long-term chasing project, so not certain to go.

*Going preference* Form is on soft
*Star rating* ✪✪

## FRONT VIEW

**4 gr g; Trainer** Joseph O'Brien
**Bumper form** 2B, best RPR 110
**Left-handed** B
**Right-handed** 2, best RPR 110

Was favourite but proved no match for Blue Sari at Gowran in January, going down by 11 lengths. Appeared to be moving sweetly entering the straight when brought down at Naas (favourite again) in February.

*Going preference* Unknown
*Star rating* ✪

## BARNES DES MOTTES

**4 bb g; Trainer** Elizabeth Doyle
**Bumper form** (left-handed) 1, best RPR 106

With a trainer who often has a decent bumper performer. This one landed the eventful Naas bumper in which Front View was brought down and did so in the style of a strong stayer, pulling clear to win by four lengths. A Racing Post Rating of just 106 gives you an idea of the level, though, and he's going to have to improve a great deal to be competitive.

*Going preference* Win was on good
*Star rating* ✪

## GLORY AND FORTUNE

**4 b g; Trainer** Tom Lacey
**Bumper form** (left-handed) 1, best RPR 116
**Cheltenham form** 1, best RPR 116

Another son of Fame And Glory and has experience of Cheltenham, having won a Listed junior bumper on New Year's Day by four and a half lengths from a couple of previous winners. That was an excellent start and he is highly regarded, but trainer (who has a good record in bumpers) is keen not to overrace him as he's a huge horse who needs to grow into his frame.

*Going preference* Win was on good to soft
*Star rating* ✪

## METICULOUS

**5 b g; Trainer** Joseph O'Brien
**Bumper form** (left-handed) 142, best RPR 131

Bigger price than a few with sexier profiles as he has been beaten on two of his three bumper starts, but on the last of them he went down by only a length and a quarter to Envoi Allen, so he has much better form in the book than most. He's another son of Fame And Glory, so you'd imagine he's going to stay very well in a strongly run race and he is out of Refinement, who made the first four at four Cheltenham Festvials, including the bumper twice.

*Going preference* Has raced only on good/yielding
*Star rating* ✪✪✪✪

## KING ROLAND

**5 br g; Trainer** Harry Fry
**Bumper form** (left-handed) 1, best RPR 128

Ten-length point winner who won by more than twice as far on his bumper debut for Harry Fry at Uttoxeter in December in a first-time hood. Did it all on the bridle there and is obviously pretty useful, but the ground was heavy and it doesn't look like he has beaten much.

*Going preference* Won on heavy
*Star rating* ✪✪

## MT LEINSTER

**5 b g; Trainer** Willie Mullins
**Bumper form** 1235, best RPR 128
**Left-handed** 35, best RPR 125
**Right-handed** 12, best RPR 128

Has gained plenty of experience with four starts so far and wasn't disgraced when fifth to Envoi Allen at Leopardstown on the latest of them in February. On RPRs, though, he hasn't quite matched the form of his 22-length debut success at Ballinrobe in September. That was the only time he has faced deep ground, so it's not impossible that he will be a force if we get a soft-ground festival.

*Going preference* Probably wants it soft
*Star rating* ✪✪

## SANTA ROSSA

**5 b m; Trainer** Dermot McLoughlin
**Bumper form** 11, best RPR 116
**Left-handed** 1, best RPR 113
**Right-handed** 1, best RPR 116

Mare who won the Grade 2 Leopardstown bumper in February taken by last year's

## CHAMPION BUMPER RESULTS AND TRENDS

| | FORM | WINNER | AGE & WGT | Adj RPR | SP | TRAINER | BEST RPR LAST 12 MONTHS (RUNS SINCE) |
|---|---|---|---|---|---|---|---|
| 18 | 11 | Relegate D | 5 10-12 | 126$^{-25}$ | 25-1 | W Mullins (IRE) | won Leopardstown Gd2 bumper (2m) (0) |
| 17 | 811 | Fayonagh D | 6 10-12 | 140$^T$ | 7-1 | G Elliott (IRE) | won Fairyhouse Listed bumper (2m) (0) |
| 16 | 1121 | Ballyandy CD | 5 11-5 | 146$^T$ | 5-1 | N Twiston-Davies | won Newbury Listed bumper (2m½f) (0) |
| 15 | -11 | Moon Racer CD | 6 11-5 | 140$^{-7}$ | 9-2f | D Pipe | won Cheltenham bumper (2m½f) (0) |
| 14 | 3/2-1 | Silver Concorde D | 6 11-5 | 132$^{-15}$ | 16-1 | D Weld (IRE) | won Leopardstown bumper (2m) (0) |
| 13 | 1 | Briar Hill D | 5 11-5 | 117$^{-27}$ | 25-1 | W Mullins (IRE) | won Thurles bumper (2m) (0) |
| 12 | 21 | Champagne Fever D | 5 11-5 | 144$^{-1}$ | 16-1 | W Mullins (IRE) | won Fairyhouse bumper (2m) (0) |
| 11 | 21 | Cheltenian D | 5 11-5 | 126$^{-13}$ | 14-1 | P Hobbs | won Kempton class 5 mdn bumper (2m) (0) |
| 10 | 1 | Cue Card | 4 10-12 | 126$^{-15}$ | 40-1 | C Tizzard | won Fontwell class 6 bumper (1m6f) (0) |
| 09 | 2-11 | Dunguib D | 6 11-5 | 147$^T$ | 9-2 | P Fenton (IRE) | won Navan Gd2 bumper (2m) (0) |

**WINS-RUNS:** 4yo 1-28, 5yo 5-146, 6yo 4-54 **FAVOURITES:** -£4.50

**TRAINERS IN THIS RACE (w-pl-r):** Willie Mullins 3-6-41, Gordon Elliott 1-0-4, Philip Hobbs 1-1-8, Nigel Twiston-Davies 1-0-7, Anthony Honeyball 0-1-3 **FATE OF FAVOURITES:** 3062221704 **POSITION OF WINNER IN MARKET:** 2060061230

winner Relegate. Did it well enough by just over three lengths but will have to step up a good deal on that.

*Going preference* Has raced only on good/yielding

*Star rating* ✪✪

## VERDICT

*This is the ultimate guessers' race as there will be so few crossing form lines and, as always, it's a feat just to name the winner on these pages. Looking back, last year's book managed to name six of the first seven home but not the winner, who was trained by Willie Mullins! Still, Relegate was only fourth in the betting from the Mullins quintet at 25-1, so it seems she wasn't fancied by many anyway. This race has been won by a stack of outsiders and, as exciting as a couple of horses have looked in their limited racecourse appearances to date, I can't be considering a bet at single-figure odds. The one I may throw a few quid at on the day is Joseph O'Brien's **METICULOUS**, who has at least got some valuable experience, ran the favourite close enough last time and shapes as though he will stay well given a proper test of stamina.*

### Key trends

🏇 Won last time out, 10/10

🏇 Aged five or six, 9/10

🏇 Adjusted RPR of at least 126, 9/10

🏇 Off the track for at least 32 days, 9/10 (three not seen since Christmas or earlier)

🏇 Won a bumper with at least 13 runners, 7/10

🏇 Won a bumper worth at least £4,000 or €4,000 to the winner, 7/10

### Other factors

🏇 Ireland has won six of the last ten and 19 of the 26 runnings

🏇 Willie Mullins has the best record with nine victories (three in the last ten years) but is often mob-handed. On four of the occasions he has won, he saddled just one runner; on the other five, the winner was not his most fancied in the market

🏇 Five of the last ten winners were bred in Ireland

NOTES

PAUL KEALY
ON THE KEY
CONTENDERS

## 1.30 JLT Novices' Chase

🏇 2m4f  🏇 Grade 1  🏇 £150,000

**ITV/RTV**

As usual the final make-up of the field will depend on running plans for the Arkle and RSA, although this race over the intermediate distance is a legitimate target in its own right following its promotion to Grade 1 status in 2014 and is no longer an easier touch. Ireland has won seven of the eight runnings but Britain has two tailor-made candidates in Defi Du Seuil – the 2017 Triumph Hurdle winner for Philip Hobbs – and Colin Tizzard's Lostintranslation, who have locked horns twice already this season with the score standing at one-all. A weight swing on the second occasion may have tipped the scales for Defi Du Seuil but they are closely matched. Leading novices such as La Bague Au Roi, Topofthegame, Le Richebourg and Delta Work look set to head elsewhere, which opens the door here for lesser lights such as Winter Escape, Hardline and Real Steel.

### DEFI DU SEUIL
**6 b g; Trainer** Philip Hobbs
**Chase form** 5121, best RPR 156
**Left-handed** 52, best RPR 156
**Right-handed** 11, best RPR 156
**Cheltenham form** (all) 111152, best RPR 156
**At the festival** 17 Mar 2017 Held up, headway before 3 out, tracked leaders going well before 2 out, led on long run to last, ran on strongly to go clear run-in, won Triumph Hurdle by five lengths from Mega Fortune

Unbeaten as a juvenile hurdler in Britain two seasons ago when he powered home by five lengths in the Triumph Hurdle and followed up in the Aintree version. Second season over hurdles was a write-off as he ran only twice and beat just two horses, and his return over fences in November this term wasn't that promising either, as he was 25 lengths last of five to Lalor. A step up in trip has done the trick, though, as he beat Topofthegame at Exeter over 2m3f on his next start (although runner-up lost 20 lengths at the start) and has subsequently had two good battles with Lostintranslation. He lost the first of them, going down by a length and a quarter when conceding 3lb in the Dipper at Cheltenham, but then gained revenge off levels in the Grade 1 Scilly Isles at Sandown, emerging victorious by just under a length. There is obviously not much between the two, but Defi Du Seuil also looked all over the winner at Cheltenham and may have hit the front too soon. Barry Geraghty waited until after the last at Sandown, and that might be the

key to him at the trip. Won all four hurdles starts at Cheltenham, so plenty going for him.

*Going preference* Seems to go on any
*Star rating* ✪✪✪✪✪

### LOSTINTRANSLATION
**7 b g; Trainer** Colin Tizzard
**Chase form** 2312, best RPR 155
**Left-handed** 231, best RPR 155
**Right-handed** 2, best RPR 155
**Cheltenham form** (all) 71, best RPR 155
**At the festival** 13 Mar 2018 Looked well, held up towards rear, headway approaching 3 out, ridden after 2 out, stayed on but not pace to get on terms, finished seventh, beaten eight and a quarter lengths by Summerville Boy in Supreme Novices' Hurdle

Was rated only 134 when seventh as a 40-1 chance in last season's Supreme Novices' Hurdle, so did as well as could have been expected, especially since he has always had the size and scope to be a chaser. Has done well over fences, despite winning only one of four starts. Jumped really well when a length-and-a-half second to the still unbeaten subsequent dual Grade 1 winner La Bague Au Roi on his debut at Newbury in November and probably wouldn't have been beaten much further but for a terrible blunder three out (broke the fence) when third to her back there next time. Got off the mark in Grade 2 Dipper Chase at Cheltenham next time when battling back past Defi Du Seuil, who had swept by him two out, to win by just over a length. Runner-up had challenge delayed and reversed the form in the Grade 1 Scilly Isles next time at Sandown, but they are obviously closely matched.

*Going preference* Goes on any
*Star rating* ✪✪✪✪

## WINTER ESCAPE

**8 b g; Trainer** Aidan Howard
**Chase form** 31115, best RPR 157
**Left-handed** 5, best RPR 145
**Right-handed** 32111, best RPR 157
**Cheltenham form** (hurdles) 05, best RPR 142
**At the festival** 17 Mar 2017 Mid-division, headway turning in, soon ridden, challenged for 2nd at the last, kept on same pace, finished fifth, beaten two and three-quarter lengths by Arctic Fire in County Handicap Hurdle

Was always fairly highly regarded when with Alan King but arguably failed to deliver on his promise. Did run fifth in the County Hurdle a couple of seasons ago, but left King after dreadful chase debut at Kempton in November last season, when he was tailed off and beaten 54 lengths. New lease of life with Aidan Howard this term, though,

winning three in a row over fences, the last two in Grade 3s. In the last of those he gave chunks of weight to short-priced favourite A Plus Tard at Punchestown and earned a Racing Post Rating of 157, which puts him right up with the best of the likely runners here. Unfortunately he was well below that form when only fifth of six to La Bague Au Roi at Leopardstown in February, after which it was reported he broke blood vessels. Remains to be seen what effect that has on him and whether he is sent over given his owner has the favourite in Defi Du Seuil, but he did seem to be getting his act together and he has every right to be a player if back on song.

*Going preference* Handles most ground
*Star rating* ✪✪

## HARDLINE

**7 b g; Trainer** Gordon Elliott
**Chase form** 12113, best RPR 152
**Left-handed** 13, best RPR 152
**Right-handed** 121, best RPR 152

Spent nearly all of hurdles career over 2m and

*Lostintranslation (right) and Defi Du Seuil: closely matched after two clashes this season*

was a Grade 2 winner in that sphere but has developed into a better chaser and certainly saw out 2m3½f well when beating Getabird by half a length in Limerick Grade 1 over Christmas. Not disgraced when third to La Bague Au Roi in Leopardstown Grade 1 over 2m5f in February and certainly entitled to make the trip to Cheltenham on the back of that. Where he goes is anyone's guess as he is in four races, including the four-miler, but this would appeal as the best fit and it may be the weakest of the four in terms of quality.

*Going preference* Goes on any
*Star rating* ✪✪

## CAMELIA DE COTTE
**7 b m; Trainer** Willie Mullins
**Chase form** 114111, best RPR 143
**Left-handed** 14, best RPR 134
**Right-handed** 1111, best RPR 143

Rich Ricci-owned mare who has been mopping up against her own sex over fences since August, winning five times. On the only occasion she ventured out of mares' company she was beaten 11 lengths into fourth by Le Richebourg in Tipperary Grade 3, but that was no disgrace and she has improved again since. Was rated only 123 over hurdles last season, but feature of her chase performances has been her slick jumping and, while her best form has come on right-handed tracks, if anything she has a tendency to go out to her left. Has the Arkle as a possible target as well but most of her form is at around 2m4f.

*Going preference* Has won on good and heavy
*Star rating* ✪✪✪

## MR WHIPPED
**6 br g; Trainer** Nicky Henderson
**Chase form** (left-handed) 31, best RPR 152
**Cheltenham form** (all) P3, best RPR 143
**At the festival** 16 Mar 2018 Midfield, effort and headway on bend after 2 out, chased leaders, 8th and no impression when pulled up before last in Albert Bartlett Novices' Hurdle won by Kilbricken Storm

Promising as a novice over hurdles if a bit raw and his one-length Leamington Novices' Hurdle win from Paisley Park certainly looks a lot better now. Seemingly slightly outstayed by Red River when first tried over 3m last term and found the Albert Bartlett all too much. Made fair enough chase debut when a close third to Count Meribel at Cheltenham in November, although was hanging under pressure and awkward at the last, perhaps feeling the quickest ground he has raced on. Did better next time when winning four-runner novice on heavy ground at Haydock, winning with more in hand from Springtown Lake (conceded 5lb) than the length and three-quarters margin suggested. Has only just turned six, so there's still plenty of promise, but even this might be a year early and he's probably soft ground dependent.

*Going preference* Goes well on soft/heavy
*Star rating* ✪✪

## REAL STEEL
**6 b g; Trainer** Willie Mullins
**Chase form** F1, best RPR 147
**Left-handed** F, best RPR 143
**Right-handed** 1, best RPR 147
**Cheltenham form** (hurdles) 0, best RPR 102
**At the festival** 16 Mar 2018 Held up in rear, struggling and behind after 2 out, never a threat, finished 11th, beaten 50 and a half lengths by Kilbricken Storm in Albert Bartlett Novices' Hurdle

Another who found the Albert Bartlett far too tough at this early stage of his career and trailed home a long way behind. That was his only attempt at 3m and he won't be having another one any time soon as he is only in the Arkle and this race. Had just been headed but certainly wasn't beaten when coming down two out in race won by Paloma Blue over 2m1f at Leopardstown in December, and then largely jumped well to get off the mark over 2m5½f at Fairyhouse the following month, winning his beginners' chase by ten lengths. Untried in Graded company over fences but wouldn't have been beaten far in the Future Champions Novice Hurdle at Leopardstown last season had he not fallen at the last, so no reason to think he won't be up to the grade. Both wins have come on right-handed tracks, but that Leopardstown run over hurdles was as good as anything he has done that way round.

*Going preference* Seems versatile enough
*Star rating* ✪✪

## KILDISART

**7 b g; Trainer** Ben Pauling
**Chase form** 211, best RPR 154
**Left-handed** 1, best RPR 154
**Right-handed** 21, best RPR 146
**Cheltenham form** 1, best RPR 154

Steadily progressive performer who won twice over hurdles last season, the second time in a handicap off a mark of 135 at Kempton. Started chase career well with half-length second to Wenyerreadyfreddie at Ascot in November and then went back there to defeat the more experienced Activial by a short-head (in receipt of 11lb). He then went into handicap company in the novice chase on trials day at Cheltenham and, despite being surprisingly uneasy in the market, he stayed on strongly up the hill to defeat Highway One O One by two lengths off a mark of 141. His trainer was of the opinion he wouldn't go up more than 4lb for that success, so the novice handicap on day one was mentioned, but the handicapper had other ideas and raised him 6lb, so his choice is now this race or the Plate. He did earn a Racing Post Rating of 154 for that, so might not be badly handicapped off 147, but it also puts him bang in the mix for this race, which is something his price doesn't quite suggest.

*Going preference* Twice a non-runner because of good ground and handles soft well

*Star rating* ✪✪✪

## PRAVALAGUNA

**7 b m; Trainer** Willie Mullins
**Chase form** 411, best RPR 144
**Left-handed** 41, best RPR 144
**Right-handed** 1, best RPR 136
**Cheltenham form** (hurdles) P
**At the festival** 13 Mar 2018 Held up in last pair, badly hampered 5th, pushed along 7th, weakened after 3 out, pulled up before last in OLBG Mares' Hurdle won by Benie Des Dieux

A 50-1 shot when pulled up in the Mares' Hurdle last season, she has taken well to fences in two starts this term, winning her last two in comfortable fashion. She may have been getting plenty of weight in the Opera Hat at Naas in February but she coasted clear of her rivals to win by 14 lengths. That was over 2m and she is in the Arkle, but the JLT is the race that looks like it might cut up the most and she does have winning form at 2m4f.

*Going preference* Handles anything
*Star rating* ✪✪

## OTHERS TO CONSIDER

There are plenty of horses fairly high up in the betting who haven't been mentioned in the detailed comments and could be major factors if they run, but they all have other far more obvious targets and there seems no point repeating their profiles in these pages. Hopefully the profiles here give a better idea of what the final field will look like as well but the big names had better get a mention as they are still entered. **Delta Work** and **Topofthegame** are in the first three in the betting for the RSA and **Le Richebourg** likewise for the Arkle. **La Bague Au Roi** probably isn't going anywhere given her past performances at Cheltenham, while **Champagne Classic** and **Vinndication** also look like three-milers now, the latter especially so.

## VERDICT

*At the time of writing the only two horses at the head of the betting who look certain to run are Defi Du Seuil and Lostintranslation. It's easy enough to argue both will end up even shorter than they are now and I would just prefer previous festival winner Defi Du Seuil of the pair as he is likely to be given more of a waiting ride than he got when beaten by his rival at Cheltenham in the Dipper. However, once you start to rule out all those near the front of the market who are likely to head elsewhere, you realise it is 20-1 bar two and there must be some each-way value in there. It might be with* **KILDISART**, *who is improving and won the novice handicap on the trials day card last time out. That race has produced plenty of festival winners over the past decade and, as he won in commanding enough fashion to be handicapped out of the novice on day one, this looks his most likely port of call. His peak RPR is only 2lb behind Defi Du Seuil and 1lb below Lostintranslation and I can't see why he is five times the price.*

## JLT NOVICES' CHASE RESULTS AND TRENDS

| | FORM WINNER | AGE & WGT | Adj RPR | SP | TRAINER | BEST RPR LAST 12 MONTHS (RUNS SINCE) |
|---|---|---|---|---|---|---|
| 18 | 11211 **Shattered Love** | 7 10-11 | 168-3 | 4-1 | G Elliott (IRE) | won Leopardstown Gd1 nov ch (3m) **(0)** |
| 17 | 1-411 **Yorkhill** C, D | 7 11-4 | 163-7 | 6-4f | W Mullins (IRE) | won Fairyhouse nov ch (2m) **(1)** |
| 16 | 7-11F **Black Hercules** D, BF | 7 11-4 | 169-2 | 4-1c | W Mullins (IRE) | won Warwick Listed nov ch (3m) **(1)** |
| 15 | -1121 **Vautour** C, D | 6 11-4 | 165-10 | 6-4f | W Mullins (IRE) | won Leopardstown Gd2 nov ch (2m3f) **(0)** |
| 14 | 11321 **Taquin Du Seuil** C, D | 7 11-4 | 167-6 | 7-1 | J O'Neill | won Haydock Gd2 nov ch (2m5f) **(0)** |
| 13 | 21241 **Benefficient** D | 7 11-4 | 161-12 | 20-1 | A Martin (IRE) | won Leop Gd1 Arkle nov ch (2m1f) **(0)** |
| 12 | 1-111 **Sir Des Champs** C, D | 6 11-4 | 161-8 | 3-1 | W Mullins (IRE) | won Limerick Gd2 nov ch (2m3½f) **(1)** |
| 11 | 4-122 **Noble Prince** D | 7 11-4 | 164-6 | 4-1 | P Nolan (IRE) | 2nd Leop Gd1 Arkle nov ch (2m1f) **(0)** |

**WINS-RUNS:** 5yo 0-5, 6yo 2-29, 7yo 6-31, 8yo 0-11, 9yo 0-4 **FAVOURITES:** -£1.34

**TRAINERS IN THIS RACE (w-pl-r):** Willie Mullins 4-1-14, Gordon Elliott 1-0-1, Paul Nolan 1-0-1, Alan King 0-1-1, Colin Tizzard 0-0-3, Dan Skelton 0-0-1, David Pipe 0-1-3, Harry Fry 0-0-1, Henry de Bromhead 0-1-3, Noel Meade 0-2-3, Nicky Henderson 0-3-10, Nigel Twiston-Davies 0-3-6, Paul Nicholls 0-0-9, Philip Hobbs 0-1-4, Nick Williams 0-1-1, Tom George 0-0-1

**FATE OF FAVOURITES:** 20241112 **POSITION OF WINNER IN MARKET:** 22741112

*Key trends*

🏇Ran over hurdles at a previous festival, eight winners in last eight runnings

🏇Adjusted RPR of at least 161, 8/8

🏇Distance winner, 7/8 (exception had won over further)

🏇Rated within 8lb of RPR top-rated, 6/8

🏇Won a Graded chase, 6/8

🏇Graded winner over hurdles, 6/8

*Other factors*

🏇Six winners won last time out – of the two exceptions, one was beaten a short head on their previous start and the other fell when likely to win

## 2.10 Pertemps Network Final (Handicap Hurdle)  ITV/RTV
### 3m · Grade 3 · £100,000

Cheltenham took steps to rectify a perceived lack of quality in this staying handicap hurdle by changing the conditions – as of 2016, horses were eligible to run in the final only if they finished in the first six in one of the qualifiers.

A rating of at least 135 has been needed to get into the race since 2013. Six-year-olds have the best recent record, having won four of the past six runnings (and Southfield Theatre went close in 2014 when beaten a nose).

Favourites have a poor record. Fingal Bay in 2014 is one of only two market leaders to have won in the past 21 runnings, although 9-2 favourite Glencoe went down by just a nose behind 6-1 second favourite Delta Work in last year's renewal.

This had long been dominated by the home contingent but that stranglehold was broken in 2016 by Pat Kelly's Mall Dini and it has been one-way traffic since then for the Irish courtesy of Presenting Percy (for the same connections) and Gordon Elliott's Delta Work. Remarkably, Davy Russell has been on board all three of those Irish winners.

■ **ONES TO WATCH** Gordon Elliott's **Sire Du Berlais** has run in the same qualifiers at Naas and Leopardstown contested by stablemate Glenloe before last year's second here. **Aaron Lad** won over course and distance in December and has been kept back by his shrewd trainer Richard Newland, who has another possible in **Abolitionist**.

## PERTEMPS FINAL RESULTS AND TRENDS

| | FORM WINNER | AGE & WGT | OR | SP | TRAINER | BEST RPR LAST 12 MONTHS (RUNS SINCE) |
|---|---|---|---|---|---|---|
| 18 | 33243 **Delta Work** | 5 10-10 | 139ᵀ | 6-1 | G Elliott (IRE) | 4th Leopardstown hcap hdl (3m) (1) |
| 17 | 11541 **Presenting Percy** | 6 11-11 | 146⁻⁴ | 11-1 | P Kelly (IRE) | won Fairyhouse hcap hdl (2m4f) (0) |
| 16 | 31433 **Mall Dini** | 6 10-11 | 139⁻⁷ | 14-1 | P Kelly (IRE) | won Thurles mdn hdl (2m6½f) (3) |
| 15 | 21-41 **Call The Cops** (5x) D | 6 10-12 | 138⁻⁵ | 9-1 | N Henderson | won Doncaster class 2 hcap hdl (3m½f) (0) |
| 14 | 120-1 **Fingal Bay** C, D | 8 11-12 | 148ᵀ | 9-2f | P Hobbs | won Exeter class 2 hcap hdl (2m7½f) (0) |
| 13 | -2222 **Holywell** | 6 11-4 | 140⁻⁵ | 25-1 | J O'Neill | 2nd Warwick class 2 hcap hdl (3m1f) (0) |
| 12 | 5P504 **Cape Tribulation** D | 8 10-11 | 142⁻³ | 14-1 | M Jefferson | 5th Haydock Gd3 hcap hdl (3m) (1) |
| 11 | 28700 **Buena Vista** CD | 10 10-3 | 138⁻⁴ | 20-1 | D Pipe | won Pertemps Final (3m) (6) |
| 10 | -8508 **Buena Vista** | 9 10-1 | 133⁻¹ | 16-1 | D Pipe | 5th Haydock Listed hcap hdl (3m1f) (2) |
| 09 | 26211 **Kayf Aramis** D | 7 10-5 | 129⁻⁷ | 16-1 | V Williams | won Warwick class 3 nov hdl (3m1f) (0) |

**WINS-RUNS:** 5yo 1-12, 6yo 4-59, 7yo 1-65, 8yo 2-49, 9yo 1-23, 10yo 1-15, 11yo 0-10, 12yo 0-1 **FAVOURITES:** -£4.50

**FATE OF FAVOURITES:** 0000010002 **POSITION OF WINNER IN MARKET:** 0596013652

### Key trends
- Winning form between 2m4f and 2m6f, 8/10
- Carried no more than 11st 4lb, 8/10
- Six to ten runs over hurdles, 8/10 (exceptions 22-plus)
- Aged six to eight, 7/10
- Officially rated 133 to 142, 7/10
- Off track between 19 and 48 days, 7/10
- Won a Class 2 or higher, 6/10

### Other factors
- Five winners had yet to win over 3m
- Four winners had run at the festival before
- Last year Delta Work became the first successful five-year-old since Pragada in 1988, while Buena Vista in 2011 was the first aged older than nine to oblige since 1981

## 2.50 Ryanair Chase  ITV/RTV
*2m4½f  •Grade 1  •£350,000*

Min has been unlucky to come up against Altior on both visits to the festival and Willie Mullins could sidestep a third clash by sending him here instead of the Queen Mother Champion Chase. Min was beaten seven lengths both times by Altior, in the 2016 Supreme Novices' Hurdle and last year's Champion Chase, but clearly has claims to be 'best of the rest' and has proved his class and versatility with Grade 1 wins this season over 2m4f and 2m1f. Colin Tizzard's Fox Norton, the 2017 Champion Chase runner-up, could also swerve that race in search of a festival win. Another leading British hope is Waiting Patiently, the impressive winner of last year's Ascot Chase who was well beaten by Cyrname (reportedly unlikely to be supplemented here) when going for a repeat. Henry de Bromhead could run last year's winner Balko Des Flos and Monalee, while Mullins' other options include 2017 winner Un De Sceaux, Footpad and Al Boum Photo.

### MIN
**8 b g; Trainer** Willie Mullins
**Chase form** 1112122411, best RPR 176
**Left-handed** 1121221, best RPR 176
**Right-handed** 141, best RPR 167
**Cheltenham form** (all) 22, best RPR 176
**At the festival** 15 Mar 2016 Tracked leader, mistake 3rd, challenged after 2 out, soon ridden, kept on but readily outpaced by winner, finished second, beaten seven lengths by Altior in Supreme Novices' Hurdle
14 Mar 2018 Looked well, travelled well, held up, hit 8th, headway when hampered 4 out, led approaching 2 out, ridden when joined last, headed soon after, kept on but outpaced final 120yds, finished second, beaten seven lengths by Altior in Champion Chase

A measure of how difficult a race the Ryanair is to weigh up is the fact the ante-post favourite is considered more likely to run in the Champion Chase, where he will be a bigger price to dethrone the brilliant Altior. Willie Mullins, you would think, simply has to run something in the Champion and he is not short of other options for this race. Min is dealt with in more detail on page 152, but

he has won over 2m4f and would obviously be a major player, although I fear the trip may be slightly beyond his best.

*Going preference* Handles everything
*Star rating* ✪✪✪

### MONALEE
**8 b g; Trainer** Henry de Bromhead
**Chase form** 1F12F321, best RPR 167
**Left-handed** F122, best RPR 163
**Right-handed** 1F31, best RPR 167
**Cheltenham form** (all) 22, best RPR 163
**At the festival** 17 Mar 2017 Raced keenly, chased leaders, led on bend between last 2, ridden and headed approaching last, kept on under pressure run-in, unable to go with winner final 100yds, finished second, beaten three and a half lengths by Penhill in Albert Bartlett Novices' Hurdle
14 Mar 2018 Looked well, raced keenly, tracked leaders, pressed leader from 7th, led 3 out, ridden and headed when hit 2 out, kept on for clear 2nd but soon held by winner, finished second, beaten seven lengths by Presenting Percy in RSA Chase

There were plenty who thought he should have run in the JLT last season instead of the

## OWNER'S VIEW
**Rich Ricci on Min** "We'll play to the horse's strengths and see where we go. Min has a lot of ability and he seems to be stronger and less keen this year. Altior is a great horse but you never know. I wouldn't mind taking him on again in the Champion Chase"
*Min hit his peak RPR of 176 in last year's Champion Chase but was still seven lengths behind Altior; his best RPR over 2m4f is 172*

RSA, but you can't say he didn't stay 3m when second to Presenting Percy, who is now a fairly warm Gold Cup favourite. Went off favourite for the 3m Growise Champion Novice Chase at Punchestown on his next start and had just about hit the front when coming down two out in an eventful race eventually won by The Storyteller. Started this campaign by finishing third over 2m3½f to Snow Falcon at Down Royal in November (gave 7lb to the winner and second) and then was runner-up in the Savills Chase, although well trounced by Kemboy. Conceivably he could go for the Gold Cup as he has been placed in two 3m races at the festival, but the extra distance of that race may well find him out and this is probably a better fit. On balance, he has a bit to find wherever he ends up, but at least goes to Cheltenham in good heart, having run out a comfortable winner of the 2m4f Red Mills Chase at Gowran in February.

*Going preference* Handles all going
*Star rating* ✪✪✪

## FOOTPAD

**7 b g; Trainer** Willie Mullins
**Chase form** 11111F2, best RPR 172
**Left-handed** 1111F2, best RPR 172
**Right-handed** 1, best RPR 164
**Cheltenham form** (all) 341, best RPR 172
**At the festival** 18 Mar 2016 Behind, ridden after 2 out to go pace, headway soon after, switched left slightly between last 2, went 3rd approaching last, stayed on, not pace to trouble front pair, finished third, beaten seven and a quarter lengths by Ivanovich Gorbatov in Triumph Hurdle
14 Mar 2017 Held up, headway approaching

last, soon chasing leaders and ridden, not quicken, kept on under pressure run-in but not pace of leaders, finished fourth, beaten ten and a half lengths by Buveur D'Air in Champion Hurdle
14 Mar 2018 Raced in 3rd place, chased clear leaders approaching 5th, blundered 6th, headway before 4 out, went 2nd before 3 out where upsides, led on bend before 2 out, drew clear from last, stayed on strongly and well in command after, won Racing Post Arkle Chase by 14 lengths from Brain Power

Another who has the Champion Chase as a viable option and has been dealt with in more detail on page 153, largely because he has yet to race over further than 2m1f over fences. However, he won twice over nearly 2m4f over hurdles in France and was third in a 3m Grade 1 at Punchestown in April 2017. The gloss has been taken off his novice season now with the 2m novices not looking a great bunch and two defeats this term leave him with questions to answer wherever he goes.

*Going preference* Softer the better
*Star rating* ✪✪✪

## WAITING PATIENTLY

**8 b g; Trainer** Ruth Jefferson
**Chase form** 111111U2, best RPR 174
**Left-handed** 111, best RPR 158
**Right-handed** 111U2, best RPR 174

Potentially brilliant young chaser who has been treated with kid gloves, running only three times in each of his first two seasons over fences. You can't say it didn't work, though, as he won all six of those and improved his Racing Post Rating with every single start. The realisation that he was indeed a Grade 1 horse came when he toyed with Art Mauresque

Un De Sceaux: has finished in the first two in all 17 completed chases

on his second outing last term at Kempton, winning with ridiculous ease by eight lengths. He was stepped into Grade 1 company for the first time in the Ascot Chase after that and, given a patient ride, swept through to collar a back-to-form Cue Card after the second-last. He swerved Cheltenham for the second year in a row and didn't make his return until the King George at Kempton, where he was taken out of the race by the fall of Bristol De Mai with a circuit to go. He came up short in his Ascot Chase defence when thrashed 17 lengths into second by new superstar Cyrname, but the race was run in record time, which tells you all you need to know about the ground conditions. Doubtful he will run if it's similar at Cheltenham.

*Going preference* Softer the better
*Star rating* ✪✪✪

## UN DE SCEAUX

**11 b g; Trainer** Willie Mullins
**Chase form** F1111F1221112112112, best RPR 174
**Left-handed** 11F2112, best RPR 174
**Right-handed** F11121211112, best RPR 174
**Cheltenham form** 12112, best RPR 174
**At the festival** 10 Mar 2015 Raced with zest, made most, shaken up approaching last, quickened clear final 110yds, ran on well, won Racing Post Arkle by six lengths from God's Own 16 Mar 2016 Tracked leader, hit 4th, led after 4 out, ridden when headed before 2 out, soon held by winner, kept on same pace, finished second, beaten three and a half lengths by Sprinter Sacre in Queen Mother Champion Chase
16 Mar 2017 Jumped boldly, held up in touch, racing keenly when progress to lead 5th, 5 lengths clear from 8th, reached for 11th, ridden after last, kept on gamely, won Ryanair Chase by one and a half lengths from Sub Lieutenant
15 Mar 2018 Sweating, tracked leaders, racing freely when leading 5th, headed after 3 out, ridden between last 2, kept on from last but no impression on winner, finished second, beaten four and a half lengths by Balko Des Flos in Ryanair Chase

Remarkably tough, consistent and enthusiastic 11-year-old who has still not finished out of the first two in 17 completed chases and has looked as good as ever this season. Got warm in the preliminaries last year and was sweating on the track, which may or may not have contributed to the loss of his Ryanair crown, but whatever the case it was surprising to see how easily Balko Des Flos swept past him after the third-last. To his credit, he stuck on for second and then went on to add Grade 2 and Grade 1 prizes to his haul at Fairyhouse and Punchestown, at the latter course surprising his better-fancied stablemate Douvan. He has been restricted to just one start so far this term, but he helped to provide a thrilling spectacle on a dank day at Sandown in December, when he almost gave Altior a race in the Tingle Creek. Although beaten four lengths in the end, he was a full 15 lengths clear of Saint Calvados in third, and that's probably a fair reflection of his superiority over most 2m chasers when the ground is riding deep. Looking back at his Ryanair success in 2017, that did come in a substandard renewal and, having been tanking along in front going to the last, he was pretty much all out to win by a length and a half and the trip does look to be right at the end of his stamina range. He will doubtless give it his best shot and be a sight to behold in the early stages as usual, but no surprise if a couple with younger legs prove too good for him this time.

*Going preference* Acts on any, brilliant when it's deep
*Star rating* ✪✪✪

## TOP NOTCH

**8 b g; Trainer** Nicky Henderson
**Chase form** 311112311411, best RPR 169
**Left-handed** 31123, best RPR 165
**Right-handed** 1111411, best RPR 169
**Cheltenham form** (all) 2552, best RPR 165
**At the festival** 13 Mar 2015 In touch, hit 5th, led over 2f out on long run to last, headed final 100yds, continued to challenge and stayed on, always held, finished second, beaten a neck by Peace And Co in Triumph Hurdle
15 Mar 2016 Midfield, headway approaching 3 out, 5th when mistake 2 out, ridden and outpaced before last, stayed on same pace run-in, finished fifth, beaten nine and three-quarter lengths by Annie Power in Champion Hurdle
16 Mar 2017 Tracked leaders, left upsides leader 4 out, every chance when mistake 2 out and dropped 3 lengths, ran on after last but always being held by winner final 100yds, finished second, beaten a length by Yorkhill in JLT Novices' Chase

Proper terrier of a horse who seems to be have been around for ages but is still only eight. Has been to three festivals and finished second twice, but missed last year following a rare below-par display when beaten 20 lengths by Waiting Patiently in the Ascot Chase at a course where he usually runs really well. He didn't suffer any long-term harm, though, as he reappeared at Sandown on the final day of the season to win the Grade 2 Oaksey Chase. Not for the first time in his career he started this campaign back over hurdles and put in a fair enough run to be third to current Stayers' Hurdle favourite Paisley Park. Next time out he was a pretty commanding five-length winner from Black Corton in a Listed chase at Kempton, a run that should have put him spot on for the Ascot Chase again in mid February.

*Going preference* Has won on all sorts
*Star rating* ✪✪✪

## POLITOLOGUE

**8 gr g; Trainer** Paul Nicholls
**Chase form** 11214F111241144, best RPR 173
**Left-handed** 124F241, best RPR 173
**Right-handed** 11111144, best RPR 170
**Cheltenham form** (all) U044, best RPR 161
**At the festival** 16 Mar 2017 Tracked leaders, disputing close 4th after 3 out, ridden and held between last 2, kept on same pace, finished fourth, beaten ten lengths by Yorkhill in JLT Novices' Chase
14 Mar 2018 On toes, sweating, in touch, headway 8th, led soon after 4 out, ridden and headed after 3 out, still every chance next, soon held, faded run-in, finished fourth, beaten 23 lengths by Altior in Champion Chase

Top-class chaser who has won Grade 1s at 2m and 2m4f. Was outclassed by Altior in Champion Chase last season, finishing a distant fourth, but ran the race of his life in a first-time tongue-tie in the 2m4f Melling Chase at Aintree to just edge out Min, who had been 16 lengths in front of him at Cheltenham. Seemingly returned as good as ever this season when giving Charbel 6lb and a half-length beating in the 1965 Chase at Ascot in November. Was sent off at just 5-1 for the King George after that despite it being his first attempt at 3m and he was going as well as anything leaving the back straight

despite having made one thunderous error. Ultimately he didn't stay, though, and he lost his unbeaten record on right-handed tracks as a chaser by finishing fourth to stablemate Clan Des Obeaux. Beaten 20 lengths when fourth in the Ascot Chase in February and needs to do a lot better than that, but has never really shone at Cheltenham.

*Going preference* Handles all but best on good to soft or slower
*Star rating* ✪✪✪

## AL BOUM PHOTO

**7 b g; Trainer** Willie Mullins
**Chase form** 1F2F1R1, best RPR 169
**Left-handed** 12F, best RPR 160
**Right-handed** F1R1, best RPR 169
**Cheltenham form** F, best RPR 160
**At the festival** 14 Mar 2018 Workmanlike, in touch, disputed 4th from 14th, ridden in close 3rd after 3 out, staying on at same pace in held 3rd when crumpled on landing and fell next in RSA Chase won by Presenting Percy

Has almost as many letters in his chase form as numbers, bur hugely capable performer when he completes. Failed to do so in last season's RSA and was probably booked for third, but then went to Fairyhouse for the 2m4f Grade 1 Ryanair Gold Cup and proved too strong for Shattered Love, who had landed quite a sizeable punt in the JLT at Cheltenham. He then went back up to 3m at Punchestown and looked set to take advantage of Monalee's fall two out only for Paul Townend to have a brain-freeze and attempt to take him round the final fence, taking Finian's Oscar with him for good measure. He looked certain to have won without that manoeuvre and may well have done so even if Monalee had stood up but we will never know for sure. What we do know is Al Boum Photo is at least as good this season as he ran out an impressive winner of a 2m5½f Listed chase at Tramore, leading five out and finding plenty in front to give Total Recall 10lb and a six-length beating. That earned him a career-best RPR of 169, but he has been unable to run since due to the ground being too quick at the Dublin Racing Festival, where he was set to run in the Irish Gold Cup. Has a Gold Cup entry too and could well go there as he definitely stays 3m. One issue is his jumping as he is not always the most fluent, but he is an improving seven-year-old and is not one to take lightly wherever he goes.

*Going preference* Best on soft
*Star rating* ✪✪✪

## FOX NORTON

**9 b g; Trainer** Colin Tizzard
**Chase form** 1123333111221112P23, best RPR 174
**Left-handed** 233331112211, best RPR 174
**Right-handed** 1112P23, best RPR 169
**Cheltenham form** 2311121, best RPR 172
**At the festival** 15 Mar 2016 Tracked leaders, pushed along and lost place after 3 out, outpaced after, slightly hampered 2 out, kept on to take 3rd final 75yds, no chance, finished third, beaten ten and three-quarter lengths by Douvan in Racing Post Arkle Chase
15 Mar 2017 Tracked leaders, slightly outpaced after 3 out, headway between last 2, strong run from last to press winner close home, just held, finished second, beaten a head by Special Tiara in Champion Chase

Top-class chaser over the years who missed 13 months after being pulled up in the 2017 King George. Hinted that the ability remains when a seven-length second to Altior in the Clarence House Chase at Ascot in January and dealt with in more detail on page 154 as he could well line up in the Champion Chase. Well beaten in Ascot Chase over 2m5f last time.

*Going preference* Handles good and soft
*Star rating* ✪✪

## BALKO DES FLOS

**8 b g; Trainer** Henry de Bromhead
**Chase form** 2133F3123214439, best RPR 174
**Left-handed** 33F2149, best RPR 174
**Right-handed** 21312343, best RPR 161
**Cheltenham form** (all) 5F1, best RPR 174
**At the festival** 18 Mar 2016 Held up, headway before 6th, tracked leaders approaching 2 out, ridden before last and not quicken, one pace after, finished fifth, beaten 15 and a half lengths by Unowhatimeanharry in Albert Bartlett Novices' Hurdle
16 Mar 2017 Led until 5th, led 7th, fell 4 out in JLT Novices' Chase won by Yorkhill
15 Mar 2018 Looked well, travelled well most of way, tracked leaders, led going best soon after 3 out, drew clear between last 2, mistake last, ridden out, won Ryanair Chase by four and a half lengths from Un De Sceaux

Capable of high-class form on his day but has

turned into a bit of an enigma and comes into the festival with more to prove than anyone could have imagined immediately after what he did to Un De Sceaux in this race last year. He has had two huge paydays in his life, winning the Galway Plate in 2017 and this race last year, but has won only one of his other 13 chase starts and has been a complete disappointment in three of them this term. Was beaten 43 lengths when fourth of six to Road To Respect at Down Royal on his return in November, but did at least show a bit more when third of five to Min at Punchestown next time. However, he was never travelling in the Savills Chase at Leopardstown, trailing home 27 lengths ninth of 11. Connections don't seem worried about pressing on as he was all set to run in the Irish Gold Cup in February until the ground was deemed too fast. Incidentally, at this time last year he was thought to need quick ground, but he sailed through the mud at Cheltenham and it more and more looks like it depends on what mood he is in. To that end it's worth remembering he was a highly creditable fifth in the Albert Bartlett here when a rag in 2016, was still bombing along when coming down four out in Yorkhill's JLT in 2017 and then hacked up in the Ryanair last year. If he takes to the place again he can't be left out of calculations.

*Going preference* Acts on any
*Star rating* ✪✪

## SHATTERED LOVE

**8 b m; Trainer** Gordon Elliott
**Chase form** 11211125220, best RPR 159
**Left-handed** 110, best RPR 159
**Right-handed** 11212522, best RPR 159
**Cheltenham form** (all) 01, best RPR 159
**At the festival** 15 Mar 2017 Held up, pushed along briefly approaching 4 out, struggling when not fluent 3 out, soon eased, finished 12th, beaten 52 and three-quarter lengths by Willoughby Court in Ballymore Novices' Hurdle
15 Mar 2018 Close up, hung left when mounting challenge turning in, led soon after 2 out, drawing clear when mistake last, stayed on strongly, ridden out, won JLT Novices' Chase by seven lengths from Terrefort

Dual Grade 1 winner as a novice who won five of her first seven starts over fences and landed a massive gamble when winning the

JLT by seven lengths from Terrefort last year. Second to Al Boum Photo at Fairyhouse when going for a third straight Grade 1 in April and was probably over the top when only fifth of 11 in the eventful Champion Novice Chase won by The Storyteller at Punchestown later that month. Still winless since, but ran right up to form when second under a penalty to Snow Falcon at Down Royal in November and when running Min to a length and a half at Punchestown in December. Bitterly disappointing when beating only one home in the Savills Chase, though, and has something to prove after that. Needs to improve on last year's form to be a factor anyway, even taking into account her 7lb sex allowance, and may well need soft ground to be at her best, so plenty of negatives.

*Going preference* Only one of nine wins on faster than soft/heavy and that was at odds of 1-6 in mares' beginners' chase
*Star rating* ✪✪

## TOUT EST PERMIS
**6 gr g; Trainer** Noel Meade
**Chase form** 1273F587111, best RPR 157
**Left-handed** 51, best RPR 157
**Right-handed** 1273F8711, best RPR 153

Has won only four of 11 chase starts, but that includes the last three and he has been a big improver this term. Started progress with six-length Galway success off mark of just 128 in October, but the following month ran out an easy winner of the Troytown at Navan off a 10lb higher mark. Confirmed he has every right to be considered a Graded performer with short-head success from 2017 Ryanair runner-up Sub Lieutenant at Thurles in January and, while he needs much more than that to be competitive, he is going the right way pretty quickly.

*Going preference* Seems versatile
*Star rating* ✪✪

## ASO
**9 bb g; Trainer** Venetia Williams
**Chase form** 2221356142184345116, best RPR 166
**Left-handed** 222561421834511, best RPR 166
**Right-handed** 1346, best RPR 156
**Cheltenham form** (all) 0542831, best RPR 166

**At the festival** 13 Mar 2015 Mid-division, headway approaching 2 out, soon ridden to chase leaders, weakening when squeezed up before last, finished 11th, beaten 21 lengths by Wicklow Brave in County Hurdle
15 Mar 2016 Mistake 1st, not fluent 3rd and dropped to rear, mistake 3 out, under pressure and outpaced after, plugged on but no danger run-in, finished fifth, beaten 14 lengths by Douvan in Racing Post Arkle Chase
16 Mar 2017 Tracked leaders 4th, ridden to chase winner after 3 until last, stayed on but no extra, finished third, beaten seven and a half lengths by Un De Sceaux in Ryanair Chase

Managed only one run last season when fifth in the Old Roan Chase, but absence clearly hasn't done him any harm as he returned with wins at Newbury and Cheltenham. Dotted up by 13 lengths at the Berkshire track on return from 13 months off and then shrugged off 8lb rise in Grade 3 handicap over the Ryanair course and distance, leading from around halfway and not really looking in any danger despite winning by only two lengths. That was his first win at Cheltenham but he has run several cracking races on the course, including when fifth in the Racing Post Arkle at 66-1 in 2016 and third in this race a year later at 40-1. Was rated only 152 then but is officially an 11lb better horse now, and given his affinity with the track it's easy to see him going much better than he did when a distant last in the Ascot Chase in February.

*Going preference* Handles most ground
*Star rating* ✪✪✪

## THE STORYTELLER
**8 ch g; Trainer** Gordon Elliott
**Chase form** 1371515463, best RPR 161
**Left-handed** 7163, best RPR 161
**Right-handed** 135154, best RPR 161
**Cheltenham form** 1, best RPR 161
**At the festival** Looked well, in touch, ridden in 5th turning in, hit next, disputing 2 length 2nd jumping last, led final 100yds but drifting right, stayed on well, driven right out, won Brown Advisory & Merriebelle Stable Plate by a length and three-quarters from Splash Of Ginge

Took really well to this place last year and landed massive gamble in the Plate. Undoubtedly fortunate to win eventful 3m Grade 1 at Punchestown after that and has run

## RYANAIR CHASE RESULTS AND TRENDS

| | FORM WINNER | AGE & WGT | Adj RPR | SP | TRAINER | BEST RPR LAST 12 MONTHS (RUNS SINCE) |
|---|---|---|---|---|---|---|
| 18 | -1232 **Balko Des Flos** D | 7 11-10 | 172-6 | 8-1 | H de Bromhead (IRE) | 2nd Gd1 Christmas Chase (3m) **(0)** |
| 17 | -1611 **Un De Sceaux** C, D | 9 11-10 | 178T | 7-4f | W Mullins (IRE) | won Cheltenham Gd1 chase (2m½f) **(0)** |
| 16 | 11-12 **Vautour** CD | 7 11-10 | 184T | Evensf | W Mullins (IRE) | 2nd Gd1 King George VI Chase (3m) **(0)** |
| 15 | -418U **Uxizandre** C | 7 11-10 | 170-5 | 16-1 | A King | Won Cheltenham Listed chase (2m) **(2)** |
| 14 | 21-25 **Dynaste** C, D, BF | 8 11-10 | 179T | 3-1f | D Pipe | 2nd Gd1 Betfair Chase (3m1f) **(1)** |
| 13 | 2-151 **Cue Card** C, D | 7 11-10 | 174-2 | 7-2 | C Tizzard | won Gd1 Ascot Chase (2m5½f) **(0)** |
| 12 | 121-1 **Riverside Theatre** D | 8 11-10 | 176T | 7-2f | N Henderson | won Gd1 Ascot Chase (2m5½f) **(0)** |
| 11 | 1-4FP **Albertas Run** CD | 10 11-10 | 176-1 | 6-1 | J O'Neill | won Gd1 Melling Chase (2m4f) **(3)** |
| 10 | P1362 **Albertas Run** C, D | 9 11-10 | 171-3 | 14-1 | J O'Neill | won Ascot Gd2 chase (2m3f) **(3)** |
| 09 | 14-16 **Imperial Commander** C, D | 8 11-10 | 165-19 | 6-1 | N Twiston-Davies | won Paddy Power Gold Cup (2m4½f) **(1)** |

**WINS-RUNS:** 6yo 0-3, 7yo 4-19, 8yo 3-38, 9yo 2-27, 10yo 1-12, 11yo 0-5, 12yo 0-4 **FAVOURITES:** £3.25

**TRAINERS IN THIS** Willie Mullins 2-3-11, Alan King 1-2-8, Colin Tizzard 1-0-5, Henry de Bromhead 1-1-4, Nicky Henderson 1-2-13, Paul Nicholls 0-1-10, Gordon Elliott 0-1-2, Noel Meade 0-1-1, Enda Bolger 0-0-1, Tom George 0-0-1, Jessica Harrington 0-0-2, Ruth Jefferson 0-0-1

**FATE OF FAVOURITES:** 2241213112 **POSITION OF WINNER IN MARKET:** 2821218113

no more than okay in four starts this season, the last three in Grade 1s. Is going to have to improve to take a hand, but would appreciate a strong pace to chase and with this contest looking likely to attract a good field he may well get it. Not discounted at a price.

*Going preference* Handles any
*Star rating* ❂❂❂

## OTHERS TO CONSIDER

There are plenty who haven't been mentioned who are short enough, but surely the likes of **Road To Respect**, **Kemboy**, **Frodon** and **Bellshill** will be going for Gold, while **Cyrname** never even got an entry as connections believe he can't go left-handed and they have indicated he won't be supplemented even after his dominant Ascot Chase success.

## VERDICT

*It's hard to know what is going to run, but with Altior likely to scare off a few in the Champion Chase we could be in for a big field here. It's not a race I'm particularly keen on ante-post, but if pushed I'd take a chance on* **THE STORYTELLER** *at a big price.*

### Key trends

🏇 Adjusted RPR of at least 170, 9/10

🏇 Rated within 6lb of RPR top-rated, 9/10

🏇 No more than four runs since October, 9/10

🏇 Course winner, 8/10

🏇 No more than 11 runs over fences, 8/10

🏇 Top-two finish in at least one of last two starts, 8/10

### Other factors

🏇 Three of the six beaten favourites had won a Grade 1 chase last time out

🏇 Five winners had recorded a top-four finish in a Grade 1 or 2 chase over 3m-plus (three of the other five achieved that subsequently)

🏇 The first five winners (2005-2009) had either won or been placed in the BetVictor Gold Cup or Caspian Caviar Gold Cup, but none of the last nine had run in either

## 3.30 Sun Racing Stayers' Hurdle ITV/RTV
### 3m  Grade 1  £325,000

Paisley Park has emerged as the rising star among the stayers and, as long as Apple's Jade is not unexpectedly diverted here, he holds an outstanding chance for Emma Lavelle after taking the division by the scruff of the neck with victory in the Grade 1 Long Walk at Ascot and, most impressively of all, the Grade 2 Cleeve over this course and distance. Last year's winner Penhill was well beaten into second by stablemate Faugheen at Punchestown in April and has not been seen again since, although both his festival victories have come after lengthy breaks (323 days last year and 78 days before the 2017 Albert Bartlett Novices' Hurdle). Supasundae, last year's runner-up, looks set to return and the list of possibles also includes Faugheen, although the 2015 Champion Hurdle winner has much to prove after a disappointing campaign.

### PAISLEY PARK
**7 b g; Trainer** Emma Lavelle
**Hurdles form** 12201111, best RPR 172
**Left-handed** 220111, best RPR 172
**Right-handed** 11, best RPR 156
**Cheltenham form** 01, best RPR 172
**At the festival** 16 Mar 2018 Raced keenly in midfield, lost place after 6th, behind 8th, finished 13th, beaten 53 and three-quarter lengths by Kilbricken Storm in Albert Bartlett Novices' Hurdle

Fair novice hurdler last term without ever suggesting he was going to turn into the superstar he is now close to being, and was tailed off at a big price in the Albert Bartlett. That was very early in his career, though, and he has gone from strength to strength this season and is now the highest-rated three-mile hurdler in Britain or Ireland. Began his rise to the top in October with a commanding victory in a 2m4f Aintree handicap and then went on to Haydock, where he got up in the dying strides to win by a half a length. That saw him nudged up to an official mark of 152, but handicaps were out anyway and he went straight for the Grade 1 Long Walk Hurdle at Ascot, which he won by two lengths from West Approach. That looked an unsatisfactory race with favourite Call Me Lord clearly not staying, second favourite Unowhatimeanharry falling at the eighth and third favourite and the previous year's winner Sam Spinner trying to refuse at the second and getting rid of Joe Colliver. However, Paisley Park confirmed the form in no uncertain terms when powering clear of his field to win the Grade 2 Cleeve Hurdle. In doing so he extended his margin of victory over runner-up West Approach to 12 lengths and did so while giving him 6lb. That was a real eye-opening run and it earned him an official mark of 168 and a Racing Post Rating of 172. To put the latter into context, an RPR of 170 in a three-mile race over hurdles has been achieved only 24 times since 2006 and the results were 21 wins and three runners-up spots in this race. It's a full 10lb higher than Penhill needed to run to in a messy race last year and, if Paisley Park can repeat it, he is far and away the most likely winner. There was a fierce pace in the Cleeve set by Lil Rockerfeller and Sam Spinner, which obviously suits him very well, but both are probable runners again and they are not likely to do much different.

*Going preference* Has won on soft but said not to want it too deep
*Star rating* ✪✪✪✪✪

### PENHILL
**8 b g; Trainer** Willie Mullins
**Hurdles form** 16111411212, best RPR 162
**Left-handed** 61111, best RPR 162
**Right-handed** 114122, best RPR 160
**Cheltenham form** 11, best RPR 162
**At the festival** 17 Mar 2017 Held up, headway when slightly hampered 2 out and forced wide, good progress entering straight between last 2, led approaching last, ran on strongly to draw clear final 100yds, won Albert Bartlett Novices' Hurdle by three and a half lengths from Monalee

15 Mar 2018 Looked well, held up in last place, headway approaching 2 out, led narrowly between last 2, ridden run-in, edged left, asserted towards finish, won going away, won Stayers' Hurdle by two lengths from Supasundae

High-quality performer who ran nine times in his novice season but has been raced far more sparingly since. The experience he gained during that novice campaign, plus a lengthy Flat career, meant he was properly prepared for the Albert Bartlett, which can be a brutal affair, and he swept around the outside turning for home looking as though he had just joined in before taking Monalee's measure at the last. Defeat followed to Champagne Classic at Punchestown on his final outing of that campaign, after which he wasn't sighed again until last season's Stayers' Hurdle. Given very soft ground and the emergence of what looked like a star in Sam Spinner, Penhill was allowed to go off at 12-1, but he proved much the best and sprinted up the hill to beat Supasundae by two lengths. You could argue the race played to the strengths of a horse with Flat speed as the gallop was ordinary, but the runner-up was a 2m Grade 1 hurdler, so it wouldn't be too wise to crib the form, even if it is hard to put a big figure on it. Unfortunately he has run only once more since and he again met defeat at Punchestown, when rider Paul Townend allowed Faugheen far too much rope and never looked like getting to the 13-length winner in the Champion Stayers Hurdle. Fitness and wellbeing have to be taken on trust again, but he's done it once already.

*Going preference* Versatile
*Star rating* ✪✪✪

---

## TRAINER'S VIEW

**Emma Lavelle on Paisley Park** "We bought him as a three-year-old store. He has always been a nice horse but he has just kept improving. We thought he was well handicapped off a mark of 140 at the start of the season, but it was hard to imagine he could do what he did [in the Cleeve]. He has got better and better and he takes very little out of himself in his races" *Has improved from an RPR of 143 as a novice to 172 now*

## SUPASUNDAE

**9 b g; Trainer** Jessica Harrington
**Hurdles form** 3174812412321221222, best RPR 165
**Left-handed** 1782412212222, best RPR 165
**Right-handed** 341312, best RPR 165
**Cheltenham form** (all) 6712, best RPR 160
**At the festival** 11 Mar 2015 Took keen hold, led after 3f to just over 1f out, faded, finished sixth, beaten seven and a half lengths by Moon Racer in Champion Bumper
15 Mar 2016 Tracked leaders, hit 5th, ridden after 2 out, soon outpaced, 5th and held when hit last, no extra, finished seventh, beaten 14 lengths by Altior in Supreme Novices' Hurdle
15 Mar 2017 Chased leaders, not fluent 4 out, challenging 2 out, ridden to lead approaching last, stayed on well, won Coral Cup by two lengths from Taquin Du Seuil
15 Mar 2018 Slightly on toes, sweating, midfield, headway 2 out, upsides between last 2, pushed along approaching last, continued to challenge run-in, outpaced by winner towards finish, finished second, beaten two lengths by Penhill in Stayers' Hurdle

High-class and versatile performer who will be competing at his fifth Cheltenham Festival at the age of nine. Was better than ever last season when the pick of his form included a half-length second to Apple's Jade in the 3m Christmas Hurdle at Leopardstown and 2m Grade 1 victories in the Irish Champion Hurdle and Punchestown Champion Hurdle. He also finished second in this race and the Aintree Hurdle, but this season there have been signs of decline. He was expected to need the run when second to Apple's Jade in the Hatton's Grace on his return in December, so even a 20-length defeat could be forgiven, but he didn't exactly step up dramatically when second to Sharjah in a messy Ryanair Hurdle back at 2m at Leopardstown over Christmas. Another thumping defeat by Apple's Jade folllowed in the Irish Champion in February and it seems clear he no longer has the speed to be a factor in the top 2m contests. Whether he still has the class to be competitive over 3m is the issue, though, as he is going to need to be at least 10lb better than any of this season's three runs to have a shot.

*Going preference* Handles any, likes decent ground
*Star rating* ✪✪

## FAUGHEEN

**11 b g; Trainer** Willie Mullins

**Hurdles form** 1111111112111P2612F, best RPR 177

**Left-handed** 1111P26F, best RPR 177

**Right-handed** 11111121112, best RPR 173

**Cheltenham form** 116, best RPR 170

**At the festival** 12 Mar 2014 Prominent, tracked leader after 6th, not fluent next, led and mistake 3 out, drew clear before last, ridden out, won Neptune Investment Management Novices' Hurdle by four and a half lengths from Ballyalton 15 Mar 2015 Made all dictating steady pace, jumped right and not fluent 2 out, quickened off bend between last 2, about 3 lengths clear last, kept on well towards finish, won Champion Hurdle by a length and a half from Arctic Fire 13 Mar 2018 Led, headed after 1st, raced in 2nd place, mistake 4th, led after 3 out, leant on rival soon after, headed just before 2 out, ridden and

weakened between last 2, finished sixth, beaten 22 lengths by Buveur D'Air in Champion Hurdle

Brilliant in his early years and won 12 of first 13 starts over hurdles including a Neptune and Champion Hurdle at the festival. Looked to be on the brink of legendary status after recording a Racing Post Rating of 177 with a 15-length drubbing of Arctic Fire in the 2016 Irish Champion Hurdle, but unfortunately he has been plagued with problems since and it was a full 665 days until he made another appearance. That he did so with a 16-length defeat of fellow former Champion Hurdle winner Jezki gave hope that he could return to the top even as he apporoached double digits, but he was pulled up on his next start when never travelling at odds of 2-11 and had no answer to Supasundae in the Irish Champion Hurdle. The regard in which he is held by racing fans in Britain and Ireland is such that he still went off second favourite for the Champion Hurdle, but he was a spent force just after three out and trailed home sixth. He did have one final salvo when winning the Champion Stayers Hurdle at Punchestown by 13 lengths from Penhill and if you can believe that form he ought to be a player here, but he did seem to be given an enormous amount of rope and it is probably best taken with a pinch of salt. Has run twice this season, showing he no longer has the speed for 2m when comfortably seen off by stablemate Sharjah in the Morgiana at Punchestown and then taking a heavy fall two out in the Christmas Hurdle at Leopardstown. In fairness, he certainly hadn't been asked

*Faugheen: would be bidding to become the first 11-year-old winner since Crimson Embers in 1986*

for his full effort then and was going better than those behind him, but it's a big ask to bounce back from that and he isn't getting any younger. The last 11-year-old to win this was Crimson Embers in 1986.

*Going preference* Handles anything
*Star rating* ✪✪✪

## BLACK OP

**8 br g; Trainer** Tom George
**Hurdles form** (left-handed) 412213, best RPR 156
**Cheltenham form** (all) 2233, best RPR 156
**At the festival** 14 Mar 2018 Looked well, tracked leaders, hit 3rd, ridden and not quicken after 2 out, rallied to take 2nd approaching last where mistake, stayed on for pressure run-in, edged right final 150yds, no impression on winner final 75yds, finished second, beaten two and three-quarter lengths by Samcro in Ballymore Novices' Hurdle

Decent if a little clumsy as a novice last season, finishing second to Santini at the trials meeting in January and then to Samcro in the Ballymore, when he kicked the final hurdle out of the ground but still stayed on really strongly and finished well clear of the rest. Form of last season's novices has taken several knocks this term, though, and the only horse in the first nine to win from the Ballymore this term up to the start of February was seventh-placed Aye Aye Charlie, who did so at odds of 1-12 in a Kelso novice hurdle. Black Op did at least win his Grade 1 at Aintree last term, but he was sent chasing to start with this season only to find the fences getting in his way. He made several mistakes on both starts, particularly at Cheltenham in the Dipper, when he did well to finish as close as he did to JLT market leaders Lostintranslation and Defi Du Seuil. Switched back to hurdles in the Cleeve at Cheltenham, the anticipated improvement for the step up to 3m didn't materialise and he was beaten 14 lengths into third by Paisley Park. There is an argument to say he chased the strong pace too closely and that he would prefer softer ground, but he is going to need to step up dramatically on that to trouble the winner.

*Going preference* Handles soft very well
*Star rating* ✪✪

## MIDNIGHT SHADOW

**6 b g; Trainer** Sue Smith
**Hurdles form** (left-handed) 1222U7120110, best RPR 155
**Cheltenham form** 010, best RPR 155

Scottish Champion Hurdle winner (handicap, off mark of just 134) last year and a much-improved performer this term for a step up in trip. Won decent 2m4f handicap hurdle at Aintree in December and followed up by surprising short-priced Wholestone in the 2m4½f Relkeel at Cheltenham on New Year's Day, showing much the best turn of foot in a steadily run race. Pretty weak in the market when stepped up to 3m for the Cleeve Hurdle on trials day at Cheltenham in January and, while he wouldn't have been beaten so far had he not been brought to a standstill at the last, he still would have suffered a heavy defeat. That might not be his form, but he certainly hasn't answered the stamina question for 3m and he needs to improve for it.

*Going preference* Handles good and soft
*Star rating* ✪

## BACHASSON

**8 gr g; Trainer** Willie Mullins
**Hurdles form** 111128U1, best RPR 148
**Left-handed** 18U, best RPR 148
**Right-handed** 11121, best RPR 148
**Cheltenham form** (all) UF, best RPR 124
**At the festival** 18 Mar 2016 Held up in rear, hampered 8th, headway approaching 2 out, ridden to go pace after flight, disputing 5th about 6 lengths off the pace and keeping on for pressure when blundered and unseated rider last in Albert Bartlett Novices' Hurdle won by Unowhatimeanharry
16 Mar 2018 Fell 2nd in Gold Cup won by Native River

Has done his fair share of winning, mostly at a lower level, but looked a chaser going places last year when recording a Racing Post Rating of 165 with an easy 13-length drubbing of A Toi Phil and Champagne West at Tramore. Had a Ryanair entry last season (as he does this) but instead went for the Gold Cup and fell at the second. That was his second failure to complete at Cheltenham as he unseated at the last in the 2016 Albert Bartlett, but on the first occasion he was in fifth at the time and running well, so the track is not an issue. Has been seen only once since the Gold Cup, winning at Punchestown but by only just over two lengths from a horse conceding him 8lb who was well beaten next time. Obviously has ability and interesting to see where he goes, but will be an outsider wherever that is.

*Going preference* Seems versatile
*Star rating* ✪✪

## BACARDYS
**8 bb g; Trainer** Willie Mullins
**Hurdles form** F11P1F0, best RPR 155
**Left-handed** 111PF, best RPR 155
**Right-handed** F10, best RPR 155
**Cheltenham form** (all) 3PF, best RPR 155
**At the festival** 16 Mar 2016 Held up in midfield, progress over 4f out to track leaders 3f out, ridden and no impression 2f out, stayed on final furlong to take 3rd final 100yds, finished third, beaten two lengths by Ballyandy in Champion Bumper
15 Mar 2017 Held up, badly hampered and lost ground 5th, no danger, well behind when pulled up before last in Neptune Investment Management Novices' Hurdle won by Willoughby Court
15 Mar 2018 Midfield, lost place after 3 out, pushed along and outpaced between last 2, soon switched left, staying on in disputing 5th about 4 lengths off pace when fell last in Stayers' Hurdle won by Penhill

Talented performer at his best who has won five of his 15 starts but also had his fair share of mishaps, having fallen in a point, two hurdles and two chases. Had his first crack at chasing last term but didn't really take to it and fell on second start, after which he was switched back to hurdles in the Stayers', in which he also fell. However, he was running on at the time and was only a couple of lengths down at the last, which he flew but instead of landing running he stumbled and fell. He probably wouldn't have won, but he'd have been in the mix for the places. Unfortunately he didn't go on from there as he was tailed off in the Punchestown version in April and has had two goes at chasing again this term, finishing well beaten in a beginners' event at Naas and then falling three out at Leopardstown in December. He's had a break since and this is his only entry.

*Going preference* Act on any
*Star rating* ✪✪

## BAPAUME
**6 b g; Trainer** Willie Mullins
**Hurdles form** 61212312383P521432, best RPR 156
**Left-handed** 611232383213, best RPR 156
**Right-handed** 21P542, best RPR 156
**Cheltenham form** 3, best RPR 143
**At the festival** 17 Mar 2017 Held up, headway between last 2, nodded and took narrow 2nd last, stayed on under pressure run-in but outpaced by winner, lost 2nd near finish, finished third, beaten five lengths by Defi Du Seuil in Triumph Hurdle

Useful hurdler on his day without really looking top class. Was third in the Triumph Hurdle two seasons ago and has shown mild improvement this term, winning a Grade 2 at Auteuil in June and then running Presenting Percy to a length and a quarter in the Galmoy Hurdle in January. Won't have the Gold Cup favourite to worry about this time, but will have other hurdlers with better form and only outside place claims at best.

*Going preference* Seems best on soft
*Star rating* ✪✪

## WEST APPROACH
**9 b g; Trainer** Colin Tizzard
**Hurdles form** 935201235U3PP22, best RPR 155
**Left-handed** 935012353PP2, best RPR 155
**Right-handed** 2U2, best RPR 153
**Cheltenham form** (all) 302353P363P2, best RPR 155
**At the festival** 18 Mar 2016 Midfield until weakened 3 out, finished 11th, beaten 50 lengths by Unowhatimeanharry in Albert Bartlett Novices' Hurdle
16 Mar 2017 Chased leaders, losing place when mistake 2 out, soon weakened, behind when pulled up before last in Stayers' Hurdle won by Nichols Canyon
15 Mar 2018 Looked well, held up, effort to challenge for held 4th approaching 2 out, faded between last 2, finished sixth, beaten 21 and a quarter lengths by Shattered Love in JLT Novices' Chase

Much less talented half-brother to 2016 Stayers' Hurdle winner Thistlecrack who has produced a mixed bag over the last few seasons. Was chasing last season, and early this, but reverted to hurdles after finishing a distant fifth in the Ladbrokes Trophy at Newbury. The switch seems to have revitalised

## STAYERS' HURDLE RESULTS AND TRENDS

| | FORM WINNER | AGE & WGT | Adj RPR | SP | TRAINER | BEST RPR LAST 12 MONTHS (RUNS SINCE) |
|---|---|---|---|---|---|---|
| 18 | 4112- **Penhill** CD, BF | 7 11-10 | 159[-10] | 12-1 | W Mullins (IRE) | won Gd1 Albert Bartlett Nov Hurdle (3m) **(1)** |
| 17 | -312F **Nichols Canyon** CD | 7 11-10 | 170[-2] | 10-1 | W Mullins (IRE) | won Punchestown Gd1 hurdle (2m) **(2)** |
| 16 | -2111 **Thistlecrack** CD | 8 11-10 | 176[T] | Evensf | C Tizzard | won Gd2 Cleeve Hurdle (3m) **(0)** |
| 15 | -1234 **Cole Harden** | 6 11-10 | 162[-7] | 14-1 | W Greatrex | 2nd Newbury Gd2 hdl (3m½f) **(2)** |
| 14 | 1-111 **More Of That** C | 6 11-10 | 165[-14] | 15-2 | J O'Neill | won Gd2 Relkeel Hurdle (2m4½f) **(0)** |
| 13 | 22/21 **Solwhit** | 9 11-10 | 169[-5] | 17-2 | C Byrnes (IRE) | 2nd Punchestown Hurdle (2m4f) **(1)** |
| 12 | 1-111 **Big Buck's** CD | 9 11-10 | 182[T] | 5-6f | P Nicholls | won Gd1 Liverpool Hurdle (3m½f) **(3)** |
| 11 | 11-11 **Big Buck's** CD | 8 11-10 | 180[T] | 10-11f | P Nicholls | won Gd1 World Hurdle (3m) **(3)** |
| 10 | 11-11 **Big Buck's** CD | 7 11-10 | 180[T] | 5-6f | P Nicholls | won Gd1 Liverpool Hurdle (3m½f) **(2)** |
| 09 | 1-U11 **Big Buck's** CD | 6 11-10 | 170[-7] | 6-1 | P Nicholls | won Gd2 Cleeve Hurdle (3m) **(0)** |

**WINS-RUNS:** 5yo 0-5, 6yo 3-29, 7yo 3-40, 8yo 2-26, 9yo 2-17, 10yo 0-8, 11yo 0-4, 13yo 0-1 **FAVOURITES:** -£2.43

**TRAINERS IN THIS RACE (w-pl-r):** Paul Nicholls 4-3-17, Willie Mullins 2-2-20, Colin Tizzard 1-0-2, Jonjo O'Neill 1-0-2, Warren Greatrex 1-0-3, Alan King 0-2-1, Gordon Elliott 0-0-1, Harry Fry 0-1-2, Nicky Henderson 0-2-12, Neil King 0-1-2, Jessica Harrington 0-1-3, Nigel Twiston-Davies 0-1-4, Jedd O'Keeffe 0-0-1, Tom George 0-0-1

**FATE OF FAVOURITES:** 4111P22135 **POSITION OF WINNER IN MARKET:** 3111436145

him as he was second at 40-1 to Paisley Park in the Long Walk Hurdle at Ascot and then again to the same horse in the Cleeve, albeit beaten a long way second time. Has won only one of 15 starts over hurdles and it's hard to know what you're going to get with him, but paid out would seem most unlikely.

*Going preference* Acts on any
*Star rating* ooooo

## WHOLESTONE

**8 br g; Trainer** Nigel Twiston-Davies
**Hurdles form** 3F112113426123231529, best RPR 159
**Left-handed** 3F11211342612321529, best RPR 159
**Right-handed** 3, best RPR 149
**Cheltenham form** 1211312329, best RPR 159
**At the festival** 17 Mar 2017 Midfield, headway after 3 out, every chance and challenging between last 2, not quicken and switched left approaching last, kept on under pressure and edged right run-in but no impression, finished third, beaten seven and a half lengths by Penhill in Albert Bartlett Novices' Hurdle
15 Mar 2018 Midfield, headway 2 out, chasing leaders but unable to quicken approaching last, stayed on to take 3rd final 75yds, not pace of front two, finished third, beaten five lengths by Penhill in Stayers' Hurdle

Usually admirably consistent performer who has twice finished third to Penhill at the festival, first in the Albert Bartlett and then

### Key trends

- Aged six to nine, 10/10
- Ran no more than four times since August, 10/10
- Top-two finish on last completed start, 9/10
- Adjusted RPR of at least 165, 8/10
- Previously ran at the festival, 8/10
- Not out of the first two in all completed hurdle starts that season, 8/10
- Won a Graded hurdle over at least 3m, 7/10
- Ran between nine and 20 times over hurdles, 7/10

### Other factors

- A five-year-old has never won (one of the five to have run in the past ten seasons was placed)
- Four of the seven Irish winners since the mid-1980s prepped in the Boyne Hurdle at Navan
- The record of Cleeve Hurdle winners is 17214213

when beaten five lengths in last season's Stayers' Hurdle. Started his season well enough with a conditions win at Aintree over 2m4f in November, but beaten a long way in the Long Distance Hurdle at Newbury three weeks later when weakening rapidly. Done for speed by Midnight Shadow when attempting to win his second Relkeel Hurdle at Cheltenham in January and then beaten out of sight in the Cleeve at the end of that month. That was the first time he had finished out of the first three at Cheltenham, but the race had turned into a real test and, despite a couple of novice wins at 3m in 2016, he has always looked as though the trip was at the end of his stamina range. Won't find it any easier next time.

*Going preference* Acts on any
*Star rating* ✪

## SAM SPINNER
**7 b g; Trainer** Jedd O'Keeffe
**Hurdles form** 121121153UU4, best RPR 164
**Left-handed** 12112153U4, best RPR 162
**Right-handed** 1U, best RPR 164
**Cheltenham form** 54, best RPR 156
**At the festival** 15 Mar 2018 Set steady pace, not fluent 2 out, headed between last 2, still well there last, hung left under pressure run-in, stayed on same pace final 150yds, finished fifth, beaten six and a quarter lengths by Penhill in Stayers' Hurdle

Real enigma who looked like he had the staying division at his mercy last season, having won two of the races Paisley Park has won this season in commanding fashion, a Grade 3 handicap at Haydock and the Grade 1 Long Walk Hurdle at Ascot. Never looked in danger at Ascot having set a solid pace, but was then given a three-month break before the festival. That may not have helped but rider Joe Colliver clearly didn't go fast enough in front early and the race turned into a sprint, which suited others better than him. However, he couldn't redress the balance when only third at Aintree on his final start and this term has been little short of disastrous. He was beaten when he unseated in the Long Distance at Newbury and then slowed right into the first two hurdles at Ascot in the Long Walk, unshipping Colliver at the second of them. He did at least show more and have more of a cut at his hurdles in the Cleeve, but he was still beaten 24 lengths into fourth and it's hard not to conclude that he blew his big chance.

*Going preference* Likes soft ground
*Star rating* ✪

## OTHERS TO CONSIDER
As with a lot of the races there are a few who have been left out deliberately who are shorter in the ante-post betting, but that's largely due to trainers keeping their options open. There is next to no chance of **Apple's Jade** (second favourite) running, for instance, while it would also be a surprise if **Benie Des Dieux** did not attempt to retain her OLBG Mares' Hurdle crown. **Samcro** has been under a cloud all season and has yet to try 3m, although trainer Gordon Elliott now says Cheltenham is not out of the question and he was a market mover after that. **Top Notch** is surely going for the Ryanair and **Melon** must be Champion Hurdle-bound. Others worthy of a mention are the popular **Lil Rockerfeller**, who helped make it such a test in the Cleeve, and **Kilbricken Storm**, who won last season's Albert Bartlett. There has also been talk of **Presenting Percy** being supplemented and he was only 2-1 'with a run' with one firm after missing the Red Mills Chase at Gowran. That would be an incredibly unpopular move and still has to be considered unlikely.

## VERDICT
*On RPRs **PAISLEY PARK** is very much the one to beat and if he can repeat the form of his Cleeve Hurdle success he will surely win and make it a perfect five for the season. The problem with trying to find one with which to oppose him is that so many have some sort of negative against them, so perhaps last year's winner **Penhill** is the biggest danger. Still, I've not given up hope of **Black Op** doing better and if the ground is on the soft side I'd expect him to make the frame.*

## 4.10 Brown Advisory & Merriebelle Plate   ITV/RTV
*2m4½f handicap chase*   *Grade 3*   *£110,000*

Gordon Elliott's The Storyteller ended a five-year sequence of winners at double-figure odds when he justified 5-1 favouritism last year. He was only the fifth successful market leader in the history of this race (established in 1951 and traditionally known as the Mildmay of Flete), which has been the biggest graveyard for favourites at the festival.

The last two successful favourites before The Storyteller both came from the Pipe stable – Majadou (trained by Martin) in 1999 and Salut Flo (trained by David) in 2012. Their yard has won the race seven times in the past 21 runnings, including David Pipe's three wins since 2010, and is always to be respected.

Some of the bigger stables struggle to get runners at the lower end of the handicap and Paul Nicholls has not won in 31 attempts.

Nicky Henderson has been more successful, with two winners, a third and a fourth from his last 17 runners. Venetia Williams is another trainer to note, having won three times in the last 12 runnings.

■ **ONES TO WATCH** Venetia Williams has a good candidate in **Cepage**, runner-up to Frodon in the Caspian Caviar Gold Cup in December. Another with strong course form and a progressive profile is **Siruh Du Lac**, whose trainer Nick Williams has hit the target in handicaps at the past two festivals.

### BROWN ADVISORY & MERRIEBELLE STABLE PLATE RESULTS AND TRENDS

| | FORM WINNER | AGE & WGT | OR | SP | TRAINER | BEST RPR LAST 12 MONTHS (RUNS SINCE) |
|---|---|---|---|---|---|---|
| 18 | -2137 **The Storyteller** D | 7 11-4 | 147-7 | 5-1f | G Elliott (IRE) | 7th Leopardstown Gd1 nov ch (2m5f) (0) |
| 17 | 14322 **Road To Respect** | 6 10-13 | 145-16 | 14-1 | N Meade (IRE) | 3rd Leopardstown Gd1 nov ch (2m1f) (2) |
| 16 | -F2P1 **Empire Of Dirt** D | 9 10-11 | 142-13 | 16-1 | C Murphy (IRE) | 2nd Punchestown hcp ch (2m6f) (2) |
| 15 | 7/157 **Darna** D | 9 10-11 | 140-6 | 33-1 | K Bailey | won Sedgefield class 3 hcp ch (2m3½f) (2) |
| 14 | P18-P **Ballynagour** D | 8 10-9 | 140-1 | 12-1 | D Pipe | 8th Cheltenham Gd3 hcap ch (2m5f) (1) |
| 13 | 4P61P **Carrickboy** | 9 10-5 | 136-13 | 50-1 | V Williams | won Chepstow class 2 hcap ch (2m3½f) (1) |
| 12 | 112/0 **Salut Flo** | 7 10-10 | 137-5 | 9-2f | D Pipe | 12th Atlantic4 Gold Cup hcap ch (2m5f) (0) |
| 11 | 152F1 **Holmwood Legend** (5x) D | 10 10-6 | 130-5 | 25-1 | P Rodford | won Sandown class 3 hcap ch (2m4½f) (0) |
| 10 | -3144 **Great Endeavour** D | 6 10-1 | 135-11 | 18-1 | D Pipe | 4th Fontwell class 3 nov ch (2m6f) (1) |
| 09 | 20272 **Something Wells** | 8 10-7 | 139-1 | 33-1 | V Williams | 2nd Ascot class 2 hcap ch (2m5½f) (2) |

**WINS-RUNS:** 5yo 0-2, 6yo 2-19, 7yo 2-44, 8yo 2-60, 9yo 3-47, 10yo 1-32, 11yo 0-15, 12yo 0-5, 13yo 0-1 **FAVOURITES:** +£1.50

**FATE OF FAVOURITES:** 2231022PP1 **POSITION OF WINNER IN MARKET:** 0001060871

*Key trends*

🐎 Won between 2m3f and 2m5f, 10/10

🐎 Carried no more than 10st 13lb, 9/10

🐎 No more than 12 runs over fences, 9/10

🐎 Won a Class 3 or higher, 8/10

🐎 Officially rated 135 to 145, 8/10

*Other factors*

🐎 None of the last ten winners had been placed in one of the big 2m4f-2m5f handicaps run at Cheltenham that season

🐎 Ireland has won the last three runnings but their last winner before them was Double-U-Again in 1982

🐎 Five of the last seven winners had been well beaten on their previous start (two pulled up, three unplaced)

🐎 Two winners were trained by David Pipe and had not run since the turn of the year

## 4.50 Dawn Run Mares' Novices' Hurdle RTV
🏇2m1f  🏇Grade 2  🏇£90,000

All three runnings of this newest addition to the festival line-up have gone to Willie Mullins, whose strength in the mares' division has long been evident in his dominance of the senior version of this race. He is always the trainer most likely to turn up a new star mare but he does not have a standout candidate this time and this could be the year he is forced to relinquish his grip on the trophy. The leading Irish hope this time is the Henry de Bromhead-trained Honeysuckle, who was a six-length winner at Fairyhouse in January in the same Grade 3 contest used as a stepping stone by two of Mullins' three winners. Her regular rider is Rachael Blackmore, who has never won at the festival but is challenging for the Irish championship this season. Nicky Henderson has strong contenders in Elusive Belle and Epatante, plus Lust For Glory, and Mullins also has a number of possibles, including Chante Neige, Masons Daughter, Relegate, Salsaretta and Sancta Simona.

### DAWN RUN MARES' NOVICES' HURDLE RESULTS

| | FORM WINNER | AGE & WGT | Adj RPR | SP | TRAINER | BEST RPR LAST 12 MONTHS (RUNS SINCE) |
|---|---|---|---|---|---|---|
| 18 | F2-11 **Laurina** D | 5 11-7 | 155T | 4-7f | W Mullins (IRE) | won Fairyhouse Gd3 nov hdl (2m2f) (0) |
| 17 | 21111 **Let's Dance** D | 5 11-7 | 153T | 11-8f | W Mullins (IRE) | won Leopardstown Gd2 nov hdl (2m4f) (0) |
| 16 | 11 **Limini** D | 5 11-7 | 148-4 | 8-11f | W Mullins (IRE) | won Fairyhouse Gd3 nov hdl (2m2f) (0) |

**WINS-RUNS:** 4yo 0-3, 5yo 3-19, 6yo 0-18, 7yo 0-5, 8yo 0-1 **FAVOURITES:** +£2.67

**TRAINERS IN THIS RACE (w-pl-r):** Willie Mullins 3-0-8, Henry de Bromhead 0-0-3, John Kiely 0-0-1, Jessica Harrington 0-0-1, Nicky Henderson 0-1-5, Paul Nicholls 0-0-1, Warren Greatrex 0-0-1

**FATE OF FAVOURITES:** 111 **POSITION OF WINNER IN MARKET:** 111

*Sancta Simona: one of a handful of possible runners for Willie Mullins*

## 5.30 Fulke Walwyn Kim Muir Handicap Chase — RTV
🐎3m2f   🐎Amateur riders   🐎£70,000

The best amateur jockeys are always in demand for this contest and Jamie Codd is the main man with four wins in the last ten runnings, most recently aboard Cause Of Causes in 2016. Non-claiming riders have the edge in quality and others to note include Patrick Mullins (second last year, with Codd third), Derek O'Connor and Sam Waley-Cohen. Last year's winning rider on Missed Approach was Noel McParlan, another non-claimer.

A number of the larger stables target this race and their runners always merit respect. Eight of the past 17 winners have come from the Pipe stable, Nicky Henderson and Donald McCain. David Pipe, whose father Martin won this race on three occasions, had the first two in 2011 and landed the spoils again in 2015, while Henderson has had three successes, including a couple of 1-2s, and McCain has had two winners and a runner-up.

The last seven runnings have been won by horses rated between 137 and 142 (three were rated 137 and one was rated 138). Irish trainers had a modest record until recently but have won twice in the past five runnings and had the second and third last year.

■ **ONES TO WATCH Mall Dini**, runner-up last year and a close fifth in 2017, looks set for another crack. **Glenloe**, another who just missed out last year in the Pertemps Final (won by Mall Dini in 2016), is a likely sort. **Impulsive Star**, representing the Waley-Cohen family, is on a good mark after winning the Grade 3 Classic Handicap Chase at Warwick in January.

### KIM MUIR HANDICAP CHASE RESULTS AND TRENDS

| | FORM WINNER | AGE & WGT | OR | SP | TRAINER | BEST RPR LAST 12 MONTHS (RUNS SINCE) |
|---|---|---|---|---|---|---|
| 18 | -P632 **Missed Approach** | 8 11-5 | 138-2 | 8-1 | W Greatrex | 8th Scottish Grand National (4m1f) (3) |
| 17 | 45683 **Domesday Book** | 7 11-4 | 137-6 | 40-1 | S Edmunds | 3rd Leicester class 3 hcap ch (2m4f) (0) |
| 16 | 8-005 **Cause Of Causes** C | 8 11-9 | 142-6 | 9-2 | G Elliott (IRE) | 5th Naas Gd2 ch (2m) (0) |
| 15 | 30-6P **The Package** CD | 12 11-4 | 137T | 9-1 | D Pipe | 6th Cheltenham Gd3 hcap ch (3m3½f) (1) |
| 14 | 13280 **Spring Heeled** (2ow) | 7 11-8 | 140-5 | 12-1 | J Culloty (IRE) | 2nd Limerick hcap ch (3m) (2) |
| 13 | 34136 **Same Difference** | 7 11-0 | 137-2 | 16-1 | N Twiston-Davies | 3rd Newbury class 2 nov ch (3m) (1) |
| 12 | -37P9 **Sunnyhillboy** C | 9 11-11 | 142-1 | 13-2f | J O'Neill | 3rd Irish Grand National (3m5f) (3) |
| 11 | 31-32 **Junior** | 8 11-6 | 134-4 | 10-3f | D Pipe | 3rd Cheltenham Gd3 hcap ch (3m3½f) (0) |
| 10 | 0-311 **Ballabriggs** D | 9 11-12 | 140T | 9-1 | D McCain | won Ayr class 2 hcap ch (3m1f) (0) |
| 09 | 14339 **Character Building** D | 9 11-12 | 139-10 | 16-1 | J Quinn | 3rd Cheltenham class 2 hcap ch (3m2½f) (1) |

**WINS-RUNS:** 6yo 0-10, 7yo 3-46, 8yo 3-59, 9yo 3-57, 10yo 0-32, 11yo 0-15, 12yo 1-11, 13yo 0-2 **FAVOURITES:** £1.83

**FATE OF FAVOURITES:** 0311200UU2 **POSITION OF WINNER IN MARKET:** 5311063203

### Key trends
🐎Officially rated 134 to 142, 10/10

🐎Rated within 6lb of RPR top-rated, 9/10

🐎Aged seven to nine, 9/10

🐎Ran over at least 3m last time out, 8/10

🐎Won over at least 3m, 8/10

🐎No more than 11 runs over fences, 8/10

🐎Ran at a previous festival, 8/10

🐎Finished in first three in either or both of last two starts, 6/10

🐎Won a handicap chase, 6/10

### Other factors
🐎Ireland has won two of the last five runnings (Spring Heeled in 2014 and Cause Of Causes in 2016). The last Irish-trained winner before them was Greasepaint in 1983

## 1.30 JCB Triumph Hurdle — ITV/RTV
🏇 2m1f   🏇 Grade 1   🏇 £125,000

For every Cheltenham there is an Irish banker and this year's could be Sir Erec, whose trainer Joseph O'Brien has the strongest team of juvenile hurdlers in Ireland or Britain. Fakir D'Oudairies laid claim to being the best of them with a Grade 2 win on Cheltenham's trials day but the following weekend Sir Erec put up an equally sparkling display with a six-length victory over stablemate Gardens Of Babylon in the Grade 1 Spring Juvenile Hurdle, the chief Irish trial for the Triumph. With all three in the ownership of JP McManus, the thinking is that Fakir D'Oudairies will be sent into battle against older novices in the Supreme on the opening day, leaving Sir Erec as the stable number one here, possibly backed up by Gardens Of Babylon and Band Of Outlaws, also trained by O'Brien. British hopes are led by Grade 1 Finale winner Quel Destin for Paul Nicholls, while other Irish challengers could include Carlo Biraghi for Fozzy Stack and the Willie Mullins-trained Tiger Tap Tap.

### SIR EREC
**4 b c; Trainer** Joseph O'Brien
**Hurdles form** (left-handed) 11, best RPR 146

Unusually good horse to be sent hurdling as a four-year-old after running a two-and-a-half-length third to Stradivarius, and is still a colt. Made the perfect start to hurdles career in 28-runner three-year-old maiden at Leopardstown over Christmas when winning by a neck from Tiger Tap Tap, although did not always impress with his jumping. That aspect of his game was much better second time in the Grade 1 Spring Juvenile Hurdle back at the same track as he stormed to Triumph Hurdle favouritism and a six-length victory, making all of the running. There is no doubt he was extremely impressive, but the race was a little bit unsatisfactory all he same as he managed to pinch three lengths at the start and was allowed to set his own pedestrian gallop. Indeed, he went so slow that the winner of the other Grade 1 novice on the card would have reached the second-last almost 100 yards ahead of him if they'd set off at the same time. Allowing a horse with his Flat ability such an easy time was always likely to see him in an extra-special light, especially as his jumping was never put under any pressure, and he clearly had too much speed for his rivals. Whether he gets such an easy time again is another matter and may well depend on the size of the field, but it is always just as likely that he is the best horse in the race by a long way anyway. Given his Flat rating of 109, it would be no surprise if that's exactly what he is.

*Going preference* Won on good ground over hurdles and heavy on the Flat
*Star rating* ✪✪✪✪✪

### FAKIR D'OUDAIRIES
**4 b g; Trainer** Joseph O'Brien
**Hurdles form** 2611, best RPR 147
**Left-handed** 261, best RPR 147
**Right-handed** 1, best RPR 116
**Cheltenham form** 1, best RPR 147

Didn't win in five starts in France, two of them chases (fell in one), but unbeaten in two outings over hurdles for Joseph O'Brien, who has such a remarkably strong hand in the juvenile hurdle division. He was a comfortable

## TRAINER'S VIEW
**Joseph O'Brien on Sir Erec** "Making the running wasn't ideal [in the Spring Juvenile Hurdle] but he did it very well. Stamina is probably his forte but he quickened well from the second-last. It was only his second run over hurdles, whereas Fakir D'Oudairies has more experience, if not quite the same engine as this fellow" *Ireland's four Triumph winners in the past six years all ran in the Spring and Our Conor in 2013 was the only one to achieve an RPR there as high as Sir Erec's*

winner on his Cork debut in January and was then sent to Cheltenham on trials day, where he was backed from 16-1 overnight to 4-1 by post time and never gave his punters any worry as he dotted up by 13 lengths. He was awarded a Racing Post Rating of 147 for that, which is 1lb superior to that given to Sir Erec at Leopardstown, but he has been bought by JP McManus, who has others he can run here as well, and by all accounts he is seen as the one most likely to run in the Supreme Novices' Hurdle.

*Going preference* Has won on soft and good to soft
*Star rating* ✪✪✪

## QUEL DESTIN
**4 ch g; Trainer** Paul Nicholls
**Hurdles form** 54F1211111, best RPR 137
**Left-handed** 54121111, best RPR 137
**Right-handed** F1, best RPR 130
**Cheltenham form** 1, best RPR 130

One of the shortest-priced British contenders at the time of writing in a race dominated by the Irish and no doubt he is a tough and game performer with plenty of experience. Ran four times over hurdles in France, winning on final start, and has since won the last five of his six outings for Paul Nicholls, including the Grade 1 Finale Junior Hurdle at Chepstow, where he really put his head down and outbattled the odds-on Adjali. The only problem is Adjali was thrashed by Fakir D'Oudairies in the Cheltenham trial, so it really doesn't look like top juvenile form. He warmed up with an impressive win in the Victor Ludorum at Haydock, but there was always the chance main rival Torpillo had been overrated by beating poor horses twice at Sandown and it certainly looked that way. In the end Quel Destin was only left with the 120-rated Capone to beat, so he should have done it easily. The handicapper has given him an official mark of 146, which makes him only 2lb inferior to Sir Erec's Irish mark, but you can bet your life that's not how the market will see it on the day.

*Going preference* Has won on good and heavy
*Star rating* ✪✪

## CARLO BIRAGHI
**4 ch g; Trainer** Fozzy Stack
**Hurdles form** (right-handed) 1, best RPR 130

Ran only three times on the Flat for Fozzy Stack in Ireland and the last one was in the Irish Derby, in which he was beaten only nine and a half lengths. Gelded shortly after and returned in January to run out fairly impressive winner of a 22-runner maiden hurdle at Punchestown. They went a fair old lick in that race, so he showed he could jump at speed and his jumping was really good until he wandered around going to the last. That could be put down to greenness, though, and he obviously has promise.

*Going preference* Looks versatile
*Star rating* ✪✪✪

## TIGER TAP TAP
**4 ch g; Trainer** Willie Mullins
**Hurdles form** (left-handed) 24, best RPR 135

Didn't go unabcked against Sir Erec on debut at Leopardstown and ran him to a neck, the pair having pulled eight lengths clear. However, well and truly put in his place when only fourth to that rival in the Spring Juvenile and, while he almost certainly could have done with a stronger gallop, the same could have been said of a couple in front of him. Has it to prove now.

*Going preference* Hurdles form on good, won on soft on Flat in France
*Star rating* ✪✪

## PIC D'ORHY
**4 b g; Trainer** Paul Nicholls
**Hurdles form** (left-handed) 112122, best RPR 138

The real unknown quantity and may well make his British hurdles debut in the Triumph itself. Doesn't really need much more experience as he ran six times over them at Auteuil (and also in a chase, in which he fell) and never finished out of the first two. Ran in some of the biggest juvenile contests in France, so obviously very highly regarded by his former yard.

*Going preference* Has run only on very soft or heavy ground
*Star rating* ✪✪✪

## BAND OF OUTLAWS
**4 b g; Trainer** Joseph O'Brien
**Hurdles form** 311, best RPR 129
**Left-handed** 1, best RPR 129
**Right-handed** 31, best RPR 118

Yet another string to the mighty bow of Joseph O'Brien and propelled himself towards the head of the market by showing a tidy turn of pace to win a Naas novice in February. That was his third start over hurdles following a maiden third at Cork and a win at Limerick, each time on soft/heavy ground, but this was certainly an improvement and may have come about because of the good ground. He was a miler on the Flat and won a Premier handicap off a mark of 88 on good to firm at the Curragh last summer, although he has also won on soft. The Naas race was fairly steadily run, so it's hard to put a massive figure on it and Racing Post Ratings awarded a figure of just 129. No doubt O'Brien would love the British handicapper to reciprocate as that would make this one a warm order for the Fred Winter, but he does look more about speed than stamina and there's always a chance he'll go straight to Aintree.

*Going preference* Has won on good to firm on the Flat and soft/heavy over hurdles
*Star rating* ✪✪✪✪

*Band Of Outlaws: part of Joseph O'Brien's strong team of juveniles*

## GARDENS OF BABYLON
**4 b g; Trainer** Joseph O'Brien
**Hurdles form** 122, best RPR 141
**Left-handed** 2, best RPR 138
**Right-handed** 12, best RPR 141

Yet another Joseph O'Brien-trained/JP McManus-owned contender and finished second to stablemate Sir Erec in the Spring Juvenile Hurdle at the Dublin Racing Festival. That was his third run over hurdles and he had earlier beaten and then been beaten by Gordon Elliott's filly Surin, who was just behind him in the Spring. There's obviously not much between that pair, but he shapes like a really strong stayer at the trip and did well to get up for second at Leopardstown. A stronger-run race and the extra furlong at Cheltenham looks certain to suit him as well as anything assuming he runs (and McManus has been mobhanded in the race before) and he might just prove the biggest danger.

*Going preference* Seemed to handle cut in two Flat runs but hurdles form on good
*Star rating* ✪✪✪

## COEUR SUBLIME

**4 b g; Trainer** Gordon Elliott
**Hurdles form** 12F4, best RPR 133
**Left-handed** F, best RPR 133
**Right-handed** 124, best RPR 128

Won Navan maiden on the Flat at odds of 16-1 for Peter Fahey in April but switched to Gordon Elliott for a hurdles campaign (for €260,000) and got off the mark at first time of asking when winning at Down Royal in November. Just edged out of Fairyhouse Grade 3 by bigger-priced stablemate Chief Justice the following month, but was throwing down big challenge and looked probable winner when coming down at the last in the Grade 2 Knight Frank Juvenile Hurdle at Leopardstown over Christmas. Chief Justice was beaten just over three lengths into second that day, so it was looking like an improved effort, but his next run was delayed when he came out of the Spring because of fast ground. Instead, with time running out for another run, he went up against older rivals a fortnight later in a Grade 3 at Gowran and finished fourth to the 149-rated Darasso, beaten 19 lengths. Not a bad effort, but one that suggested he might end up in the Fred Winter.

*Going preference* Won Flat maiden on yielding to soft and may want some ease
*Star rating* ✪✪✪

## ADJALI

**4 b g; Trainer** Nicky Henderson
**Hurdles form** 213123, best RPR 137
**Left-handed** 21323, best RPR 137
**Right-handed** 1, best RPR 136
**Cheltenham form** (hurdles) 3, best RPR 137

Joined Nicky Henderson with a decent reputation from France and cemented that with impressive first-time-out success at Market Rasen, where he scooted clear by 13 lengths. Was still a colt then, but gelded soon afterwards and then went to the Finale at Chepstow, where he ran well but was outbattled by Quel Destin, going down by a neck at odds of 4-6. Was favourite again at Cheltenham but thumped by Fakir D'Oudairies to the tune of 16 and a half lengths. He was conceding 5lb to the field that day, but that still leaves him a lot of ground to make up.

Handicapper has whacked him with a mark of 145 (was 147), so it's hard to imagine him being well enough treated for the Fred Winter.

*Going preference* Handles soft and good to soft
*Star rating* ✪✪

## LASKADINE

**4 b f; Trainer** Nicky Henderson
**Hurdles form** 11 (left-handed), best RPR 122

Unbeaten in two hurdles starts, the first a Listed fillies' affair at Auteuil in September (2m2f) and then a juvenile at Warwick in January, when she went off at odds of 30-100 and won by a length and a half. However, she only beat a 68-rated Flat maiden and is going to need a huge amount more if coming here instead of the mares' novice.

*Going preference* Has won on soft and good to soft
*Star rating* ✪

## AUTHORIZO

**4 b g; Trainer** Gordon Elliott
**Hurdles form** (right-handed) 1, best RPR 108

Half-brother to a couple of useful Flat performers and won a maiden on the level in France. Good start to hurdles career when winning 19-runner maiden against older horses by six and a half lengths at Fairyhouse, but RPR of 108 tells you how much more he needs to improve. Also has an entry in the Supreme so evidently reasonably well regarded, although powerful owners can afford scattergun entries.

*Going preference* Has won on soft and yielding
*Star rating* ✪✪

## JON SNOW

**4 b g; Trainer** Willie Mullins

A 1m4f maiden winner at Maisons-Laffitte last May, he has since joined Willie Mullins and Rich Ricci, but at the time of writing had yet to appear over hurdles. Same connections' Saldier didn't make his hurdles debut until the third week in February, though, and while he finished only fifth in the Triumph, he wound up his campaign by reversing form with the principals in the Champion Four Year Old

## TRIUMPH HURDLE RESULTS AND TRENDS

| FORM | WINNER | AGE & WGT | Adj RPR | SP | TRAINER | BEST RPR LAST 12 MONTHS (RUNS SINCE) |
|------|--------|-----------|---------|-----|---------|--------------------------------------|
| 18 | 22 Farclas | 4 11-0 | 155-3 | 9-1 | G Elliott (IRE) | 2nd Gd1 Leopardstown nov hdl (2m) (0) |
| 17 | 11111 Defi Du Seuil CD | 4 11-0 | 164T | 5-2f | P Hobbs | won Gd1 Finale Hurdle (2m) (1) |
| 16 | 14 Ivanovich Gorbatov D, BF | 4 11-0 | 149-5 | 9-2f | A O'Brien (IRE) | won Leopardstown maiden hdl (2m) (1) |
| 15 | 111 Peace And Co CD | 4 11-0 | 159T | 2-1f | N Henderson | 2nd Doncaster Gd2 hdl (2m½f) (1) |
| 14 | 12 Tiger Roll D | 4 11-0 | 150-2 | 10-1 | G Elliott (IRE) | 2nd Gd1 Leopardstown nov hdl (2m) (0) |
| 13 | 111 Our Conor | 4 11-0 | 160-3 | 4-1 | D Hughes (IRE) | won Gd1 Leopardstown nov hdl (2m) (0) |
| 12 | 12123 Countrywide Flame D | 4 11-0 | 151-6 | 33-1 | J Quinn | 2nd Gd1 Finale Hurdle (2m½f) (1) |
| 11 | 1 Zarkandar | 4 11-0 | 155-2 | 13-2 | P Nicholls | won Gd2 Adonis Nov Hdl (2m) (0) |
| 10 | 4211 Soldatino D | 4 11-0 | 150-6 | 6-1 | N Henderson | won Gd2 Adonis Nov Hdl (2m) (0) |
| 09 | 11 Zaynar D | 4 11-0 | 152-6 | 11-2 | N Henderson | won Newb class 4 nov hdl (2m½f) (1) |

**FAVOURITES:** £2.00

**TRAINERS IN THIS RACE (w-pl-r):** Nicky Henderson 3-4-16, Gordon Elliott 2-1-8, Paul Nicholls 1-2-16, John Quinn 1-0-6, Philip Hobbs 1-0-3, Alan King 0-2-15, David Pipe 0-0-5, Willie Mullins 0-6-19, Edward O'Grady 0-1-3, Gary Moore 0-0-2, Joseph O'Brien 0-0-1, Tom George 0-0-2, Tony Carroll 0-0-3

**FATE OF FAVOURITES:** 2443641114 **POSITION OF WINNER IN MARKET:** 3330261115

Hurdle at Punchestown. One to look out for in the coming days.

*Going preference Won Flat maiden on good*
*Star rating* ○○

### SURIN

**4 b f; Trainer** Gordon Elliott
**Hurdles form** 213, best RPR 130
**Left-handed** 3, best RPR 130
**Right-handed** 21, best RPR 129

Has run against Gardens Of Babylon on three occasions and obviously very closely matched with him, although he gives the impression he will be the stronger stayer. Has the option of the mares' novice too and would probably be better off there.

*Going preference Has raced only on good*
*Star rating* ○

### VERDICT

*Only nine went to post last year when there was a short-priced favourite and a small field looks likely again. **Sir Erec** is the most likely winner and has far more solid claims than last year's beaten jolly Apple's Shakira. If he gets the run of the race again it's hard to see what is going to beat him, but in the hope the contest will be more stamina-sapping this time I've backed **GARDENS OF BABYLON** each-way against him. I'm sure he's going to improve given a proper test and can't think of a British horse I want to back.*

### Key trends

🏇 Last ran between 19 and 55 days ago, ten winners in the last ten runnings

🏇 Won at least 50 per cent of hurdle races, 9/10 (exception still a maiden)

🏇 Top-three finish last time out, 9/10 (six won)

🏇 Adjusted RPR of at least 150, 9/10

🏇 By a Group 1-winning sire, 8/10

🏇 Ran two or three times over hurdles, 7/10

### Other factors

🏇 Zarkandar is the only once-raced hurdler to win in the past 30 years

🏇 Five of the last ten winners were undefeated over hurdles

🏇 Five winners had landed Graded events (two had won the Adonis at Kempton in February)

🏇 Three winners had raced on the Flat in Britain and Ireland and all had recorded an RPR of at least 83

🏇 Since the introduction of the Fred Winter Hurdle in 2005, 13 of the 14 winners have had an SP of 10-1 or shorter

## 2.10 Randox Health County Handicap Hurdle    ITV/RTV
### 2m1f    Grade 3    £100,000

This is an ultra-competitive handicap and being in the right ratings bracket has become a virtual prerequisite. Although the classy Arctic Fire defied a mark of 158 in 2017, every other winner since 2006 was rated in the 130s and six of the last eight have run off 138 or 139. Since 1970 just eight winners have carried more than 11st.

Ireland has accounted for eight of the last 12 winners, with six of them trained by a Mullins. Paul Nicholls has done best of the British trainers, winning four times in the last 15 runnings, but the one to watch recently has been Dan Skelton (a former Nicholls assistant), who won with Superb Story in 2016 and Mohaayed last year.

The Betfair Hurdle and the Ladbrokes Hurdle at the Dublin Racing Festival have been key pointers – nine of the past 18 winners had run in one of those hot contests. But also look closely at horses who have been kept out of the fray – the last three winners were returning after breaks of 124 days, 418 days and 80 days respectively.

■**ONES TO WATCH Off You Go** will have a leading chance for Charles Byrnes if he comes here after his Ladbrokes Hurdle victory. Willie Mullins has any number of possibles, including **Uradel** and **Shanning**.

## COUNTY HURDLE RESULTS AND TRENDS

| | FORM WINNER | AGE & WGT | OR | SP | TRAINER | BEST RPR LAST 12 MONTHS (RUNS SINCE) |
|---|---|---|---|---|---|---|
| 18 | -1023 **Mohaayed** D | 6 10-8 | 139-4 | 33-1 | D Skelton | 3rd Gd1 Christmas Hurdle (0) |
| 17 | 1142- **Arctic Fire** D | 8 11-12 | 158-4 | 20-1 | W Mullins (IRE) | Seasonal debutant (0) |
| 16 | 44-12 **Superb Story** D | 5 10-12 | 138T | 8-1 | D Skelton | 2nd Cheltenham Gd3 hcap hdl (2m½f) (0) |
| 15 | F580P **Wicklow Brave** D | 6 11-4 | 138-1 | 25-1 | W Mullins (IRE) | 11th Newbury Gd3 hcap hdl (2m½f) (1) |
| 14 | 8-141 **Lac Fontana** CD | 5 10-11 | 139-3 | 11-1 | P Nicholls | won Cheltenham class 2 hcap hdl (2m1f) (0) |
| 13 | 31923 **Ted Veale** | 6 10-6 | 134-2 | 10-1 | A Martin (IRE) | 3rd Boylesports Hcap Hurdle (2m) (0) |
| 12 | 10120 **Alderwood** D | 8 11-1 | 139-3 | 20-1 | T Mullins (IRE) | won Killarney hcap hdl (2m6f) (2) |
| 11 | 13-51 **Final Approach** | 5 10-12 | 139-8 | 10-1 | W Mullins (IRE) | won MCR Hcap Hurdle (2m) (0) |
| 10 | 40110 **Thousand Stars** D | 6 10-5 | 134-5 | 20-1 | W Mullins (IRE) | 14th MCR Hcap Hurdle (2m) (0) |
| 09 | 1349 **American Trilogy** D | 5 11-0 | 135-7 | 20-1 | P Nicholls | 3rd Cheltenham Gd2 nov hdl (2m½f) (2) |

**WINS-RUNS:** 5yo 4-69, 6yo 4-78, 7yo 0-61, 8yo 2-28, 9yo 0-16, 10yo 0-10 **FAVOURITES:** -£10.00

**FATE OF FAVOURITES:** 60000P0460 **POSITION OF WINNER IN MARKET:** 7040350300

### Key trends

- Achieved career-best RPR of at least 129 on a left-handed track, 10/10
- Officially rated between 134 and 139, 9/10
- Carried no more than 11st 1lb, 8/10 (both exceptions trained by Willie Mullins)
- Ran no more than 12 times over hurdles, 8/10 (both exceptions trained by Willie Mullins)
- Aged five or six, 8/10
- No previous festival form, 7/10

### Other factors

- There have been five winning novices since 1996
- Three winners ran in the (now) Ladbrokes Hurdle at Leopardstown, finishing 013, but only one ran in Newbury's Betfair Hurdle (finished unplaced)
- Paul Nicholls has had four winners, two seconds and a fourth since 2004
- Ireland has won six of the last ten, including four for Willie Mullins

## 2.50 Albert Bartlett Novices' Hurdle ITV/RTV
🏇3m 🏇Grade 1 🏇£125,000

The favourite for this staying novice hurdle often comes from one of the big stables but upsets are not uncommon and last year Nicky Henderson's 11-4 market leader Santini was only third as Kilbricken Storm became the third 33-1 shot to win in the past nine runnings. The top trainers always have an embarrassment of riches across the Grade 1 novice hurdles, however, and those with potential cards to play here include Gordon Elliott with Commander Of Fleet and Battleoverdoyen, Nicky Henderson (Birchdale and Valtor) and Willie Mullins (Relegate, Blackbow and Salsaretta). Others to note are Rockpoint for last year's winning trainer Colin Tizzard and Derrinross (Philip Dempsey).

## COMMANDER OF FLEET
**5 b g; Trainer** Gordon Elliott
**Hurdles form** 141, best RPR 145
**Left-handed** 1, best RPR 145
**Right-handed** 14, best RPR 136

Looked a horse of huge potential when storming home in a bumper at the Punchestown festival last April and did so again on hurdles debut, although was a 1-5 shot for that 2m4½f contest. Did not handle drop to 2m well when last of four in Grade 1 Royal Bond at Fairyhouse in December but then went up to 2m6f for another Grade 1 at Leopardstown's Dublin Racing Festival and stayed on well to beat Rhinestone (conceded 2lb weight for age) by half a length. Ran in one point, so has had five outings overall, but only two of this race's previous 14 winners had so little experience and this is a tough race. Against that, he'll have learned plenty at Leopardstown.

*Going preference* Seems versatile
*Star rating* ✪✪✪

## TRAINER'S VIEW
**Gordon Elliott on Commander Of Fleet**
"Jack [Kennedy] said the horse is still very green but he's improving and stays well. I imagine the Albert Bartlett is the race we'll be looking at. We decided against running Battleoverdoyen [at the Dublin Racing Festival] as he'd had three runs in a short space of time and he'll probably go straight for the Ballymore" *Elliott has yet to win this race and 13-8 favourite Death Duty was beaten two years ago*

## BIRCHDALE
**5 b g; Trainer** Nicky Henderson
**Hurdles form** (left-handed) 11, best RPR 147
**Cheltenham form** 1, best RPR 147

Won a point and two hurdles in three starts, giving him same profile as Santini, last year's beaten favourite for the same stable. Certainly nothing wrong with form of 18-length win at Cheltenham on trials day even if he may not have won had Brewin'upastorm not fallen at the last, but lightly raced sorts like this are just the sort you want to oppose in this race.

*Going preference* Has raced only on good/good to soft
*Star rating* ✪✪✪

## BATTLEOVERDOYEN
**6 b g; Trainer** Gordon Elliott
**Hurdles form** (left-handed) 11, best RPR 144

Grade 1 winner at Naas when last seen in January, making it 2-2 over hurdles, although trainer said he'd be looking to get another run into him before Cheltenham. Favourite for this in some books, but also second favourite for Ballymore, and you'd imagine Gigginstown will split up him and Commander Of Fleet.

*Going preference* Has raced only on good/yielding
*Star rating* ✪✪✪

## DERRINROSS
**8 b g; Trainer** Philip Dempsey
**Hurdles form** (right-handed) 42211, best RPR 146

Not from such a high-profile yard as the

favourites, but has been given enough experience to make him interesting, especially as on Racing Post Ratings he has achieved just as much as those ahead of him in the betting. Has won Grade 3 and 2 races on last two starts at Cork and Limerick (beat Sams Profile by further than Battleoverdoyen did) and looks tough. Trainer says they will be dreaming about this race if we get a wet spring.

*Going preference* Must have it soft according to connections
*Star rating* ✪✪✪

## LISNAGAR OSCAR
**6 b g; Trainer** Rebecca Curtis
**Hurdles form** (left-handed) 2211, best RPR 148
**Cheltenham form** 2, best RPR 133

Progressive stayer who was second on first two starts over hurdles to horses who might reoppose (Emitom and Rockpoint) but has evidently improved a great deal by winning his next two and is now a shorter price than the pair who beat him. Showed good battling qualities when beating Nicky Henderson's well-regarded Dickie Diver over 2m3½f at Chepstow in January and then took his form to a new level in February with a ten-length trial win at Haydock, where he had Rockpoint a long way behind in sixth. Short-priced favourite Kateson didn't seem to stay but there were some other promising horses in opposition and he dealt with them pretty easily.

*Going preference* Still early days but obviously has no problem with good ground
*Star rating* ✪✪✪

## RELEGATE
**6 b m; Trainer** Willie Mullins
**Hurdles form** 215, best RPR 135
**Left-handed** 15, best RPR 135
**Right-handed** 2, best RPR 119
**Cheltenham form** (bumper) 1, best RPR 135
**At the festival** 14 Mar 2018 Held up in rear, nudged along over 4f out, headway on outer over 2f out, 14th with work to do well over 1f out, good run final furlong and drifted left, stayed on to lead final 100yds, kept on well near finish, won Champion Bumper by a neck from Carefully Selected

Last year's Champion Bumper winner has been a mixed bag so far over hurdles, getting beaten at odds of 4-9 on her debut and then having to work hard enough for her 2m maiden win at Naas. Never seemed to be travelling early in 2m6f Leopardstown Grade 1 won by Commander Of Fleet but stayed on strongly late for fifth place. Unbeaten on soft last season, but yet to have it this term.

*Going preference* Soft ground looks a must
*Star rating* ✪✪✪

## ROCKPOINT
**6 b g; Trainer** Colin Tizzard
**Hurdles form** 435327202146, best RPR 137
**Left-handed** 4202146, best RPR 137
**Right-handed** 35372, best RPR 125
**Cheltenham form** 01, best RPR 135

Six-year-old who has been well and truly battle-hardened by the same stable as last year's winner Kilbricken Storm. That's because he's a second-season hurdler who took an age to break his duck, but he spent much of his time at 2m and it wasn't until he was upped in trip that he started to improve. He was strong at the end when beating Lisnagar Oscar over course and distance in December and, while only fourth dropped back in trip in the Leamington at Warwick next time, on RPRs that was his third career-best in a row. However, he finished well in the ruck behind Lisnagar Oscar at Haydock in his prep, for which he was a huge drifter and never seemed to be travelling before plodding on late for sixth. He's better than that but needs to be.

*Going preference* Best form on good
*Star rating* ✪✪

## BLACKBOW
**6 b g; Trainer** Willie Mullins
**Cheltenham form** (bumper) 5, best RPR 137
**At the festival** 14 Mar 2018 lengthy, will make a jumper, raced keenly, held up in midfield, headway 2f out, ridden and chased leaders over 1f out, kept on same pace final 100yds, finished fifth, beaten five and three-quarter lengths by Relegate in Champion Bumper

The fact that last year's Champion Bumper fifth was as short as 8-1 with a run with one firm when he had not made his hurdling debut by mid-February tells you what a guess-up

## ALBERT BARTLETT NOVICES' HURDLE RESULTS AND TRENDS

| | FORM | WINNER | AGE & WGT | Adj RPR | SP | TRAINER | BEST RPR LAST 12 MONTHS (RUNS SINCE) |
|---|---|---|---|---|---|---|---|
| 18 | 3113 | Kilbricken Storm CD | 7 11-5 | 152-11 | 33-1 | C Tizzard | won Cheltenham Gd2 nov hdl (3m) (1) |
| 17 | 11141 | Penhill D | 6 11-5 | 157-2 | 16-1 | W Mullins (IRE) | won Limerick Gd2 nov hdl (3m) (0) |
| 16 | -1111 | Unowhatimeanharry CD | 8 11-5 | 154-9 | 11-1 | H Fry | won Exeter class 2 hcap hdl (2m7f) (0) |
| 15 | 11F12 | Martello Tower D | 7 11-7 | 151-6 | 14-1 | M Mullins (IRE) | 2nd Leopardstown Gd2 nov hdl (2m4f) (0) |
| 14 | -1253 | Very Wood | 5 11-7 | 143-18 | 33 1 | N Meade (IRE) | 3rd Naas Gd2 nov hdl (2m4f) (0) |
| 13 | -1111 | At Fishers Cross CD | 6 11-7 | 161T | 11-8f | R Curtis | won Cheltenham Gd2 nov hdl (2m5f) (0) |
| 12 | 2111 | Brindisi Breeze D | 6 11-7 | 157-6 | 7-1 | L Russell | won Haydock Gd2 nov hdl (3m) (0) |
| 11 | 1-111 | Bobs Worth C | 6 11-7 | 160T | 15-8f | N Henderson | won Cheltenham Gd2 nov hdl (2m4½f) (0) |
| 10 | 12F34 | Berties Dream | 7 11-7 | 155-3 | 33-1 | P Gilligan (IRE) | 3rd Cheltenham Gd2 nov hdl (2m5f) (1) |
| 09 | -5112 | Weapon's Amnesty D, BF | 6 11-7 | 150-12 | 8-1 | C Byrnes (IRE) | 2nd Leopardstown Gd2 nov hdl (2m4f) (0) |

**WINS-RUNS:** 5yo 1-37, 6yo 5-94, 7yo 3-33, 8yo 1-13, 9yo 0-1 **FAVOURITES:** -£4.75

**TRAINERS IN THIS RACE (w-pl-r):** Willie Mullins 1-4-30, Colin Tizzard 1-1-7, Harry Fry 1-0-3, Nicky Henderson 1-3-12, Lucinda Russell 1-0-1, Noel Meade 1-0-2, Rebecca Curtis 1-0-8, Margaret Mullins 1-0-1, Evan Williams 0-0-2, Joseph O'Brien 0-0-1, Fergal O'Brien 0-0-1, David Pipe 0-1-5, Dan Skelton 0-0-3, Mouse Morris 0-0-3, Jessica Harrington 0-0-1, Nigel Twiston-Davies 0-2-9, Paul Nicholls 0-2-6, Philip Hobbs 0-0-4, Tom George 0-0-3, Gordon Elliott 0-2-5, Warren Greatrex 0-0-4, Henry Daly 0-0-3

**FATE OF FAVOURITES:** 2P121F0PU3 **POSITION OF WINNER IN MARKET:** 4012197670

this race can be. He obviously has plenty of ability and is bred to stay, but he wouldn't have anything like the right profile if he turns up on the back of just one run, which he still needs to have.

*Going preference* Seems versatile
*Star rating* ✪

### SAMS PROFILE

**5 b g; Trainer** Mouse Morris
**Hurdles form** 122, best RPR 136
**Left-handed** 2, best RPR 136
**Right-handed** 12, best RPR 136

Has entries in all three novice hurdles but was keen and jumped badly in the early stages when second to Battleoverdoyen over 2m4f when last seen and didn't jump better until the pace picked up. Looks a promising horse but would prefer to see him running at shorter for now even though the layers seem to think this is his best chance.

*Going preference* Seems to handle anything
*Star rating* ✪✪

### SALSARETTA

**6 b m; Trainer** Willie Mullins
**Hurdles form** 392F511U, best RPR 139
**Left-handed** 392FU, best RPR 127
**Right-handed** 511, best RPR 139
**Cheltenham form** F, best RPR 123
**At the festival** 15 Mar 2018 Midfield, steady

### Key trends

🐎 At least three runs over hurdles, 10/10

🐎 Won over at least 2m5f, 9/10

🐎 Adjusted RPR of at least 150, 9/10

🐎 Top-three finish in a Graded hurdle last time out, 8/10 (four won)

🐎 Aged six or seven, 8/10

🐎 Rated within 9lb of RPR top-rated, 7/10

### Other factors

🐎 Seven winners had won a Graded hurdle

🐎 Three winners had raced at least twice at Cheltenham (all had won at the course)

NOTES

headway after 2 out, under pressure keeping on moderately in 6th about 18 lengths off the pace when fell last in Trull House Stud Mares' Novices Hurdle won by Laurina

Fell in the mares' novice last season (would have been about sixth) and didn't break her duck until May, so is entitled to go for it again. Some of her form reads well, though, notably a fairly comfortable 2m4f success from Felix Desjy at Limerick in December. Took on Commander Of Fleet in 2m6f Grade 1 at Leopardstown in February, so stamina presumably considered her game, but unfortunately unseated at the second.

*Going preference* Most form is on soft
*Star rating* ✪✪

## KAPCORSE

**6 br g; Trainer** Paul Nicholls
**Hurdles form** 46761, best RPR 115
**Left-handed** 47, best RPR 110
**Right-handed** 661, best RPR 115

Hurdles form is hardly inspiring with a best Racing Post Rating of just 115 earned in October 2017. However, has won two of three chase starts and was a ten-length winner of a fair contest off a mark of 128 in December. Afterwards Paul Nicholls reasoned that he was still a lightly raced horse and might be better served going back over hurdles and he duly won a Wincanton novice in January, albeit a weak one. It would be a slightly unusual prep for this, but this is his only entry and a couple of other winners had been chasing.

*Going preference* Seems versatile
*Star rating* ✪✪✪

## VALTOR

**10 b g; Trainer** Nicky Henderson
**Hurdles form** 525723580745, best RPR 136
**Left-handed** 57235807, best RPR 136
**Right-handed** 5245, best RPR n/a
**Cheltenham form** (chase) P

Scores strongly on the experience front, having run 52 times in all, but one firm surely having a laugh making him just 10-1. Didn't win in 12 hurdles starts in France and, while now rated 160 over fences, looked to hate Cheltenham on trials day when pulled up behind Frodon.

*Going preference* Loads of form on soft
*Star rating* ✪

## EMITOM

**5 b g; Trainer** Warren Greatrex
**Hurdles form** (left-handed) 11, best RPR 137

Has won all four starts, starting with a Warwick bumper in April and another one at Ascot in November. Easy winner of two Class 4 hurdles since then, first at Ffos Las (2m4f, soft) and then dropped back to 2m at odds of 1-8 at Lingfield in January and trainer says he's probably more of a 2m4f horse for now even though he's bred to stay well. Would have made more appeal for this race or the Ballymore if he had managed to learn something over hurdles, but was denied the chance to take on Supreme favourite Angels Breath in the 2m3½f Sidney Banks at Huntingdon when the equine flu outbreak intervened.

*Going preference* Seems to handle anything
*Star rating* ✪✪

*Rhinestone: made Commander Of Fleet work hard last time*

## DOWNTOWN GETAWAY

**6 b g; Trainer** Nicky Henderson
**Hurdles form** 21, best RPR 127
**Left-handed** 2, best RPR 132
**Right-handed** 1, best RPR 127

Big reputation after winning bumper by 12 lengths and has started a shade of odds-on for both hurdles starts. Turned over by one with more experience (well-beaten favourite in Grade 2 next time) first time at Newbury but then just about got the job done at Ascot, getting up by a short head over 2m5½f. Shouldn't have a problem with the trip but still appears to need a bit more experience for a race of this nature.

*Going preference* Has raced on soft/good to soft
*Star rating* ✪✪

## CASTLEBAWN WEST

**6 b g; Trainer** Willie Mullins
**Hurdles form** 21, best RPR 137
**Left-handed** 1, best RPR 137
**Right-handed** 2, best RPR 134

Won the second of two bumper starts, but only in a five-runner race in March. Second and first in two maiden hurdles over 2m4f in December and the one he beat at Leopardstown was trounced 35 lengths by Commander Of Fleet afterwards. Has promise but not seen since and only as short as he is (14-1 in places) because of his trainer.

*Going preference* Too early to say
*Star rating* ✪

## RHINESTONE

**6 b g; Trainer** Joseph O'Brien
**Hurdles form** (left-handed) 142, best RPR 146
**Cheltenham form** (bumper) 9, best RPR 132
**At the festival** 14 Mar 2018 In touch, ridden and not quicken over 1f out, weakened inside final furlong, finished 11th, beaten 11 lengths by Relegate in Champion Bumper

Ran in four bumpers last term, culminating in the Champion Bumper at Cheltenham, where he ran creditably enough in ninth. Only scrambled home on maiden hurdle debut at Naas in November and then made a few too many errors when only 14-length fourth in Grade 2 Navan Novice Hurdle a month later. However, made this race's

favourite Commander Of Fleet pull out all the stops to beat him by half a length in a 2m6f Grade 1 at Leopardstown in February and was conceding 2lb weight for age, which won't be the case at Cheltenham. Whether he will jump so well in a big field is another matter, but he has plenty of talent.

*Going preference* Looks versatile
*Star rating* ✪✪✪

## OTHERS TO CONSIDER

This must be the hardest of the novice races in which to nail down the likely field. As well as giving Champion Bumper fifth **Blackbow** an entry, Willie Mullins has also given one to his runner-up **Carefully Selected** and he, like Blackbow, had not made his debut over hurdles by mid-February, although it didn't stop one firm offering just 8-1. Another with the completely wrong profile is Nicky Henderson's **Dickie Diver**, who is only 12-1 in places with a lot of firms despite having run in just a 2m3½f novice hurdle at Chepstow and got beaten. Mullins' **Easy Game** has all three novice entries but, having run six times between July and December, he hasn't been seen since. **Aye Aye Charlie** doesn't look trustworthy, which is why he's a second-season novice, but his peak form is as good as any of these and he has loads of experience, so wouldn't be the daftest outsider given this race's history.

## VERDICT

*A race for big, backward and largely clueless future chasers, so no wonder it's the hardest novice hurdle in which to find the winner, with a ten-year average SP for the winner of 16-1 compared to 9-1 for the Supreme and 9-2 for the Ballymore. The horses with the sexy lightly raced profiles routinely sink without trace as they're just not conditioned for the sort of battle this contest provides, so look for a horse with at least half a dozen runs to its name, whether that is in points, bumpers or over hurdles (only two of the winners had less and they had five). The two I like are **ROCKPOINT**, who is better than he showed at Haydock and will be a massive price on the day, and **DERRINROSS**, with the latter only if the ground is on the soft side.*

## 3.30 Magners Cheltenham Gold Cup ITV/RTV
### 3m2½f · Grade 1 · £625,000

Native River and Might Bite treated us to an instant classic last year with their epic duel and both of them will be back again, but they are no longer the big two. While Native River is second favourite as he bids to become the first since Best Mate to retain the crown, Might Bite's form has tailed off and a host of fresh challengers have emerged. The betting is headed by Presenting Percy, who confirmed himself as the rising star with his seven-length victory in last year's RSA Chase – the top novice proving ground. In typical low-key fashion, trainer Pat Kelly has not sent Presenting Percy to contest the season's other key races and instead King George VI Chase winner Clan Des Obeaux, Kemboy (Savills Chase) and Bellshill (Irish Gold Cup) have staked their claims with big-race victories. With previous festival winners Road To Respect and Thistlecrack also in the picture, this is shaping up as another fascinating battle for Gold.

### PRESENTING PERCY
**8 b g; Trainer** Patrick Kelly
**Chase form** 13121, best RPR 170
**Left-handed** 1, best RPR 170
**Right-handed** 1312, best RPR 163
**Cheltenham form** 11, best RPR 170
**At the festival** 16 Mar 2017 Held up, headway approaching 2 out, led and wanted to lug left before last, a little disorganised after flight, stayed on strongly to go clear final 100yds, won Pertemps Network Final Handicap Hurdle by three and three-quarter lengths from Barney Dwan
14 Mar 2018 Jumped and travelled well, held up in last pair, headway after 4 out, led before 2 out, drew clear between last 2, stayed on well, ridden out, won RSA Insurance Novices' Chase by seven lengths from Monalee

Won Pertemps Final off a mark of 146 two years ago but developed into a considerably better chaser last term, when he won three of his five starts in that sphere and also bolted up in the Grade 2 Galmoy Hurdle for good measure. Jumped well to beat De Plotting Shed on debut at Galway and, following a disappointing third of five at Punchestown on next start, took advantage of Irish handicapper's decision to award him a mark of 145 (14lb lower than he was over hurdles at the time) based on those two runs to sluice up in 3m5f handicap chase at Punchestown. After the Galmoy he then ran Our Duke to a length over an inadequate 2m4f in the Red Mills Chase at Gowran before rocking up at Cheltenham to turn the RSA Chase into a procession, winning by seven lengths from Monalee. Has been favourite for the Gold Cup pretty much ever since, but while he has thrived on racing for the past two seasons, connections have adopted kid gloves treatment this term, avoiding ground considered too fast (which he handled well as a hurdler). Finally made his return in the Galmoy Hurdle again in January, some 316 days after his previous run, and was a comfortable enough winner by a length and a quarter from Bapaume. However, he missed his intended chase prep in the Red Mills at Gowran Park (the last leg on his route to the 2018 festival), so was running out of time to get more chase experience before the big day and he'll be a rare winner indeed if he can claim Gold having not run in a single chase during his winning season.

*Going preference* Handles any
*Star rating* ✪✪✪

### OWNER'S VIEW
**Racing manager Steve Massey on Kemboy** "He was tremendous [when winning the Savills Chase in December]. I know the ground was good but the time was very good also. He had plenty left in the tank and the big thing about it, which people keep forgetting, is that he won it as a six-year-old. He was the youngest horse in the race and he's improving" *Has won on heavy but both wins this season have been on good ground*

## NATIVE RIVER
**9 ch g; Trainer** Colin Tizzard
**Chase form** 311332111131123, best RPR 178
**Left-handed** 313211113112, best RPR 178
**Right-handed** 133, best RPR 164
**Cheltenham form** (all) F9231, best RPR 178
**At the festival** 13 Mar 2015 Prominent,
blundered 6th and lost place, weakened after 3
out, finished ninth, beaten 53 lengths by Martello
Tower in Albert Bartlett Novices' Hurdle
15 Mar 2016 In touch, blundered 13th, chased
winner 19th (water), lost 2nd and ridden after
4 out, outpaced after 3 out, rallied run-in and
hung left, went 2nd final 120yds, stayed on to
close on winner near finish, finished second,
beaten one and a quarter lengths by Minella
Rocco in National Hunt Chase
17 Mar 2017 Disputed lead 2nd until 9th, led
15th, ridden after 3 out, narrowly headed 2 out,
stayed on very gamely in held 3rd from last to
regain 2nd final 50yds, lost 2nd final stride,
finished third, beaten two and three-quarter
lengths by Sizing John in Gold Cup
16 Mar 2018 Looked well, made virtually
all, jumped slightly right, ridden after 3
out, narrowly headed next, regained narrow
advantage last, stayed on strongly, edged right,
driven out, very game, won Gold Cup by four
and a half lengths from Might Bite

Reigning Gold Cup holder who turned in a
really brave performance to beat Might Bite
by four and a half lengths in sticky ground
12 months ago and, unlike his great rival, he
doesn't seem to have gone backwards after
that tough battle. He may not have quite
recaptured that form so far this season, but
he wasn't a million miles from it in the Betfair
Chase at Haydock when beaten four lengths
by Bristol De Mai, who is near unbeatable
around there even when the ground is on
the quick side, as it was. Native River did
not shine in the King George at Kempton,
finishing a 13-and-a-half-length third to Clan
Des Obeaux, but he looked ill at ease on the
track from the start and it is testament to his
willing attitude that he kept plugging away
and finished strongly in the straight. He was
due to run in the Denman Chase at Newbury
after that, as he had last season, but the
abandonment of that card due to equine flu
and the rescheduling of the race at Ascot put
paid to that as Colin Tizzard doesn't want to
run him right-handed again. Goes up against

a batch of young, improving rivals on what
will be his fifth visit to the festival and you
get the impression he will need it soft to be a
major player again, but if it is whatever beats
him will know it has been in a battle.

*Going preference* Softer the better
*Star rating* ✪✪✪

## KEMBOY
**7 b g; Trainer** Willie Mullins
**Chase form** 214F1111, best RPR 172
**Left-handed** 41, best RPR 172
**Right-handed** 21F111, best RPR 163
**Cheltenham form** (all) 54, best RPR 151
**At the festival** 15 Mar 2017 In touch, well
there 3 out, still close up 2 out, ridden and
outpaced before last, stayed on run-in but no
impression, finished fifth, beaten nine and a
quarter lengths by Willoughby Court in Neptune
Investment Management Novices' Hurdle
15 Mar 2018 Held up, blundered 9th, ridden
and headway to challenge for 4th after 3 out,
not pace to get on terms with leaders, no extra
from last, finished fourth, beaten 14 and a half
lengths by Shattered Love in JLT Novices' Chase

Could manage only a distant fourth to
Shattered Love in last season's JLT but has
the look of a massive improver since,having
won his final two starts last season and both
outings this term. Started his run with a 3m
Grade 3 success over Tombstone on heavy
ground at Limerick and then took advantage
of a handicap mark of 147 when dropped to
2m5f to win a valuable 18-runner handicap
at Punchestown. On his return in November
he continued his progress, although arguably
didn't need to improve to win the Clonmel Oil
Chase (2m4f, good) by three lengths from
Alpha Des Obeaux. The improvement was
very much in evidence at Leopardstown for
the Grade 1 Savills Chase over Christmas,
though, as he tanked through the race, took
it up at halfway and sprinted clear of the
best chasers in Ireland (Presenting Percy
notwithstanding) to win by seven and a half
lengths. That race was unsatisfactory to the
eye of many experts as they went slowly,
David Mullins rode his rivals to sleep once
he decided to pick up the pace and favourite
Road To Respect took a stumble at the third-
last before running on late. However, it was
still an impressive performance from a young

chaser on a roll and, while he arguably still has the stamina question to answer for 3m2½f, it's worth remembering Willie Mullins ran him in the Irish National (3m5f, fell first) and would have sent him for the Ladbrokes Trophy but for travel problems. He has pretty much the perfect profile for a second-season chaser going into the race. Mullins, of course, has yet to win the Gold Cup, but it took Nicky Henderson more than 30 years and it will happen one day.

*Going preference* Seems versatile, although the softer it is, the more stamina becomes an issue

*Star rating* ✪✪✪✪

## CLAN DES OBEAUX

**7 b g; Trainer** Paul Nicholls
**Chase form** 4125142123411, best RPR 177
**Left-handed** 41241234, best RPR 167
**Right-handed** 51211, best RPR 177
**Cheltenham form** (all) 2622, best RPR 139
**At the festival** 18 Mar 2016 Tracked leaders, ridden and outpaced between last 2, jumped left and not fluent last, kept on under pressure but no danger, finished sixth, beaten 15 lengths by Ivanovich Gorbatov in Triumph Hurdle

Has always been highly regarded by Paul Nicholls and started to show signs he was coming of age in his second season over fences last term. Only win was in a conditions chase at Haydock over 2m5f, but his third to Might Bite and Bristol De Mai at Aintree represented a career best and he stepped up again on his return in the Betfair Chase when beaten just under nine lengths into fourth by Bristol De Mai at Haydock. Native River (second), Thistlecrack (third) and Might Bite (fifth) were all in the field too, so Clan Des Obeaux obviously had it to do if he was going to reverse form in the King George at Kempton, where they all met again. Harry Cobden must have been half confident, though, as given the choice of Clan Des Obeaux or his shorter-priced stablemate Politologue he went

with the former. Clan Des Obeaux did indeed reverse the form, with Cobden giving him a balls-of-steel ride to hold on to him right until the final fence having looked as though he was running all over runner-up Thistlecrack from just after three out. Afterwards Cobden said he knew Clan Des Obeaux doesn't do anything in front, which has to be the worry up Cheltenham's unforgiving hill. Still, he looked brilliant in the rescheduled Denman Chase at Ascot (easy task on paper) and is another youngster going into the race in career-best form with a cracking profile.

*Going preference* Seems to go on anything
*Star rating* ✪✪✪✪

## ROAD TO RESPECT

**8 ch g; Trainer** Noel Meade
**Chase form** 143221112143132, best RPR 170
**Left-handed** 132211432, best RPR 170
**Right-handed** 411231, best RPR 170
**Cheltenham form** 14, best RPR 167
**At the festival** 16 Mar 2017 Jumped left at

times, prominent when hit 1st, settled midfield after 3rd, headway from 8th, led approaching 2 out, drew clear between last 2, not fluent last, kept on well, pushed out, won Brown Advisory & Merriebelle Stable Plate Handicap Chase by six lengths from Baron Alco

16 Mar 2018 Mid-division, took closer order after 16th, went 3rd 4 out, ridden when hit next, lost 3rd between last 2, not fluent last, stayed on same pace, finished fourth, beaten 12 and a half lengths by Native River in Gold Cup

Won a big-field handicap at the meeting two seasons ago and has subsequently proved himself a proper Grade 1 performer, although seemingly outstayed when a 12-and-a-half-length fourth to Native River and Might Bite in last year's Gold Cup. However, that was on very soft ground and he travelled just as well as the front two until they went for home, so there's always a chance he will last a bit

*Kemboy: latest big hope for Willie Mullins as he tries to break his Gold Cup duck*

longer this time. Form has been a mixed bag since as he was well held by Bellshill when third in the Punchestown Gold Cup in April, returned for an easy win in the JNwine.com Champion Chase at Down Royal but has suffered two further defeats since. The chances are he'd have been no better than a four- or five-length second to Kemboy had he not stumbled three out in the Savills Chase, and it was disappointing he could not gain revenge over Bellshill in a depleted Irish Gold Cup back at Leopardstown in February. It's true he was beaten only a short-head and his jumping was terrible, but the quickish ground (good to firm in places) should have been far more in his favour than the winner's. Questions to answer now and fair chance there are some better horses in this year's contest.

*Going preference* Handles most but decent ground suits well
*Star rating* ✪✪

## BELLSHILL

**9 b g; Trainer** Willie Mullins
**Chase form** 11F315141, best RPR 172
**Left-handed** F341, best RPR 169
**Right-handed** 11151, best RPR 172
**Cheltenham form** (all) 003, best RPR 157
**At the festival** 11 Mar 2015 Settled towards rear, effort into midfield well over 2f out, ridden and no headway soon after, finished tenth, beaten 16 and a half lengths by Moon Racer in Champion Bumper
15 Mar 2016 Tracked leaders, not fluent 4th, pushed along after next, ridden after 3 out, soon outpaced, weakened after next, finished 13th, beaten 31 and a half lengths in Supreme Novices' Hurdle won by Altior
15 Mar 2017 Held up, steady progress from 15th, went 11 lengths 2nd briefly 3 out, soon ridden, stayed on same pace from next, finished third, beaten ten lengths by Might Bite in RSA Novices' Chase

Slowly developed into the top-class chaser many always hoped he would become and last two seasons have been his best. Having been an easy winner of the Bobbyjo Chase on his belated return at Fairyhouse last February, he put up a really brave run under a big weight in the Irish National (fourth, demoted to fifth) before seeing off Djakadam for his first Grade 1 success over fences. This season he was a respectable fourth to Kemboy on his

return and then bagged his second Grade 1 when outjumping and outbattling Road To Respect by a short-head in the Irish Gold Cup. There's no doubt he has the form claims to be a player on the pick of his efforts, but he does have a Cheltenham question mark as he was well beaten when Ruby Walsh's choice in the Champion Bumper, beat only one home in Altior's Supreme and was a distant third to Might Bite in the RSA. That was his best run around there, and it coincided with the soft ground he probably needs on an undulating track, but he still got left for dead by Whisper from two out. He has obviously improved since, but he'll need to run around 20lb better than he has on his previous visits to Cheltenham and that's doubtful even if he gets soft ground and surely impossible if he doesn't.

*Going preference* Goes on all but particularly effective on soft
*Star rating* ✪✪

## THISTLECRACK

**11 b g; Trainer** Colin Tizzard
**Chase form** 11112432, best RPR 174
**Left-handed** 11123, best RPR 174
**Right-handed** 142, best RPR 174
**Cheltenham form** (all) 71112, best RPR 178
**At the festival** 17 Mar 2016 Midfield, headway approaching 7th, went 2nd before 3 out, led on bit just before 2 out, always travelling strongly, effortlessly went clear run-in, impressive, won Stayers' Hurdle by seven lengths from Alpha Des Obeaux

Real superstar of a staying hurdler three seasons ago who has had his problems since being sent chasing and has missed the last two festivals. He has run in three King Georges, but Kempton in December 2016 was the scene of his last victory and he has run only four times in two seasons since being outbattled by the ill-fated Many Clouds on that sad day in January 2017. Last season he beat only one home on his reappearance over hurdles in the Long Distance Hurdle at Newbury and then failed to show his old sparkle when fourth in the King George, although he wasn't beaten far. This term has been much more like it, with third place to Bristol De Mai in the Betfair Chase and then second to Clan Des Obeaux in the King George, showing much of his old dash as he turned for home going very well. However, he was soon off the bridle, with the winner seemingly running all over him after the third-last, and while he battled on gamely, he just wasn't strong enough at the end. That's the problem for a horse of his age because, no matter how good he was over hurdles, he has always seemed to need to put too much effort into his jumping and that spent energy will add up as the Gold Cup goes on. The race is run over a furlong further than he has ever been and it must be doubtful whether he can get up the hill. The Gold Cup is not really a race for horses of his age either, and better 11-year-olds (Kauto Star and Denman for a start) have not been able to win at that age. The last winner older than ten was the 12-year-old What A Myth in 1969 and racing is far more competitive now.

*Going preference* Handles all but definitely won't get home if it's soft or heavy
*Star rating* ✪✪

## AL BOUM PHOTO

**7 b g; Trainer** Willie Mullins
**Chase form** 1F2F1R1, best RPR 169
**Left-handed** 12F, best RPR 160
**Right-handed** F1R1, best RPR 169
**Cheltenham form** F, best RPR 160
**At the festival** 14 Mar 2018 In touch, disputed 4th from 14th, ridden in close 3rd after 3 out, staying on at same pace in held 3rd when crumpled on landing and fell next in RSA Novices' Chase won by Presenting Percy

Very capable performer who is sometimes a sticky jumper but is nevertheless improving in all departments. Was a well-held third when coming down two out in Presenting Percy's RSA Chase, but bounced back to beat JLT winner Shattered Love in a Fairyhouse Grade 1 afterwards and would almost certainly have won the Champion Novice Chase at Punchestown had Paul Townend not thought he had to bypass the last fence. His progress continued this season when he gave 10lb and a comfortable six-length beating to Total Recall in a 2m5½f Listed chase at Tramore in January, but he hasn't been seen since as the ground was considered too fast for him in the Irish Gold Cup. Has the option of this and the Ryanair and, having shown career-best form

on his last three starts, is definitely worth considering wherever he goes.

*Going preference* Handles soft/heavy well
*Star rating* ✪✪✪

## MIGHT BITE

**10 b g; Trainer** Nicky Henderson
**Chase form** 521F111112157, best RPR 174
**Left-handed** 521111215, best RPR 174
**Right-handed** F117, best RPR 169
**Cheltenham form** (all) 15712, best RPR 174
**At the festival** 15 Mar 2017 Led 2nd, pushed clear after 4 out, 12 lengths up 2 out, soon ridden, mistake last, idling when veered right 1f out, headed final 130yds, ran on again final 90yds, led final stride, won RSA Novices' Chase by a nose from Whisper
16 Mar 2018 Pressed winner virtually throughout, took narrow advantage 2 out until last, soon ridden, kept on for clear 2nd but outstayed by winner final 160yds, finished second, beaten four and a half lengths by Native River in Gold Cup

Brilliant if wayward as a novice and best remembered for nearly throwing away a ten-length lead on the run-in of the 2017 RSA Chase. There were no signs of any quirks last season, but he had to work hard to win his King George in what was a weak renewal and then found himself outstayed/outbattled by Native River in the Gold Cup. There were no signs the race had left its mark when he bounced right back to win the Bowl at Aintree in April, but two runs this term have been terrible, finishing last in the Betfair Chase and then weakening out of contention as soon as he made a mistake six out in the King George. Has looked both times as though he didn't fancy it any more, but connections have given him a wind operation and intend to bring him back fresh. Hard not to think his chance has been and gone, though.

*Going preference* Handles any
*Star rating* ✪

## FRODON

**7 b g; Trainer** Paul Nicholls
**Chase form** 411101F115323213501211, best RPR 177
**Left-handed** 41101531501211, best RPR 177
**Right-handed** 1F112323, best RPR 160
**Cheltenham form** (all) 3801150211, best RPR 177

**At the festival** 18 Mar 2016 In touch, ridden and outpaced on bend between last 2, kept on under pressure run-in but no danger, finished eighth, beaten 16 and three-quarter lengths by Ivanovich Gorbatov in Triumph Hurdle
15 Mar 2018 Close up, struggling after 13th, outpaced in last after 4 out, no danger after, finished fifth, beaten 36 and a half lengths by Balko Des Flos in Ryanair Chase

Wonderfully battle-hardened performer who has run in more chases (22) than nearly every horse among the Gold Cup entries yet is one of the youngest in the field at the age of seven. He has done his share of winning, too, scoring ten times, the last four under Bryony Frost, with whom he has forged a fine partnership. Most of his form has come in handicaps at around 2m4f-2m5f but he has put in some really good weight-carrying performances, with a victory off a mark of 164 in December one of the highlights. Loves Cheltenham and won his first Graded non-handicap when seeing off Elegant Escape by three-quarters of a length in the Cotswold Chase on trials day in January. His stamina had been questionable beforehand, but he saved one of his biggest jumps for the last and had enough in reserve at the end. That race was run over 151 yards further than advertised, so he doesn't have much further to go in the Gold Cup itself, but whether the form is strong enough is another matter. Blew out in last season's Ryanair, but had a long campaign and a hard race in February and he'll be fresher this time. Easy enough to see him going well for a long way, but suspect others will be stronger when it matters.

*Going preference* Handles anything
*Star rating* ✪✪✪

## ELEGANT ESCAPE

**7 b g; Trainer** Colin Tizzard
**Chase form** 22121331212, best RPR 167
**Left-handed** 2133212, best RPR 167
**Right-handed** 2211, best RPR 160
**Cheltenham form** (all) 5732, best RPR 167
**At the festival** 17 Mar 2017 Prominent, chased leader approaching 6th, mistake 3 out, every chance 2 out, soon ridden, weakened before last, finished seventh, beaten 26 lengths by Penhill in Albert Bartlett Novices' Hurdle
14 Mar 2018 Led, dived at 1st, headed 3rd,

tracked leader until 7th, raced in 3rd most of the way until ridden after 4 out, outpaced after 3 out, left 4th next, stayed on into 3rd soon after last but no chance with front pair, finished third, beaten 14 lengths by Presenting Percy in RSA Novices' Chase

Distant third to Presenting Percy in the RSA Chase last term but has had a good second season, finishing runner-up in the Ladbrokes Trophy and then winning the Welsh National off a mark of 151. Landed a massive gamble there, in similar style to stablemate Native River a couple of seasons earlier, but then just couldn't get to Frodon when second in the Cotswold Chase. Clearly a strong stayer, but needs to prove he is more than that and you suspect he will have little chance unless the mud is flying.

*Going preference* Handles all but needs a test, so a bog is preferable
*Star rating* ✪✪

## MONALEE

**8 b g; Trainer** Henry de Bromhead
**Chase form** 1F12F321, best RPR 167
**Left-handed** F122, best RPR 163
**Right-handed** 1F31, best RPR 167
**Cheltenham form** (all) 22, best RPR 163
**At the festival** 17 Mar 2017 Raced keenly, chased leaders, led on bend between last 2, ridden and headed approaching last, kept on under pressure run-in, unable to go with winner final 100yds, finished second, beaten three and a half lengths by Penhill in Albert Bartlett Novices' Hurdle
14 Mar 2018 Raced keenly, tracked leaders, pressed leader from 7th, led 3 out, ridden and headed when hit 2 out, kept on for clear 2nd but soon held by winner, finished second, beaten seven lengths by Presenting Percy in RSA Novices' Chase

Decent novice hurdler and novice chaser who has been second at the last two festivals. Gave Presenting Percy most to do in the RSA last season but was still beaten seven lengths in the end. Was just about disputing the lead and by no means done for when falling two out in an eventful Champion Novice Chase at Punchestown (2-1 favourite) on his final start last term and restricted to just two outings this season, first of all when a beaten favourite behind Snow Falcon at Down Royal. Stepped up on that when second to Kemboy in the Savills Chase at Leopardstown but was still

## GOLD CUP RESULTS AND TRENDS

| | FORM WINNER | AGE & WGT | Adj RPR | SP | TRAINER | BEST RPR LAST 12 MONTHS (RUNS SINCE) |
|---|---|---|---|---|---|---|
| 18 | 113-1 **Native River** D | 8 11-10 | 177$^T$ | 5-1 | C Tizzard | won Newbury Gd2 chase (2m7½f) (0) |
| 17 | -3211 **Sizing John** | 7 11-10 | 172-12 | 7-1 | J Harrington (IRE) | won Gd1 Irish Gold Cup (3m½f) (0) |
| 16 | 111F1 **Don Cossack** | 9 11-10 | 185$^T$ | 9-4f | G Elliott (IRE) | won Gd1 Punchestown Gold Cup (3m1f) (4) |
| 15 | 3/111 **Coneygree** C | 8 11-10 | 173-9 | 7-1 | M Bradstock | won Newbury Gd2 chase (2m7½f) (0) |
| 14 | 1-876 **Lord Windermere** C | 8 11-10 | 161-24 | 20-1 | J Culloty (IRE) | 7th Gd1 Lexus Chase (3m) (1) |
| 13 | 321-1 **Bobs Worth** C, D | 8 11-10 | 178-6 | 11-4f | N Henderson | won Gd3 Hennessy Gold Cup (3m2½f) (0) |
| 12 | -P731 **Synchronised** | 9 11-10 | 175-12 | 8-1 | J O'Neill | won Gd1 Lexus Chase (3m) (0) |
| 11 | 13-31 **Long Run** | 6 11-10 | 184-2 | 7-2f | N Henderson | won Gd1 King George VI Chase (3m) (0) |
| 10 | 1-P25 **Imperial Commander** C | 9 11-10 | 181-15 | 7-1 | N Twiston-Davies | 2nd Gd1 Betfair Chase (3m) (1) |
| 09 | 2-1U1 **Kauto Star** CD | 9 11-10 | 188-1 | 7-4f | P Nicholls | won Gd1 King George VI Chase (3m) (0) |

**WINS-RUNS:** 6yo 1-3, 7yo 1-20, 8yo 4-38, 9yo 4-40, 10yo 0-17, 11yo 0-9, 12yo 0-2 **FAVOURITES:** £4.25

**TRAINERS IN THIS RACE (w-pl-r):** Nicky Henderson 2-3-10, Paul Nicholls 1-4-21, Colin Tizzard 1-1-4, Gordon Elliott 1-0-3, Jessica Harrington 1-0-2, Jonjo O'Neill 1-2-6, Nigel Twiston-Davies 1-0-4, Mark Bradstock 1-0-4, Noel Meade 0-1-3, Venetia Williams 0-1-4, Willie Mullins 0-5-16, Henry de Bromhead 0-0-2, Tony Martin 0-1-1, Brian Ellison 0-0-1, Harry Fry 0-0-1

**FATE OF FAVOURITES:** 1F13150142 **POSITION OF WINNER IN MARKET:** 1313172143

beaten seven lengths. Consistent but perhaps just lacks the class for a Gold Cup and stamina not certain either, hence an entry and shorter price for the Ryanair. Prepped over 2m4f with a win in the Red Mills, too.

*Going preference* Handles all ground
*Star rating* ⊙⊙

## OTHERS TO CONSIDER

*It might seem strange not to give a full profile to one of the joint-highest-rated horses in the field, but we are all pretty sure what **Bristol De Mai** is about these days and it's hard to see him being a factor, which is why he is 33-1 when, if the race was at Haydock, he'd be just about favourite. He has been placed at a festival, though, and stranger things have happened. **Anibale Fly** was third last year, so is worth a mention. It will be surprising if anything else wins.*

## VERDICT

*It is easy to see why **Presenting Percy** is favourite as he carried all before him in the staying novice division last season and some of those he trounced have become his biggest dangers. He needs to show he has improved from his novice campaign, though, while the likes of **KEMBOY** and **AL BOUM PHOTO** have already done that. I've backed both in the hope Willie Mullins will shake the monkey off his back this season and land a first Gold Cup.*

### Key trends

- Grade 1 chase winner, 10/10
- Aged between seven and nine, 9/10
- Adjusted RPR of at least 172, 9/10
- Won over at least 3m, 9/10
- Two to five runs that season, 8/10 (both exceptions ran just once)
- Won a Graded chase that season, 8/10
- No more than 12 starts over fences, 8/10
- Won or placed previously at the festival, 8/10
- Within 12lb of RPR top-rated, 8/10

### Other factors

- In 2015, Coneygree became the first winner not to have run at a previous festival since Imperial Call in 1996. He was also the first novice to win since Captain Christy in 1974
- Six of the last ten winners had run in the King George or Savills Chase (formerly Lexus) that season

## 4.10 St James's Place Foxhunter Chase — ITV/RTV

*3m2½f    Amateur riders    £45,000*

Nine horses since 1956 have won the race twice – three of them (Salsify, On The Fringe and Pacha Du Polder) in the last seven runnings – and the 12-year-old Pacha Du Polder now has a shot at the hat-trick for Paul Nicholls.

Pacha Du Polder ended the run of six consecutive Irish winners from 2011. Since the first Irish-trained victory in 1983 there have been ten subsequent wins.

Seventeen of the last 27 winners have been aged nine or younger, but the last four were ten or 11.

■ **ONES TO WATCH** Enda Bolger, who has trained the winner three times, has leading contenders **Stand Up And Fight** and **Gilgamboa**. Among the other former track stars are **Ucello Conti** and **Shantou Flyer**, while those to emerge from point-to-pointing include **Hazel Hill** and **Burning Ambition**.

### FOXHUNTER CHASE RESULTS AND TRENDS

| | FORM WINNER | AGE & WGT | Adj RPR | SP | TRAINER | BEST RPR LAST 12 MONTHS (RUNS SINCE) |
|---|---|---|---|---|---|---|
| 18 | 114-3 **Pacha Du Polder** CD, BF | 11 12-0 | 145-5 | 25-1 | P Nicholls | won Foxhunter Chase (3m2½f) (2) |
| 17 | -3341 **Pacha Du Polder** CD | 10 12-0 | 143-8 | 16-1 | P Nicholls | 3rd Uttoxeter Listed hcap ch (3m2f) (2) |
| 16 | 11-17 **On The Fringe** CD, BF | 11 12-0 | 148T | 13-8f | E Bolger (IRE) | won Aintree Fox Hunters ch (2m5f) (2) |
| 15 | -1122 **On The Fringe** | 10 12-0 | 144T | 6-1 | E Bolger (IRE) | 1st Punchestown hunt ch (2m7f) (4) |
| 14 | -6213 **Tammys Hill** BF | 9 12-0 | 139-9 | 15-2 | L Lennon (IRE) | 2nd Down Royal hunt ch (2m7f) (2) |
| 13 | -1221 **Salsify** CD | 8 12-0 | 143-6 | 2-1f | R Sweeney (IRE) | won Foxhunter Chase (3m2½f) (5) |
| 12 | -11P1 **Salsify** | 7 12-0 | 132-14 | 7-1 | R Sweeney (IRE) | won Leopardstown hunt ch (3m) (0) |
| 11 | 44-21 **Zemsky** | 8 12-0 | 125-23 | 33-1 | I Ferguson (IRE) | won Musselburgh class 6 hunt ch (3m½f) (0) |
| 10 | 2-121 **Baby Run** | 10 12-0 | 144-7 | 9-2jf | N Twiston-Davies | won Warwick class 6 hunt ch (3m½) (0) |
| 09 | 11 **Cappa Bleu** | 7 12-0 | 130-14 | 11-2 | S Crow | won Chaddesley Corbett open (3m) (0) |

**WINS-RUNS:** 6yo 0-3, 7yo 2-17, 8yo 2-33, 9yo 1-41, 10yo 3-50, 11yo 2-48, 12yo 0-33, 13yo 0-7, 14yo 0-4 **FAVOURITES:** £-1.63

**TRAINERS IN THIS RACE (w-pl-r):** Enda Bolger 2-1-6, Paul Nicholls 2-1-14, Fergal O'Brien 0-0-3, Colin McBratney 0-2-3, Gordon Elliott 0-0-3, James Joseph Mangan 0-2-4, Warren Greatrex 0-2-4, Willie Mullins 0-0-1

**FATE OF FAVOURITES:** 0142153148 **POSITION OF WINNER IN MARKET:** 2103142160

*Key trends*

🐎 Ran between 20 and 41 days ago, 10/10

🐎 Won over at least 3m, 9/10

🐎 Top-three finish last time out, 9/10

🐎 Adjusted RPR of at least 130, 9/10

🐎 Aged seven to ten, 8/10 (both exceptions were previous winners)

🐎 Rated within 9lb of RPR top-rated, 7/10

*Other factors*

🐎 The record of the previous year's winner is 4U1141

🐎 Three were back-to-back winners – Salsify (2012-13), On The Fringe (2015-16) and Pacha Du Polder (2017-18). The last one before them was Double Silk in 1993-94

🐎 Four winners had competed at a previous festival and all had finished in the first five

🐎 Those aged 12 or older are winless in the last ten years. The 13-year-old Earthmover (2004) is the only winner from this category since 1990

## 4.50 Grand Annual Handicap Chase — RTV
### 2m½f · Grade 3 · £110,000

The quality of this 2m handicap chase has improved year on year and seven of the last eight winners were rated at least 140. Le Prezien defied a mark of 150 (11st 8lb) when winning for Paul Nicholls last year and you have to go back to Stopped (11st 12lb) in 1980 to find a better weight-carrying performance.

The last five winners carried at least 11st, following a 14-year run where no winner carried more than 10st 13lb.

Le Prezien was the fourth winner in the past 15 runnings for Nicholls, although he has also had five beaten favourites. The race's full title has commemorated Nicky Henderson's father Johnny since 2005 and the trainer won the following year with Greenhope and again in 2012 with Bellvano (both 20-1 shots). He has also had four runner-ups and three thirds from a total of 37 runners.

Four of the last ten winners were officially novices. This has been a good race for novices with 12 winners, rated from 129 to 140, since 1983.

■ **ONES TO WATCH Whatswrongwithyou** could get in on a low mark for Nicky Henderson. Other interesting novices who could run here are **Ballywood** (Alan King), **Knocknanuss** (Gary Moore) and **Us And Them** (Joseph O'Brien).

### GRAND ANNUAL HANDICAP CHASE RESULTS AND TRENDS

| | FORM WINNER | AGE & WGT | OR | SP | TRAINER | BEST RPR LAST 12 MONTHS (RUNS SINCE) |
|---|---|---|---|---|---|---|
| 18 | P-238 **Le Prezien** C, D | 7 11-8 | 150-2 | 15-2 | P Nicholls | 3rd BetVictor Gold Cup hcap ch (2m4½f) (1) |
| 17 | 63-3P **Rock The World** C, D | 9 11-5 | 147-2 | 10-1 | J Harrington (IRE) | 2nd Punchestown hcap ch (2m) (2) |
| 16 | 63-3P **Solar Impulse** D | 6 11-0 | 140-8 | 28-1 | P Nicholls | 3rd Haydock class 2 ch (2m½f) (1) |
| 15 | 5-604 **Next Sensation** D | 8 11-2 | 143-5 | 16-1 | M Scudamore | 4th Newbury class 2 hcap ch (2m½f) (0) |
| 14 | -3439 **Savello** D | 8 11-5 | 147-2 | 16-1 | A Martin (IRE) | 3rd Leopardstown hcap ch (2m1f) (1) |
| 13 | -S312 **Alderwood** C, D | 9 10-11 | 140T | 3-1f | T Mullins (IRE) | 2nd Punchestown hcap ch (2m) (0) |
| 12 | -1621 **Bellvano** D | 8 10-2 | 138T | 20-1 | N Henderson | won Kelso class 2 nov ch (2m1f) (0) |
| 11 | U6483 **Oiseau De Nuit** CD | 9 10-13 | 145-3 | 40-1 | C Tizzard | 3rd Newbury Gd2 ch (2m1f) (0) |
| 10 | 222F5 **Pigeon Island** C, D | 7 10-1 | 129T | 16-1 | N Twiston-Davies | 2nd Cheltenham Gd2 nov ch (2m5f) (2) |
| 09 | 423F2 **Oh Crick** (10h) C, D | 6 10-0 | 130-13 | 7-1 | A King | 2nd Hereford class 3 nov ch (2m3f) (0) |

**WINS-RUNS:** 5yo 0-5, 6yo 2-23, 7yo 2-48, 8yo 3-54, 9yo 3-41, 10yo 0-29, 11yo 0-15, 12yo 0-2 **FAVOURITES:** -£6.00

**FATE OF FAVOURITES:** 0P0012430F **POSITION OF WINNER IN MARKET:** 2800197062

*Key trends*

🐎Distance winner, 10/10

🐎No more than 12 runs over fences, 9/10

🐎Aged nine or under, 10/10

🐎Officially rated 138 to 150, 8/10 (the last eight)

🐎Yet to win that season, 8/10

🐎Top-three finish on at least one of last two starts, 8/10

🐎Carried no more than 11st 2lb, 7/10

🐎Had run at a previous festival, 7/10

🐎No more than four runs since August, 6/10

*Other factors*

🐎Six winners had won at the course – two of the exceptions had been placed in this race previously

🐎There have been four winning novices

🐎The record of the previous year's winner is 5B009

🐎The last five winners have carried at least 11st

## 5.30 Martin Pipe Conditional Jockeys' Hcap Hurdle — RTV
### 2m4½f — £70,000

This handicap hurdle for conditional riders has taken over from the Grand Annual as the final race of the festival and it won't be an easy 'getting out stakes' for punters, with six of the last seven winners having been sent off at double-figure odds.

Big guns Willie Mullins, Paul Nicholls and Gordon Elliott have won seven of the last eight runnings between them. The Mullins and Elliott winners have had the shortest SPs (9-2 favourite, 7-1, 11-1 and 12-1 twice) with the others sent off at 14-1 or bigger.

Elliott's two wins have come in the most recent renewals with Champagne Classic and Blow By Blow, both in the Gigginstown colours. Having also won with Sir Des Champs and Don Poli, and with this race earning a reputation as a proving ground for future top chasers, the Gigginstown runners are worth a close look.

The minimum rating needed to get into the race since 2016 has been 135. Runners rated between 133 and 139 have won seven of the ten last runnings.

Although the race is open to four-year-olds and upwards, only five- and six-year-olds had been successful until Blow By Blow (seven) last year. Five- and six-year-olds have also been placed 20 times.

David Pipe has yet to win the race named in honour of his father, having had the beaten favourite three times and two unplaced second favourites.

■**ONE TO WATCH Dallas Des Pictons**, trained by Gordon Elliott and owned by Gigginstown, has the ideal profile. The six-year-old has won his last two hurdle starts, latterly a valuable 3m handicap at the Dublin Racing Festival in early February.

### MARTIN PIPE HANDICAP HURDLE RESULTS AND TRENDS

| | FORM WINNER | AGE & WGT | OR | SP | TRAINER | BEST RPR LAST 12 MONTHS (RUNS SINCE) |
|---|---|---|---|---|---|---|
| 18 | 32161 Blow By Blow D | 7 11-10 | 144·1 | 11-1 | G Elliott (IRE) | won Thurles Gd3 nov hdl (2m4f) (0) |
| 17 | 23213 Champagne Classic D | 6 11-3 | 138·9 | 12-1 | G Elliott (IRE) | won Thurles mdn hdl (2m6½f) (1) |
| 16 | 4-235 Ibis Du Rheu | 5 11-7 | 139·4 | 14-1 | P Nicholls | 3rd Lanzarote hcap hdl (2m5f) (1) |
| 15 | -5123 Killultagh Vic D | 6 11-1 | 135·5 | 7-1 | W Mullins (IRE) | 3rd Leopardstown Gd2 nov hdl (2m4f) (0) |
| 14 | 2-211 Don Poli | 5 11-5 | 143·4 | 12-1 | W Mullins (IRE) | won Clonmel Gd3 nov hdl (3m) (0) |
| 13 | -4251 Salubrious D | 6 11-5 | 141·9 | 16-1 | P Nicholls | won Musselburgh cl 3 hcap hdl (2m4f) (0) |
| 12 | 135P1 Attaglance | 6 11-3 | 139ᵀ | 20-1 | M Jefferson | won M Rasen class 3 hcap hdl (2m3f) (0) |
| 11 | 1-1 Sir Des Champs | 5 11-3 | 134ᵀ | 9-2f | W Mullins (IRE) | won Navan hdl (2m) (0) |
| 10 | -445U Pause And Clause D | 6 11-10 | 137·3 | 14-1 | E Lavelle | 4th Haydock Listed hcap hdl (3m1f) (2) |
| 09 | -4134 Andytown C, D | 6 11-2 | 133·6 | 25-1 | N Henderson | won Chelt class 3 cond hcap hdl (2m5f) (1) |

**WINS-RUNS:** 4yo 0-1, 5yo 3-65, 6yo 6-75, 7yo 1-49, 8yo 0-26, 9yo 0-9, 10yo 0-6, 12yo 0-1 **FAVOURITES:** -£4.50

**FATE OF FAVOURITES:** 3010P03000 **POSITION OF WINNER IN MARKET:** 0610862676

### Key trends
🏇Officially rated 133-144, 10/10

🏇Aged five or six, 9/10

🏇Top-three finish in at least one of last two starts, 9/10

🏇No more than eight hurdle runs, 9/10

🏇Rated within 6lb of RPR top-rated, 8/10

🏇Had won that season, 8/10

### Other factors
🏇Willie Mullins (three) and Gordon Elliott (two) account for the five Irish-trained winners, four of whom were owned by Gigginstown

🏇Seven of the ten winners carried between 11st 1lb and 11st 5lb